Pitfalls & Progress

Paul Ottley

A Schiel & Denver Paperback

Pitfalls & Progress

First published in 2011 by Schiel & Denver Publishing Limited
10685-B Hazelhurst Drive Suite 8575
Houston, Texas USA 77043

www.schieldenver.com

ISBN 978-1-84903-090-8

Printed in the United States of America and United Kingdom.

Typeset by Schiel & Denver Publishing Limited.

All papers used by Schiel & Denver Publishing are natural
recyclable products made from wood grown in well-managed
forests. The manufacturing processes conform to the
environmental regulations of the country of origin.

Introduction

I would like you to spend just a little time with me as I give you the gist behind the topic of this book.

I had to ponder the topic for a while before I decided to start this writing journey. Then it became evidently clear to me that I was definitely on the right track. Now I'm onto something good that will benefit us all.

One day as I decided to pen this my next novel, I had to first take a good look around my writing area. There I noticed on the wall a business diploma, and right behind it was an old replica of a piece of art that says 'dream'. All of a sudden, all sorts of ideas started to flood my head. Immediately I knew I was on to something important, and that I was right on the target with the topic.

This was the right time for me to demonstrate to you, the reader, that it is okay to have ambitious tendencies, and of course pursue them from any angle that you please.

One thing you may be mindful of is that there certainly will be difficult times. As road signs indicate to us a bumpy road ahead, so too will you experience bumps during your journey. This is to warn you about uncertainties, because one thing for sure is we have to prepare for the very best, and keep focusing on what it is that you expect. Remember that where ever there are pitfalls, there may be progress if you choose to persevere.

This book is intended to help you realize there will be many difficult roads that you travel, but try not to get yourself all tangled up in the doubts and uncertainties. Instead, prepare to your full advantage, giving credit to the reason for your success.

Determine to change whatever it is that you can.

Since the beginning of time, we have been growing up in a world with great complexities. For each succeeding generation, the rules are the same just about everywhere. When you are young, no one spends any time to define the things that you are seeing. At that time, in life, it is all about having lots of fun, and so it should be, because before long, a different reality will kick in, and that's when your eyes will be opened to the ways of the world. Before, you saw things dimly, completely without focus, instead of paying attention to things of greater value.

You should really give things a chance to settle in, for as we get older we have no choice but to face the music. By then, you will appreciate life enough that you may feel like dancing, because we all know when to begin to have fun. Whatever you may choose to do, don't let the fun end. Be it work, or play, try and incorporate fun times to makes the work feel a little lighter. God knows we may have to work for quite some time in our lives, and that's whether we work for ourselves or the company down the street.

One thing I dislike to do is assuming anything, what so ever, only this time I think I will. If you are young, know that this time should not be wasted. This is the time you must take things serious enough, and learn all the rules of engagement. Don't ever wait until you are older. It is too late, because there are too many things to try to catch up on, which will only serve as a source of discouragement in so many ways.

What that does is to stifle your interest for the more important things in life that have to be first and foremost in your mind. Your thinking time is now. This is the beginning of your journey, and you may want to feel up to it, especially knowing that this is what one may call preparation for the foundation for your life.

What made it very beneficial for me was, that I knew that what I was doing earlier on would be the greatest investment in my life. Today, I have the type of support that I prepared for in earlier times. It is ever so true to know that today can certainly pave the way for tomorrow, if we make the right choices and decisions now.

I might sound like a purist, but in fact I am not. I'm just thinking of what can provide the biggest and best changes for me, as I move forward to lay the foundation for what I know is very possible.

I also understand that there will be all sorts of stumbling blocks in my way as I try to establish my priorities. One thing I know there is absolutely no way to avoid some of these things. So what I do is to acknowledge its presence, and move along with my plans. After all, the goals that I set are all very important to me, otherwise I wouldn't waste time on any of them.

One of the things that I really like is the ability to make a choice. So despite my obstacles, I am determined not to allow them to impede my progress. To me, they're like life and death, which are a part of the realities of life.

I try to weigh my options carefully so as to enable me to side step the pitfalls. That should be our only major concern in anything that we do. You see, I just want to be successful in all that I may do, whatever it may be. With that type of attitude, I know I must succeed.

I really don't like to hear no as my answers. Otherwise you are sure to hear me ask why not. I want answers and I am looking for them wherever I can find them. When I receive my answers, I use them as a validation that I am on the right track. The answers give me a sense of direction, and free me up to go full steam ahead. I know the way is clear by the answers that I receive.

Most people will tell you that they are like me. They are simply fastidious when coming to what they want. Nothing but the best will do for them, but also take note that what happens to be their best, may not be yours. It's all based on opinion. As you must have heard people say time and time again, keep your opinions to yourself. That's because we make the type of decisions that will affect our lives personally. Hey, don't knock me. That is just what I wished for. Luckily, it is what I have gotten.

One thing that I know for sure is that I write because I want to inspire you. I cannot force you to do anything, but what I can do is to show you the sweeter side of what you may be considering.

The fact is, there are many people out there that are thinking of acquiring big things, even though they have started with small steps, which is not really a bad way to start. What people want us to do, is to follow through to the end. Just make sure that the end is just what you expected so you may be at least happy.

Whatever you may do, do it with a good level of planning, so that when the end comes you will see all of your plans manifest themselves in a way that you can be proud of. Now, who wouldn't want that. Everyone likes good reports, especially when you know that you are the master of them. I don't know about you, but for me, whenever I do something that both I and those that are privy to my accomplishments are proud of, it's like a double blessing.

You, try it sometime, then go around to your friends and do a little show and tell, because you are very happy with the outcome. Somehow it also makes you feel more confident for any other attempts, encouraging you to do more, and to me more is always better in this regard.

Something that I have tried to do is to give the pitfalls their fair break. Acknowledge that they're there, simply because, they are going to be there, whether I want them to be or not. The thing is, I am not to going to allow them to get the better of my attention. I need that for things that are of more importance.

I have seen people give far too much attention to the wrong things, while at the same time spend too little time on what really matters. Try not to exhaust the good side of you until you are depleted and out of wind, because it really takes too much time to set things right things again. That's too much time and energy wasted which may cost you dearly.

When it comes to cost, time is one, money is the other. There is no sense in loosing from both sides, at the same time. I don't know about you, but to me, that's overwhelming to think about when it comes to the success that I expect.

Just in case you are wondering why I am so crazy about success, the answer is why not. In some of my earlier works, if you may recall that I laid out the difference between having, and not having, and just what it means for each individual. One thing I was careful to bring to your attention was that, those who use all that they have to acquire what they want, are like the cream that rises to the top. While those that live carefree lives, and do simply nothing, waste precious time with little to show for time spent.

After all, one may question why these folks may even have a question about not making it. It is simply because they did nothing with their time, and talents. For the same reason, that's why they would experience self defeat. It is simple, if we have done nothing, why should we have an expectation of getting any returns. It's like having no bank account but expecting to make a withdrawal.

Now this is exactly when we create our own pitfalls, and from here on progress seems difficult. I know of people that have rebounded from such treacherous experiences. Simply put, they were faced with the end before the beginning, placing themselves between what you call a rock and a hard place. What do you do when you are faced with such difficult situations? You better make a decision to at change that present situation before it's too late. Although it has been said it's better late than never. I would be very careful about that, because some lates can be too late. There are a plethora of things to take into consideration to avoid any of these pitfalls to hamper your life.

Have you ever stopped to realize that when you were born, you were born to be an entity? Every man and woman was born with all of their faculties that if developed, would enable them to do almost anything. That's why I said before that there should be absolutely no real excuse for not being able to take care of yourself and avoid any pitfall that may threaten to erode your life. Then progress really becomes a very sweet word.

The simple truth is that almost everyone loves having the very best that they can have. Has it ever crossed your mind that you may have to work very hard for the things that you want? Never mind about the basic needs, for example, food, water, and shelter, we all must have some of these things that are too important not to have.

Now, what if you had to purchase any of these, just what would you do? I hope you would look around to find a job to enable you to have some of these basic things, for doing without them would be carelessness.

Life is sweet. I really love it, so I try to enjoy it every day, doing whatever I can to be as happy as possible. It really doesn't take much to be happy, and I am not talking about getting up in the morning, and acting like a crazy fool jumping around like a clown. I mean find a good reason to have a real good laugh, and the thing is, you really don't have to travel far to find the joke. Take a good look at yourself, and you can surely find a million things to laugh at.

The fact is, life is not going anywhere, and we are. Before you know it, the time is come and gone right before our very eyes, leaving some of us standing, wondering what's for dinner, and by the time they think and collect themselves, it's night time, and not only that, it's also bed time. Gosh, what did I get done today as an investment into the future? Well, that answer seems to be, nothing.

My, my, up to this time I have only seen pitfalls and simply no progress. Something is unforgivably wrong. Don't sleep into the night before you get the day's work done. Use the day for everything that must be done during the day, the night comes and we will rest from it all.

It's funny how we all see things differently. I was talking to a young man recently, and in our conversation I learned that he was working three jobs just to be able to take care of his family's needs. I asked him, "When do you get to sleep?". His answer to me was,

"I don't like sleeping. I must use my life to build for better days ahead, and to secure my family's future."

I thought that was a fair answer. He had to know that first that he was strong enough to handle so much work. Now you can take whatever you can from that type of attitude, but there are people out there with a vastly different view when it comes to taking care of themselves and of their families.

I certainly learned some valuable lessons from that man. Not that I am prepared to take on his work ethic, but his passion for building himself to be able to build a solid financial foundation, is something that he can rely on when he is older. I don't know about you but this is a sure source of inspiration.

This man has not only maximized all of his efforts, avoided the pitfalls, but he made solid progress.

One of the things that I learned in some of the research that I did was, if someone wants something from me, because he or she thinks they would like it, who am I to tell them not to take it. People have to learn for themselves. Many times we have the tendency to tell others what we think they should do, and that is totally wrong.

Everyone should be expected to develop a passion for what they wish to accomplish, then you know for sure that time will be well spent.

What I have been doing is the direct opposite to what I am seeing. Here is something to consider. Try using prior results to inspire people under any circumstance. Once people see what the results look like, somehow they become more prone to jump right in and try it for their own satisfaction, and gage what happens.

Someone once said that people are creatures of habits. I am in agreement with that. If you notice when someone you know wins a lottery, what happens is the next day everybody and their grandmother goes out and purchases lottery tickets. People love results, and those type of results are indeed fascinating. All of a sudden everything turns into a wish. Now whether that wish, becomes a reality, is another thing, for it could be wishful thinking too.

I think that we should all look at the real value in the things that interests us. Other than those things that tend to want to take our money away, or what little we have, we should use things to make a solid investment in tangible things, such as a real skills. Whatever skill that happens to be your most favorite, to me that is far better than betting on some uncertain lottery that has no satisfaction other than winning, and does not come easily, as we all must have experienced. Look, from time to time, I too buy a ticket, but I try not to be habitual because it is very easy to get carried away. Like Kenny Roger's song says, "You got to know when to fold 'em", and let me tell you I know when to do just that and walk away.

I was the type of guy that was always on the prowl for something new and different I found it easy to settle for my pen, manuscript and my computer, just to be able to communicate with you in ways that can shed light on some things that you have not seen but would love to see. That may be the reason that I take real pleasure to spend the time so that you may be edified with enlightenment that will sure help you to find your way.

What I am dedicated to do here is help you to avoid all of the pitfalls, so you may celebrate your progress.

Be careful not to allow the feeling of laziness to take a hold of any of your intentions to make good of anything. Whenever you get those feelings, think of just what you are about to lose on account of that. Always count the cost. There is always something to gain and something to lose.

As I have told myself many a time, life is for changing things, and believe me there are so many things worth changing. Right as we speak, there are too many to mention, but keep them in mind, and change them whenever you can. Whatever you think about that is worthy of your attention, is also worth pursuing. That's the reason we try to encourage you to think of all the good things that you can, because those are the same ones that may be part of your plans for the future.

Little did I know that when I was a very little boy some of the things that I am now employing would be that important and extremely helpful in my present endeavors. Everything can find a suitable place in some of our preparations, so never think for a moment that your plans are good for nothing. Just remember, everything is something that can be put to good use if we consider it.

Life is not about throwing anything away. Everything comes from somewhere, and everything has its place. It's just like people, everyone has a role to play in life and it is as good and valuable as anyone else's.

There are people that really see themselves as unimportant, and that is just the way that they think. Everyone has right to their opinion. I often say to myself I might be important, but I'm sure up to doing some important things. What I do is, first make sure that whatever it is that I am doing has a place in society enough to be counted as needful and necessary. I have to know for sure that it will benefit someone in a tangle way. Then I feel that I have contributed to some cause or the other. I am not doing this just to boast, in fact I am hoping to inspire you to go way past your complacency. After all, we are alive to do things, whatever they are. I have never heard of bones walking and talking, making plans, or something like that.

Here's what I tell people, and God knows that I have said this so many times. What I would like you to do right now is look at yourself and think of the many people that are not here. They are not even on a vacation, they have no more chances, nor the opportunities we have. Sometimes I wonder about people. Do they appreciate this precious thing that they have called life? There is nothing like it! Nothing can replace it. Once it is gone it is gone forever, and that is why I encourage you to take hold of everything good, and I mean everything. I am not just talking about money because there are some things that are much more important than money. Life is one of them.

Every day I try to be better than the day before. The way I do that is I think, then think of alternatives to everything. There is a better way; we just have to first find it.

You see, when I find what I am looking for, I lay hold onto it for it's now mine, and there's one thing less to pursue the next time around.

As I move along on my way through life, here is what I keep in my mind constantly. Everything that I learned was like money in the bank, which means that some day it would serve as handy little tools of my trade. You see I count everything learned as a piece of the puzzle. Truly enough, everything you learn becomes a piece of your puzzle, ready to use when you need it.

Whatever the case, don't ever think anything is too trivial, because any time now you may recognize its importance.

I saw this gentleman building a deck for a friend of mine. While in the process, I heard him mention that he didn't like using some the materials because he thought they were too short, ,but little did he know that you don't throw anything away until the whole project is done and over with. To his great surprise, most of the materials that he wanted to get rid off became very important for his finishing touches, otherwise it would have cost him hundred of dollars, which the client wouldn't like to pay.

The general rule here is to think things through, and be very careful to avoid that impending pitfall that would cause too much frustration. Those are very simple mistakes most of us have made many times over and over again. .At the same time, those mistakes are necessary sometimes just to have us pay closer attention, while at the same time learning how to correct them.

Don't get too hard on yourself when things don't go right the first time. Just about everyone, everywhere in the world is subjected to the same situations. Why, because we are not perfect in any way, although there are some people that present themselves as perfect. Don't let them fool you. Maybe they made some of the very same mistakes that you have made, enough times, to learn the right way.

In general we should always try to keep things as simple as possible, just as long as the end results are what you expected. As long as the job is done well, and the recipients are happy it is a job well done for both you and them.

The idea is to avoid as much of the difficulties as is humanly possible. Nothing makes you feel better that to know that when night comes, and you slip into bed that, you can and will have a great night's sleep. Remember the next day you are at the task again with one intent, and that is to do as well as you did the day before or better.

I call that progress.

What else would you do in life but to prepare for better things each and every step of the way? Don't forget that every step does not mean flawless steps. After all you are just human, and I really don't know of any one that is immune from making mistakes. In fact, it is inevitable. It is all part of the regular occurrences of everyday life. So whatever you may do, please don't disappoint yourself by expecting anything different.

For most of our lives we spend quite a lot of time worrying about what may be the right thing to do. I think if you look inside yourself, you would find out just what the right things may feel like. If in fact it sits well with you, that may be your heart speaking to you, and I'm sure you will find good answers there.

We are all human beings made with all of the necessary characteristics that can shape us into fine people, capable of doing great things. So why do we sometimes doubt ourselves. It's beyond my understanding, but I promised myself that I would never give up trying to help in the very best way that I can. For me, that is trying to inspire and motivate you to go beyond your complacency, and to awake the giant that lies inside of you.

I can assure you that you will know when he awakes. You will feel a burning desire to do things, especially some of the plans that you made years ago to start building your financial foundation. Often what whips you into submission is, as you take a good look at yourself and realize that you are a little older than last year, and have not made the progress that you might have wanted to, you're aware that time has moved along, but you have not.

To me, this is the best time to light that fire inside of you, and let it burn. The hotter it feels, the more the urgency is to get going. You see, something has to be the driving force in our lives to help us to move. For most people, it is their responsibilities that drive them. It is difficult to realize that you now have a child or two, a mortgage, and a car to pay for, and yet spend most of your time playing games. This is not an investment for now nor later.

I make a conscious effort each and every day to build for a better possibility. I never like to leave things to chance, although that is very easy to do. I feel the consequence would be too great, so I plan and plan again, check and check again, until I am satisfied that I am on track and going somewhere. Now, that feels better and, I'm looking at progress down the road, and can tell you it feels great.

I'm sure you have heard too many say that some day they would like to have a house, a car, and a nice little family. I was one of those who said so. The difference is I made it happen. That's where dreams become reality. It really matters little if you keep on dreaming, and yet do nothing about it. What's the purpose of the dream?

To me, dreams are like wishes. You dream about what you want to happen and yet do nothing about it. Stop the dreaming and start working on the things that you dream about, and see the difference it makes. Once you realize the results, you are now on fire to do so much more. Isn't that something? You may even feel like calling that self motivation.

Prepare for big things. Begin with small efforts. As a matter of fact I really don't care what it all amounts to, I will plant that tree, and believe or not, I will not expect that tree to bear just one fruit. In fact, I really do expect thousands of fruits.

What I'm trying to say to you is that the present is very small compared to that of the future. If everything goes as planned, you will realize that the efforts you made today turn out to be way too big for your mind to comprehend, but that is the way it is. It's simple, nothing from nothing equals nothing.

I just think it is high time that we come to know that our life began, and the truth is, where it ends no one knows. Frankly I don't think we can waste time watching our life from a distance. That's exactly what happens when we fail to occupy our time doing nothing.

Every now and again I promise that I will give you a true story. A relative of mine on a tropical island told me, not very long ago, that they had on their plantation banana trees which bore a huge bunch of bananas. She kept an eye on it as it matured over the months. It came to the point where it was fully matured, and began to ripen. One day she asked her friend to harvest it for her. He agreed. The next day he came to bring it in for her, only to discover it was gone. The next week the other one that was ready was also gone. How unfortunate.

The fact of the matter is, there are people out there that would do simply nothing all day and when night comes they get on the prowl like night hawks. Although it was a discouragement to her, she kept on doing just what she knows how to do best, and that is to continue to plant with an expectation of a harvest.

The moral of the story is whatever they stole would be finished, leaving them with nothing. They have just created their own pitfall instead of progress.

Somehow, I think the world is changing. I hope it's for the better. People everywhere are coming to grips with the fact that they have to be more involved, and inclusive, in order to see the results that they are looking for. For a while they would rather stand around, and just imagine, what one may call of dream.

It became apparent that they are weary from doing nothing, and having nothing. I agree that by being included in the process, and preparation, creates a better way forward. Actually, it was overdue. Everyone should have the willingness to pitch in, to makes things happen better, faster, and with a bigger production.

In my work I have spoken to many younger people. It's known that they are the up and coming generation. I don't think they are aware of that, and we must be very careful to pass on that sort of information to them. How would they hear it unless we tell them?

It's far too easy not to tell them and see them be swept away with a fast moving current.

I can clearly recall the time I spent with my dad, and my mom. I simply loved spending time with them because I have learned so much, even though I really didn't appreciate their true value. Even though I was very willing, looking back I don't think I can place a value on the things that I learned. As a matter of fact, I am still implementing some of the lessons that I stored up inside of me.

I think it's our responsibility to teach those valuable lessons to the younger generation despite the fact that sometimes they rebel against paying attention. In a way, that is normal since we cannot force people to do what we wish them to do. As a matter of fact, I teach that it is wrong to tell people what they should learn, especially when it comes to learning a skill.

What I try to do is first find out what they are like. Once I find that out I move to the next level, which is to try and show them the value of the choice they've made, and find a way to make it happen for them. That's a much shorter road to a better outcome, otherwise you may waste a whole lot of time that you could of use for much better things.

What I got from my dad was a lot of the basic things , but they were real good things that can be applied almost anywhere in the world. I call that preparation for life. There are things that we just cannot do without. Those are the things that we should grab on to first. The rest will follow in a timely fashion.

If you want to make progress in life, first get rid of the potential pitfalls. That is called seeing in advance. Think of things that have to be done by you. Consider what you have to do to make progress; nothing should happen on the spur of a moment. Things like that seldom work. Everything should progress gradually to the point where you are fully satisfied.

It's like a tree. First you sow the seed that becomes a small tree. Then later it becomes a much bigger tree. Ultimately there comes the fruit, which is like the essence of your patience. We must wait for all good things to come to pass because whether we want to acknowledge it or not, there will always be times when we may feel like nothing is going to happen at all. But wait, and remember that Rome was not built in a day.

There was a time in our lives when we were so small, creeping, and rolling around, but we did not stay there. Gradually we grew into little boys and girls, and soon enough became adults. With all of the nurturing we were given by our parents or guardians, sometimes we can turned out okay.

In my case, I am more than happy for the way I turned out to be. Look, I am still thanking my parents for all of their help along life's way. Whatever they gave me was well received. I'm sure you have heard people say time and time again, that if it were not for their parents, they really don't know just what they would do. I have said so many times.

As I said previously, I was prepared for life today. That's the reason why I became what I am, a man that is always searching, always digging deeper, to find what is possible. I am very fortunate to have that sort of drive. It's the person that I am. The answer is there, we just have to ask the questions. After all, this is a personal quest.

When I remember the words seek and you shall find, knock and it shall be opened unto you, I know that happens to people who are looking for their personal best. You never stop seeking, because it's by seeking that you shall find.

Whatever the case, please don't hesitate to ask the question about anything that comes to your mind. By doing so, you are clearing the way for a great discovery that you may use as a magic key to open all of the possibilities.

I bet you didn't think that clearing the way, by asking questions, would serve as a master piece of the puzzle to guard against the impending pitfalls. Now you can prepare for progress.

It was I who ask the questions that led me to one of the greatest expeditions that I have ever taken to date, I remember well the day I embarked on that perilous journey not really knowing what lies ahead, all that I had to do was to trust in faith, especially as it was the very first time I had ever taken such a journey, there's always a first in just about every thing.

What ever the case it was very exciting for me to go through all of the steps that led me to my destination, the place where every thing that I do goes back to that place. I have heard some one said that if you stay the course with out too much distraction, you can bet on it that I will worth it in the end, and so it was for me, I am still enjoying the fruit of that journey.

It is very true about the fact that it is not where you start in fact it is where you end up that matters most. I can really attest to that for it has happened to me personally.

Some times all that we have to do is to try at least, just about every thing that I know about has had it's beginning, some times good , and some times not so good, as they say it is up to you what ever the out come may be.
Trust me it is very true, just try asking the questions and pretend that you are answering them too, because, all that I can say to you is I tried that and it works , as a matter of fact some times you do have the answers.

I think for the most part some time we just rely too much on others for all of our basic needs, in earlier chapters we talked about we were all made with all of our own faculties and is quite capable of relying more on our own self, what happens is that we get lazy, the fact if some one is constantly giving towards your needs, to some people it doesn't seem necessary to try and get by our selves.

One time all that I had to do is to pretend that I was tossed in the middle of the ocean alone with absolutely no life preserves, what would I do if no one came to rescue me, I would soon become fish meat, to my better judgment I better be able to decide on some thing fast, and that I did, not only did it but in record time too.

I love the word reliability ,there comes a time when we should realize that it is like just us and no one else, let me tell you I some how get the feeling that you would do all that you can to take care of you.

Having a sense of self is a very good thing, after all in the normal course of things we came into the world alone, so I think we should also consider that we owe it all to our selves, when it comes to making things happen, believe me I had to learn and adapt quickly enough, yes, I got help along the way as is humanly necessary, actually may be that's the reason why I am so quick to help others, it is because of those who help me to be me so progressive, I never liked pitfall I would give any thing just to avoid them.

That is the reason why we must do every thing within our power just to avoid them, because they are there, and some times for good reasons, I truly believe that things just shouldn't be too easy, every thing as it points is to challenge us, our strength, and our purpose. I'm sure many of us have seen what happens to people who have got things way too easy, some how they don't seems they appreciate it quite as much as the people who really have had to work very hard to obtain what they have.

Just the mere preciousness of life alone is enough to have us asking tough questions, if in fact what ever you are doing is just foe the good of it, shows the appreciation for life, some times I find myself doing things for the fun it provides, that is the pleasurable side of it all, looking for rewards in any place that you can find it, some how that makes it easier for the for the remainder of the time.

Find your pleasure in the things that you do , and that of course will brighten all of the dull areas thereby making exciting, and fulfilling.

One of the reasons that some of us find fulfillment in the things that occupied our times for the most part is because we love life and living so much that we just have to bring things from thoughts to action, like some one said don't just dreams act on your dreams, make it meaningful, giving you enough time to set back just a little and, if at all think of the benefits.

If you notice just living life alone is nothing but boring to say the least, I would much rather walk the streets and say hello to people I didn't even know than than make no investment in life in some sort of way or the other, because at some time there will be a pay back, I hope will make me very happy.

How long are you going to hold on to your thoughts, it's like stopping the stream from flowing, do you know just what that can cause? I have seen people hit the ceiling just for having waste their lives and as reality sets in they realized that they had simply nothing to call their own, to me that's very sad, especially living your life so unaccountably.

Look the person that said think and grow rich was very right and true, for all that he had to do was to write a message to the world, and there you go he became rich enough that he was also able to inspire the whole world. What do you want for being alive, come on and please do some thing with your life, just don't seat there and think for a moment that some one will come and throw in your lap all that you ever needed in life, after all you own your thoughts, so you can do what ever you wish with it.

If not you have just created a monumental pitfall, but no progress. Think some times I think all that we have to do is to ask ourselves is how can I make myself comfortable, with out suffering like some others do, just know why they are suffering and that alone is enough to change the way that you think, I have seen quite enough people out there that really do better but all that I can do is to wish that they would, because even a wish some time is good enough, you remember what they say ,be careful what you wish for because you just might get it.

What are you wishing for just think about some thing for long enough and low and behold it becomes a wish, and as they say a wish soon becomes a dream, isn't that good stuff? it was not even long ago some one said to me, you are always thinking, and I replied yes I am a thinker, I am following good example, because I believe if you think deep enough you can surely change things even your own life.

I really had to do just that , after spending all this time around my parents and other influential people that had a lot to do about who is me today, one of the many things that I did was listen a lot, say thank you and process all that I heard, I just didn't want to pretend that I had full control of every thing, when in fact I didn't, we have to be wise to allow others to teach us about what we just don't have.

Humility do count for a lot of things most of the time, the smart Alex one are usually the ones that is left holding the empty bag, and if not careful will hold it for the rest of their lives, what a sad picture.

How to change that is to develop your full potentials, believe me that's not really hard to do, all that you have to say to your self is, what do I want to accomplish in my lifetime, be honest with your self, and have a clear answer, one that you know you can live with, and go for it.

believe me I know many people that had simply nothing but a very humble start in life, what they was to make a good plan, one that was very realistic enough for them to sink their teeth in and gusto the results are amazing, just do your self a big favor and start thinking, not necessarily small things what ever you have the ability to accomplish, that's just what they did and I think that if they can do it so can you.

What I want you to realize is to take a good look at all of the pitfalls way back in the distance behind you, knowing that you now have made it past the danger zone avoiding all of the dangerous pitfalls for the progress that you now have. Celebrate that victory

Some how I think that every one who steps out of that the place to where he/she is most comfortable there seems to be a little question in their mind that makes them feel sort of uncomfortable, that I know for sure is very normal, for it has happened to millions of all those that are already successful, so please don't allow that sort of thing to grab you too hard, and then again it is also good to know that you are feeling that way.

With persistence and purpose you will soon enough feel like the end results are so much more than that, and may be I should just try to pass that period.

Do you want to have some of the finer things in life?, well they will never happen until you come to grips with the fact that this life is just great with all of those unevenness, and that we must constantly look at all of the factors, simply because they all would have a part to play even in your situation, some times it almost seems that we want just a little too much, when it comes to some of the things that would give us a little jolt.

As I have head several time over and over again, that we must come out of our comfort zone, and come face to face with our challengers, other wise they would most certainly adverse effect on our life in general, that's true because for some a little scare is all it takes to stop them in their tracks, while there are others like me who welcome, the scare, simply because I really love a challenge, and for that I use it build my determination ,that works for me, if you care try it some times, and see whether it could ever work for you too.

When ever I say to people that I love dealing with what is a menace to me they seems to think that I am crazy, or just what some people may call, you are sick in the head, but let me tell you just for the records, that ,that couldn't be further that the truth, and in fact I am a very realistic person ,who happens to see things globally.

May be that is why I love to aim higher, so I see further, reach higher, if at all to touch the stars if I could, okay, now this is one of my impossibilities but I will still pretend ,as both you and I have heard so many times in the past, and even right now in this present time that to pretend is a sort of working to have just what it is that you don't have, for at least it certainly keeps things fresh in your mind.

The truth of it all is that the more you think of things is the clearer you see you see it, just like the artist he/she will never be able to draw a good picture, without thinking to be able to capture in the mind first before putting it down on to the face of the canvas. I made much more progress today, as I side step the pitfalls.

Each and every day we were asked to count our blessings, because every day has some thing good in it, and for those that are in search of just what it is that they are looking for as soon as they have found it , they get the feeling that they have accomplish, may be enough for today, tomorrow is another day, and may be with much more of the same ,some times better.

Dream, imagine, grow are all part of the human spirit. Don't let it die, once it does it's like you have lost your soul, some times I liken to be like the fuel that drive the engine.

It is very important to develop ones self after all that just that we may be able to handle every challenge feeling stronger.

All along I had this feeling that I just cannot allow myself to lag behind every one else, and think it's okay, simply because we are all have to give account of our selves.

Here is what I thought every one must have and that includes me, I want to have enough to give rather to have to ask for, so when we talk about self development this is exactly what they are talking about, as some one said there comes a time when every man should be able to stand on his own.

From the time which is a few years since, it's like it has a special place in my brain, that constantly serve as a reminder to me, then I think of self reliance, it becomes very difficult for me to not to do some thing I just feel that as long as I have life, I will try at least to stay healthy, believe me that is all that I need, and the rest is sure to follow.

I read a sad story about this man who has six children, he made sure that they all had a good education at least, while he himself is a professional builder, so they are developed adequately to manager themselves, but we have forgotten that education is not common sense, if couple together it becomes a rather powerful tool.

That is just what is missing, the use of too little common sense. What I found strange was to see that all of the children have had one or two of their own children, which means that they must have gone straight from finishing school to having their babies, to me that was very unfortunate because that seems to be the perfect recipe for the greatest pitfall there will ever be, I am only praying that in the midst of this bad situation comes out some thing good, which we can call progress.

Life can be very unforgiving at times and by that time it simply would be no ones fault ours, we are to keep in mind all of these things as we go on, why wait time is moving along and of course we must too, there will be some time major set backs, but that is going to help us develop the kind of mindset that is necessary to help us build character.

For every thing that we choose t do, there will be a plus to it , some time it may not be the kind of thing that we planned for so what we may have to do is to be able to differentiate the difference. It's like the stones, the sand and the rocks all in one bottle, what would we do if we didn't have them all, life will throw all manner of things at you it is completely up to you to take what is going to work for you best.

Look, it is simple to do it this way, just stop all of the complaining, and adapt to some positive thinking and get to work, all through life we spend way too much time dwelling on the wrong things while hoping to get all of the right results, unfortunately that's not the way things work, it's like the oil spill, every one blaming every one else but them selves, I tend to look at just what may work to create the immediate fix that we all want and need now, and deal with the rest of the blame factors later, may be I am thinking wrong, but when I saw that in which I was looking and tried to pay close attention to what was called quite a disaster, was to on all account put every bit of emphasis on stopping the leak , then move to what is to be the big clean up, restore the wholesome ness of the situation, saving lives and lively hood, then we now focus on prevention. Does that sound like a plan? I hope it does.

As there are no guarantees in life so there are no saying that some thing couldn't happen or would never happen again, what is for sure is that we know now to at least try to avoid it in the future.

I look at life this way what ever can happen will happen, it is very hard to say it is for the better, simply like this it was all bad which ever way that you look at it, what we all hope for is that to see things return to a state of normalcy, every one is healthy and happy.

What I hope that we all take out of this and other similar circumstances, is for us to say to our selves and all those around us is thank God for life to see all of this, and every thing else, because is only with life we can do all of the fighting, the hating, and the swearing, which will never do us a single bit of good.

There are times when some people got heart attack and died in the middle of the situation, after it is all settled let us all prepare for a celebration, and especially giving thanks that we are all alive to say despite that pitfall we are able to count the progress.

There is always a happy ending, especially when there is progress.

One morning as I sat on the deck of my home just over the back yard garden, it's spring time and just about every thing in the garden is looking brand new, all shrubs ,and flowering trees are beginning to fill the immediate surrounding with its' presence both in beauty and some times the overwhelming fragrance, while at the same time very welcoming.

You see life is like that not every thing will give us the kind of satisfaction that we like, but if we in fact we would wait just a little while we just might have what we want. It is a sincere desire of mine that all those that wish for nothing but the very best would one day just have that wish, and much more.

What we may have to come to grips with is that life is simply not perfect, and there are times we may say to our selves, that despite it all I really love life, and I will do all that I can to muster up the strength that I need to succeed at the end.

It was only too recently I had a conversation with an individual who thought of retiring from their job, simply because they were having a sort of hard time with certain coworker who were relentless in their peskiness, what that would of done for that person was certainly going to have quite an adverse effect on their life, so I ask one of the many questions that would ask in situations like this, and that question was , okay, now have you thought of this long enough, have you in fact make plans, and put them in place, knowing just what you are going to do when that time comes, with no surprise the answer was no, what I saw coming was quite a pitfall, and xi was very happy that I have had the opportunity to have this conversation.

Every now and again we may all have times when things seems like unrealistic to say the least, but wait times can be even tougher if we just don't take of things especially using some thing that I call alternative thinking that my carve out a better way forward. What I was able to see from my vantage point was that person was looking on one side of the road, which left them exposed to being blind sided by the lack of attention of what coming on the other side of the road.

The warning has always been posted, look both sides before you cross, if at all just to avoid the potential pitfalls. One thing I am very happy for is that I was there at the perfect time just before the decision that would change to a life time of misery.

Although there is always a need to be cautious, we also have to be cautiously optimistic, there must be some thing to believe in, after all we are still human, caution should be just to help us stay on course, we must go while at the same time being fully aware of the many bumps along the way.

There were not a time when I did not experience all sorts of bumps, what I did was to use every one of them as the reason why I must succeed, because I give every thing it's fair amount of force adequately enough to make sure that it is just what I needed to be successful.

Far too often people stop themselves from achieving their objectives simply because, they are treading way too lightly, if in fact you are going to do it, do it with power, that creates assurances that will never let you down no matter what.

It is time that we realize that we just cannot keep doing things half the way, and be happy with the end results, what we are doing is setting up ourselves for a great fall, and no one can tell me this is what they really want, when you think about it there is simply no half life it's either you are alive or not, and with that realization, you do all that is with in your power just to accomplish nothing but the very best.

Some people don't get exactly what they wanted but at least they get some thing, some times it's the way it may be for a while, and I can tell you for sure it's always better to have things come in increments for some people it is the best thing for them, not every one can handle the full load all at once, I have seen people that got themselves completely out of control, simply because they couldn't handle it.

Even me, I found out the hard way in earlier times which helped me greatly as I moved along, as I have heard my mother say, son, one thing at a time it's a very good rule as many can tell those were lessons of the past, but great for now and the future those words I will never forget as long as I live, there are carefully stored up in my achieve which I can recall from time to time, and some times to be used as bench marks.

Let me help you with this if I may, one thing to keep in mind is that you should always have a good listening ear, for some times a serves as warnings against potential pitfalls, without listening is like saying you have all of the questions and answers all coming from you and that is one of your first mistakes, no one has it all, many of the people that thought so have sadly failed not only themselves but all of the people around them.

I don't know about you, but as for me I think it is my sincere goal to keep my eyes on my immediacy just that I may move way past the pitfalls as I focus on my progress, after all this is all that I work for and nothing else, all of the others factors means simply nothing to me, they are like byproduct that I don't really care to count in my inventory, call it what ever you want ,but I call it progress.

My God sustained my life so I can do all of the things that I know that I can do, and what I learnt I recalled, one to them is with

God all things are possible, that gives me the strength to press one more time.

Some people even feels that they have done it all, and now there is nothing else to do, but remember that no matter how much you have done, count it a privilege to be able to do some more, you see, life is not over and it's with you all for a good reason, as far as I am concern you just never stop doing, as the good old song says do it till you are satisfied.

I love life especially because I can do not just for me but also for others, now here is some thing that does have significance ,or could have, and that is when we are thinking of our selves to give a little thought to some one else, just to experience how good it really feels to do good.

We can go back a little to the weak and strong, it is quite general in life that there would be some that would be stronger than others, and it's also very true that as we all know that the strong will have to support the weak in some way or the other, life requires it, and in fact it is some thing that we should not hold back from doing.

What I have noticed is, that may be the world is changing for the better, and that is lovely to see, there are more people wanting to help others than ever before, I am personally happy to see that, what I think happens along the way that the need was so great that it became unbearable and unwelcome enough that people every where are taking notice, adapting to a new serge of willingness.

Isn't amazing to know that we can depend upon one another for help when we are in dire need?, it's like knowing that you can call on a family member or a real good friend, and know that you are going to get the kind of support that you desperately needed.

Actually that is one of the many reasons that I write this simple and easy to read and understand book just as a contribution to your life.

Don't get me wrong it is not that I feel I can be all things to every one, God knows that I don't have all of the answers but I can assure you that there will be a word or two that you can pick out that can shed some light on as you make your way on your journey.

Look, all that I am doing is to help you to recognize that the pitfalls are there as you focus on your progress.

As you make your way through life you are sure to meet many undulations along your way, which is actually very common as we all at one time or the other that the world is not flat, to prove that point just take a trip to the rolling hills in your area, and you will see just what they were saying.

The same is very true in life there are a plethora each and every circumstance in life, we can call them turns and twists at every corner, of course that is exactly what causes the challenges to appear, but don't be dismayed it is only the test of the time after all there must be some things in life to help to strengthen us as we move forward.

What it is ,there are far too many people trying to get every thing the easy way, lets face it just about every one would like a little break from time to time, and if can fact you can call that easy well so be it.

Where we can all get caught is when we rely on the easy factor that we refused to do any thing that poses a little challenge, as I said before a little challenge is very good for us, in fact it causes us to have a far greater sense of determination, believe me I had to face the very same things that all of the rest of the world faces on a daily basis, all because I really wanted to say well done at the end.

I would like to see you try that some time, just to see and also feel the rush that you will get right after succeeding in what ever attempt that you make, you might in fact try and get us to that all of the reasons why we struggle for it will be around both now and after we are long gone from here, that is the reason I call them pitfalls, the good thing is that we don't have to fall into the pits.

Coming to think about it why would you even think that this would be a good place for you , that's why we make choices to help avoid some of the more unpleasant things that can happen, I don't know about you but if I can help it I know that I will be making the sort of choices that would make me feel very happy in the end.

I think most people would live all of the finer things in life but are some what lazy to work towards them, the truth is I know people that can do things to change almost every thing in their lives but they just wont make a decision that would have them move to the next plateau.

I come to realize that laziness is a heck of a thing, and will affect our lives in adverse ways, that after a while may having us filling very disappointed in our selves, simply because we have so little to show for the time we are here. What is more sickening is to be here and see some people growing down rather than up, don't let that be you, there is just far too much to loose.

One of the many things that I would love to accomplish by writing this book is to help you to get excited, may be for the first time in your life for making the decision to rise from the pit to the podium where for the first time you will celebrate your accomplishments with a heart full of gratitude and pleasure, can't wait to tell the whole world of you journey from the pitfalls to great progress.

I think it is very important for us to take this very serious and not ever start to do any thing significance with out first making solid plans to be successful at what it is that we take such pleasure in, if not the whole experience will be one of greatest remorse that will plague for a long time to come.

What I have seen is that there are way too many people finding them selves starting over too many times, not only that they are wasting too much time and efforts, but it is also costing them far too much money to do, why be in such a rush that you cannot take all of the planning serious enough to make sure that at the end there would be that satisfaction that will give you much of the courage that you need for the next phase of things.

Success is not the idea but in fact it is the results, that is what drives me to do the things that I find pleasure in, what I had to do was to make sure that every thing felt just right at the very beginning so as proceeded I would be comforted by it, other wise every thing that we do would be a constant trial and error, which some way in the process would serve to be the thing that would frustrate you the most, and in fact hinder the advancement that you expected.

If you are going to build a cupboard you must think of what it is that you are attempting before you deluge ahead, not realizing that before long you my have to start all over again, some times you may have to make sure of your measurement to calculate the amount of material that you will need before proceeding.

Look, I want you to do well that is why I took the time to do all that I can to help you in almost every area of your life, and I will make you a promise that I will continue to do just that, simply because at the final draw it is not about me it is about us together finding our way in this vast and some time unforgiving place.

I must agree with you that some times it takes great amount of courage to go on, but what would you rather do go on or stand still with out trying at least.

Believe me I see some people trying at hard as they could , but with pen or pencil in hand mapping out and charting their way to fulfill that quest, those are real admirable times for me, because I get to see them doing some thing about what it is that are hoping for.

It is a real joy for me to see people trying to help them selves in almost any way that they could, it is what we call taking charge of their personal journeys holding themselves accountable for what ever the out come may be in the end.

The more we can inspire people to avoid the looming pitfalls is the more we are able to help them be prepared for the greatest progress of their lives.

As I write this message to you bear in mind that it is up to you to maximize all of your efforts just to tap into what is known as the abundant possibilities, after all if you paid attention of writings of the past you may notice that there has always been an abundance waiting for you to lay hold on it, this has been made available for us at the inception of the world, so if in fact you didn't take what is rightfully yours you may have no rights to blame any one for taking it.

With just about any thing that you want, you should also know that you should expect that you will have to work for it, and although there are some people that think working for what they need is against their policy, well think again, what if half of the population uses that method what would really happen, I don't even want to know.

For that matter what you are sure to hear people say is that is , and mind you this is only related to those that chose to pursue despite how they feel at times, other wise there can be the reason for the big disconnect.

My rule is that I don't care what others have I want to have mine, and one thing for sure I know I would have to work hard for it which is only fair, if you notice the people that worked hard for what they want in this life, does not tolerate some one coming along and snatching it from them, what ever their reasons might be, nothing can really justify that type of behavior.

All through my earlier life I was told by my parents that it is quite an honorable thing to be able to rely on my self for just what it is that I hope to accomplish, those words keep ringing in my ears even now that I am an adult, I really don't see the need to let such valuable teaching to sleep away from me, those things are very hard to come by these days, it is just as if the people responsible for these kind of teaching are gone and is not coming back.

That is why I try to look for the good in every one as I make my way through life, and as I find it I hold on to it for dear life, as if to say this is some thing too valuable to let it pass me, part of the reasons for that is I know that I don't have it all, and that I must be constantly learning, which only serves me well in my pursuit.

What I say now is that I am so rich, every time I use the word rich people usually open their eyes as wide as they can, but long before I'm finish speaking they would know that I was not referring to money as my ultimate expectation. What happens people generally fail to recognize that there are many kind of riches.

For that matter I will tell you that I am very rich in knowledge, and possesses a great amount of wisdom, which I am very happy for, but not only that, I am a much nicer person an account of that, what is even better with the knowledge that we possess we are better able to witness from a vast distance what could be pitfalls that may hamper us, leaving us with nothing but the progress that we hoped for.

I realized that if you have ambition it is easier for you to attain your goals, people tend to develop a strong sense of determination, and it's all based on their ambition, to them it's like if nothing is going to even come close enough to stop them from making it, I like those people that no matter what comes in their way they will kick it out of the way but to make it they will.

I had to do the very same thing, first thing for me was to make quite sure of what it is that I was after, they study it very well, and know for sure that it was the same thing that I spent quite a long time preparing for, and feel good in mud gut, by that time I know for sure that I was driven to succeed, and with that type of drive I find my self going steadfastly forward to the goal that I love and expect.

I don't like wasting time mulling around it's either I am on or not, and my type of attitude I usually find my self making it to the end successfully, you see, I realize that time and tide will never wait for me nor any one else.

I spent quite a lot of time with my dad in the low land on some of our properties, so from time to time we would go down to the beach, may be to do some fishing, which was mainly our real goal, but I also noticed that the waves as they came ashore, they were in succession, one after the other, properly timed with no end in sight, now that has been a few years since, but I can challenge you that if you would go back there now it's like time stood still, because the waves are still doing the very same thing, like a symphony it plays the same old sweet sounds from waves beating on the shore, a sound that will thrill you from start to finish, but the finish is not because it stops ,in fact it is because you are gone.

There is an element of willingness that embed it's self in some things, especially those things that are controlled by nature, what we got to do is to take notice of some of these things and may be learn why they are the way that they are flawless in motion, and constant in it's workings, the unison in which they work with their surroundings, I think they are providing us with a sense of togetherness that make things work very well with them selves.

If in fact we would pay attention we could learn all of the valuable lessons that will help us to be so much better in many ways.

A few years ago my dad and I had a conversation, which was more of a lecture than any thing else, I gave him my full and undivided attention: Here's what he said to me, he said son I know for a fact that I will not be here with you forever, so I want you to listen to every thing that I have to say to you, because I want you to be better than me at the end, and that is I hope you will continue to learn all that you can from every one that you have the opportunity to listen too, because that is simply the very first step to learning, if you listen you may hear I hope that you will.

What I said to him was, dad thanks for all of the lessons, I know now how to avoid the pitfalls, if ever I am going to have progress.

One thing I can tell you is that my parents are long gone form this earth, but I am still listening and learning from them, I can never thank them enough.

From here I have decided to try at least to make the very best out of life all by the choices that I make, because those choices will guide me into my future, which other wise would not have been, because life has a way of presenting us with so many things all at the same time, that if we not able to decide for our selves, and at a reasonable time frame we no doubt may suffer some major set backs.

Although some set backs do have a place in our lives, simply because they command us to take a second look, and re-assess things before they take root, it can also be the very last thing that you want to have to deal with.

Things are simply things, they are here, and we must recognize that they will always be a part of our world, so learn to live with them, and in fact allow them to be part of the decisions that we may have to make from time to time.

When it comes to deciding what to do based on what you expects, just think of your personal fulfillment, just what makes you happy, and satisfied, remember that you are now doing all that you can just to please you first long before any one else, right after that the rest of the people may have their say, simply because you know that you have given the very best that you have.

There is a reason why we make personal choices with out going to every one asking them to decide for you, what may in fact may happen is every one knows some thing about every thing, so you will be having quite an assortment of people's opinion that may or may not work for you, that is the reason that we tell you to please your self first, you see, what happen is that you know that you are giving this all that you can, by your judgment to be the ultimate best, there is so much work gone to this, all of your time efforts, money, and your labor of love to have it made fragmented by all those that just does not have a full understanding of what you have done.

Keep in mind that making all of the right choices is a simple way of, strengthening your self so you can beat, and win against the pitfalls that is ever present, and will by all account defeat you as you try to make the kind of progress that you want and deserves. Keep your eyes on the ball, if in case winning is what you are looking for. Tune out all of the distractions, despite the difficulty of doing so at times, remember you are choosing to do so for all of the good that you expect.

As you read my work I hope you will get all of what I expect you to get, that you may add to what you already have as you make your way to the progress that will bring you joy, peace, and happiness for both you and all those that matters most to you.

Let this be a note to you, that there are times you may have to turn another page in your life, that simply means that if in case many of the things that you have tried, just failed to bring you the results that you had in mind, it's okay because that is exactly when you should think of one of the other idea of yours that may prove to be the straw that will break the camel's back, it's all about winning.

Some time I feel that I am the prime example of that, like I said before I have studied, and practiced many things all in preparation to avoid the pitfalls, and so I did, and some how I get the feeling that you will too.

Just in case you have decided to do just that, credit your self for all of the times that you spent getting ready for days like this, look! have you ever tried to drive a car in a single gear? there are times when we are compelled to change, and in this case this change is for nothing but the better.

I remembered some one saying to me one day that it nothing but a waste of time to pursue a course in carpentry when in fact you wants to be a chef de cuisine, the thing is I can decide to be a one dimensional person knowing how to do just one especially when it comes to being a skill, now mind you I have heard people say that it is sort of crazy to be a jack of all trades, and a master of none.

I would advise you here and now that when ever you hear those words keep walking, for it's far better to know a little of every thing than not knowing any thing at all.

One of the many reasons that I am bringing this up to you it is very discouraging to those that might of thought of involving them selves in what ever the occupation may be, which can only serve to broaden their knowledge making them more versatile, and flexible.

I have turned many pages in my life and I am very happy that I did, for today I am reaping some of the greatest harvests in all of my life, simply because I am very adaptable to almost any situation that come my way.

One must be able to make an independent decision to at least be able to see and avoid the pitfalls before it is too late, and take full responsibility for what ever the out come may be especially when it comes to the progress that you need to make.

When it comes to the progress that you hope to make, that should be foremost on your mind, and simply nothing else, I set aside some of my fun times just to focus on my expectation, I also knew that it would take quite a lot of my attention, but as far as I am concern I just wouldn't have any other way.

I spoke with a man who fell deep into the pit a few years ago and as far as he was concern, he's had it way up to his eyes brow, and felt like giving up, simply because he was so deep down, and never thought that he would ever rise from there.

My message to you is never be afraid of what I would call the valleys of your life, I can even assure you that they can even serve you very well, as I paint you this picture I hope you may find the light there on.

There are mountains, and there are valleys, they are both serving each other very well, what ever leaves the top of the mountain slides down the sides to the valleys, all of that nutrients will be found right at the base of the sides of the mountains where one might call, the valleys where good things grow faster, stronger, and better.

There are people who are caught in the same situations, what I discovered in the lowest time, and place in your life is one of the very best place to do the best of your thinking, and planning, because you are already down the only place to go is up if you are ambitious and willing to adapt to a new level of thinking that will help you to arrive at the place of strength and courage to move on.

One of the reasons that I arrived here is because I was in that place, and the truth is I had to do all that I am now expecting of you all for your own good, so don't be afraid to listen and learn what we have gone through to be where we are today, I became as strong as a lion with great amount of determination to make it to this level.

I can assure you that if you are serious about your personal growth nothing can stand in your way if you are determine enough to make it, I listen to many people and very attentive so as to learn well, and believe me, on account of that I will tell you that I have stored up quit a lot that I can use for many applications.

The reasoning behind this is I felt that is I just wanted to be the man of the hour, rising to any opportunity that came my way, I just had to be really in charge of my own destiny, and that was the reason behind my willingness to adapt.

If in case you are going through some life's changing situations remember to stay calm and reason things carefully and patiently with a good measure of confidence that you will succeed in the end, once you clear the way it's time to realize that your pitfalls are now behind you, and you are on to the progress that is rightfully yours, especially after working so diligently to be satisfied with the out come.

Simply put, no one likes being in the valleys, but remember that we all got our start from being in the valley, we were delicate little babies when we were born that grew up to be boys, girls, young men, young women, then full blown adults who happens to have little ones of our own, all of the natural cycles of life, you see what happens to little things that grew?, and so it is, our humble beginnings , how can we forget.

I can recall what happened in real life as we walked in the valleys where we had some of the very best vegetation that has ever grown nothing but the biggest and the best of some of our plantation were found there.

Now the reason that I bring this to your attention is because thousands, and thousands of real people face that same situation on a daily basis, and for many of them had to realize that what they had to do was to start thinking and making their plans right there, that' where they were.

Some didn't make it, as they say may the best man win, in this case it was not because they had more to offer, but because may be had a little more courage, some times that is all that it takes, for with courage you will find strength, and strength will give you determination, now you are on your way.

What makes me love this part is because I have been there, I have lived that life, I can tell you that for me nothing came easy, when I hit bottom it was me, my self ,and I for a while, I had to learn to survive on my own, for that matter it was there I learned how to ask of God, you know what it feels like when you ask just to hear every one say sorry not now, but the now was what I needed to take care of first, I knew enough to realized that the rest will follow at some point in time.

My hope was realized, but not until I made a desperate plea, believe me it was now or never, this when we would find out how great God is, some one came to my rescue, and I was saved from perishing.

What ever you do in times of trouble don't give up on any thing nor any one, in fact keep hoping, and trusting some thing will happen that will change your situation from potential pitfall to a bountiful progress.

Really that's when you get to know that life has real meaning , I found that out and that's the reason I am telling you some of my real life's story just that I may inspire you when ever you get into a bind, and think that you will never make it.

What ever the cases hang on for dear life, you are sure to make it in the end if you faint not.

It is very possible that you may face some difficult times ahead as you prepare to your self for succeeding in what ever it is you are pursuing, one of the many things that can really make things difficult is that if you are the going alone kind of person you will at some point in the process get overwhelmed by the shear enormity of your endeavor, it is not that it is that big a task, it only gets bigger simply because you are doing it alone.

That can produce many set backs, if in case this is true what you may have to do is to involve others in, that can help you to do much better, two heads is always better than one, you may save your self from hardship, by realizing that your opinion do count for some thing, but there may be a much better chance for succeeding, when you factor in the opinions of others.

Your growth will come much faster and with a greater ease, than doing it alone, you may never make it with that approach, which causes you to loose interest, resources, money and every thing else, simply that's not the way to go, and as a matter of fact if you are going to escape the pitfalls, you must keep progress constantly in mind, because that is really what you are working for.

I remember from a few years ago how my father and his friends did it, there was a time my father was adding to our house to accommodate the family, so he called his friends over to give a helping hand, with no second thought they all came to his help, and donated much of their time to help him build, before you know it the job was done, and the men, they all left and went back to their own.

This was a constant thing that would happen, when their chance came he returned the favor, not only was the job done in record time ,but it was done with love, and care.

The gains were triple fold, the satisfaction, the joy, just knowing that they were helping friends, it was simply amazing to each one of them, because they know they were taking care of each other.

There's comes a time when money should not be the ultimate goal, and that is the reason I think we should bring back those a old values, like artifacts they are as good as gold, and should be treated as such, we should even consider using them as bench marks as we go forward in almost every area of our lives.

I even head my father saying to me, son all these words are true, and don't forget that, because no matter where you go in this world you will find them useful, helpful, and even necessary helping you to be able to see in advance where the pitfalls are in order that you may arrive at the progress that you expect for the efforts that you have made.

Not only the end justify the means, but what you are doing is setting your self for a life time of success, at the start every thing seems bleak, but you may notice that the closer you get the brighter it becomes, then you know that the rewards are in sight.

I know of people that have experienced that first hand, so I used them as mentors, when a question came up all that I did was go to them looking for the answers that would help to clarify things to me, all that I wanted to do was to stay on the right track.

For all of those people that don't ask, just remember the good old saying, that ask and it shall be given, those words were long before our time, and will outlast all of us, so don't forget that you may not have the answers for some of the things that you are doing, so you should be humble enough to get the answer by asking some one who knows, at least more than you.

A little while since I met a gentleman who wanted to start a business, but he realized that he just didn't have some of the basic understanding about some aspect of the business, so he came to me with the idea, just to have a good conversation relating to his business, after all he realized that I have had various business experience, and that he could trust me for some of the kind of support that he needed.

I was more than happy to spend as much time as he needed to help him in the planning stages, because that is where he was a little weak, one thing I wanted to remind my self of was we are here for each other, and I wont turn my back on him, in a general way most of do need that, starting a business is not always pleasurable to begin with, but after things get going one can have a great time, knowing that you are now on the rails going some where.

As some one said, when the going gets tough, the tough gets going, this is very true in more ways than one, I also heard some one say that business is not for the weak knee, you got to get tough, and I don't mean destructive, but rather determine to succeed, don't lay back after you have invested thousands of dollars, and loose it all because you just didn't take it seriously enough.

Keep in mind that you are now building a life time of success, that is what you are doing today if cared for will out last you, at the same time make sure that you enjoy your self to the fullest, enjoy the success that devoted work has brought.

After all you have conquered the pitfalls just to gain the progress.

I really had a great time doing what I was doing be it work or even when I was playing around doing all sorts of things, to me that was going to be the number one thing on my list , other wise things can become quite boring, and that happens to every one, that is why some one said that all work and no fun makes jack a dull boy.

I have seen people become quite intolerant and so simply because they have been working so much, and saved so little time for fun, if that is the case with you it's high time that you recognize it and get rid of it before it becomes too systemic.

What it is, I think we ought to see the true value of both sides one is that you will have to give your undivided attention to all that you do in order that you may be very satisfied with the final product, while on the other try not to let weigh too heavy on you that may even cause you to be missing all of the good times.

I love success, success gives me a brand new way of thinking, because the more I do good at any thing that I do is the more I want to do, I hope it's the same for you, it seems like I just cannot get enough thing, and as a matter of fact I don't know who can, any thing good is plain and simple good, and any one with any sort of appreciation would tell you that it makes them very happy.

Here's a very big part of just why I become so happy as I succeed in what gives me such pleasure, I had to take a good look at my self, look at where I came from, all of the things that cause me to arrived at this podium at the first place, and then I try to seek ways that I can impact other lives, that's where some of my joys came from, the fact that there are so many people that just can't find the inspiration in side of them to go beyond their complacency, thereby causing them to fall out of contention.

I have checked things very carefully and what I have discovered is that I am very indebted to all those that are still struggling, what every happened we all do have a part to play in this world, because although it doesn't seem like it but we are all connected in simply every way what ever.

Just in case you are experiencing joy today I want to share your joy, and the same is just in case you are experiencing sadness, and sorrow I want to share that with you too.

What that does is to open up my senses to your state of being, and to find out just how I could help you better able to over come just what it is that you are experiencing.

My greatest so far is knowing that I have done some thing that will serve the purpose of removing you from the brink of the pitfall, and putting you face to face with your progress, I really want to let you know that I take great pleasure in your personal growth, and accomplishment.

My advise to you, and all of you, is to take things personally, and do every thing that you can do to make your time on this earth a living legacy, it really doesn't make a bit of sense to just live get old and die.

Some thing tells me that you really didn't have a good time nor enjoyed your self, after all part of being here is that you may appreciate being here, and that despite the pitfalls, you will have the progress.

Here is what I had to do as I made my decision to do for the things that I really wanted. It became very clear to me that I had to make some of the very best choices that could ever be made, I can even say that may be responsible for saving the day for me. Just remember choices, choices, choices that will be the reason why you may make it or break it, you decide.

What both me and some one that I know had to do was to carefully analyze from thoughts to action, leaving nothing for chance, when you make a decision to some thing real important, it becomes a priority amongst other things, giving it full attention just to make sure that you are making it according to plan.

Just about any thing that you try to do with a plan will may fail, this is some thing that any one will tell you just in case you didn't already know. The fact of the matter is life requires a plan, make no mistake about it, because it is all yours to loose ,and I real don't know of any one that is in the loosing business.

It's very much the same like investing a heap of money in the stock market with out knowing any thing about what you are doing, first we should invest in knowledge, know what things are about, any thing less is like going in with your eyes closed not being able to see, the next thing you know is, you are standing at the pitfall, but remember what we said earlier, every thing requires a plan, and that was the reason you found your self at the brink.

I can tell you for sure ,and this is as real as it is day that I found my self in this same position that I am now telling you about, it was not a pretty picture, what I had to do in that moment in time was to stand still for just to regain my composure, gather my thoughts together, reconfigure my whole situation before I could try to get back on track.

The fact is because nothing, simply nothing could hold me down I was able to regain my former position, and move heading to the thing that I wanted most of and that was the progress that I wanted so badly.

People say if you want it you can, but you should prepare to work hard for it, and believe me I am always up to the challenge, nothing is too difficult for me to at least try, for it is by trying that you have a chance to succeed, there is no other way, as they test the waters, you will at least get to know how deep it is , and whether you should jump in or not.

Look, life is not perfect, as nothing else is also, we were ask to take calculated risk in every thing, especially big and, some of the more important things that we will do.

The fact is we simply cannot leave things to chance, so we must take, time and care just to avoid all of the pitfalls, if we are to have progress sustained.

There was a time in my life when I thought every thing was that easy, until I came to grips with the true reality of how it really works.

First to begin with, don't ever let any one tell you that you will wake up in the morning, full of vim and vitality ready to conquer the world, its not quite that easy, there are times when you just even want to think pass your breakfast, never mind getting things done despite it is on your list of priority to get done.

Have you ever heard of the word shackle, yes shackle that is when your mind is so lazy to think of no matter what it is you want to accomplish, and what is worse it will happen for as long as you allows it to persist.

When ever this happens, one of the best things that I can recommend to you is for you to take a break, go for a walk, or some thing like that, when you return you will feel like you are now ready to continue from where you left off with, and yes, with all of the vim and vitality that you need to push you over the top.

I can recall a time when I had to stand up and start doing the jumping jacks to get my blood warn and ready to push this thing past the finish line.

Here's what really helped me and may be it will help you also, begin by anticipating the end results, enjoying the fruit of your labor, the moment you get your self imagining that you are on your way for sweet victory, but it will not come until you get a good dose of determination, that is the key to al most any thing that we do.

You got to feel up to the challenge, and I mean feeling excited enough to make you start singing a four part harmony all by your self that is how climatic things can become, when you are all revved up, and ready to blast off.

Some of us want what we really want , and that is success, but we were wise enough to know that it was not going to come as they say by over night, the fact is if you do all of the preparation, and do things the way it should be done, there is no reason why you should not be expecting the results that you deserves.

If you are lazy, and want every thing for free, with out making any contribution on your part, there will be absolutely no harvest for you, and you will have to put up with the hand outs from other people, which can be very humbling to say the least, and for that what you have done is to place your self right at brink of the pitfall, and keep your fingers cross that the wind wouldn't blow, just remember where you are standing, the is little hopes left.

May be you will have to do like I did, if you have good ideas that make a lot of sense to you, it's like a thought, don't just sit there with is, jump around, get excited then do some thing about, sow that seed it will become a tree, and guest what, the fruits belongs to you, the whole lot of it.

This is called success, remember? you have had nothing, and now you have a harvest, that's a far cry from where you began, but wait I have a far better word to describe it, I call it progress, may be it's because I love the word, then again it's the meaning of the word that excites me, how about you.

One thing for sure before all of these wonderful things can take place, that lazy mind of yours will have to be renewed to make place a far better way of thinking, it's called the renewing of the mind, it may feel like starting all over but it's okay that's what you need any way if you are to make your way forward.

Just in case you did not know to renew the mind is telling yourself that you are now willing and ready to push the metal to the floor, and get this thing going, after all it's like a new endeavor and you must give it your full attention, there is no time to slack off any more, the time for seriousness is now, unless you do that you are no better than before, standing at the brink of the pitfall.

People may look at you and wondering why are you starting this thing again, but keep doing what it is that you are doing, because you are doing this for you, and no one else, the start is belonging to you and so is the end.

The bible says, he that started a good thing is faithful to finish it, no matter what happens this job is all yours to be finish, if you should give up this opportunity to accomplish may be what might be the greatest of all things done by you then you have disappointed your self, and you will regret it for quite a long time.

The fact is why do we want to start some thing, first it's because we see some thing good in it, and all of the other obvious reasons, that any one can have. It could be that you have found your place in this world, doing what you like, and also some thing that will help to carve out a good future for you and your family.

Just remember that you are not alone in this, there are as many people that have lived like you, having to change from one thing to another because it was just what they had to do in order to get what it is that they wanted. Look, don't be afraid to of any change, they may bring you the greatest surprises that you have ever had.

Some times it's like walking a new road in a new area, some place that you have never traveled before, new things to see, including a change of perspectives all that is good for it will inspire all over again, that's the way I felt when I made real adjustments in my life, today I am reaping all of the benefits that the change brought, and loving every bit of it. the thing that is so special about of it is that I made the kind of progress that I am very happy for.

I work hard and I earn well, progress will not come unless you do.

Lets face it most people that work would tell you that they do it for all of the benefits it brings especially the financial aspect of it, because it is the one that most people would tell you that this is what they wish for the most, they would even say things like how else would I pay my bills.

Since this so important, let us spend a little time exploring just how to achieve financial freedom, some times it's easy , and other times it's not depending what the circumstances may be, so think well before you decide.

For some people building financial wealth is just to make sure that can take care of them selves and that of their families, but if you're like me perhaps you might even consider some of the others that are not as fortunate as you, and prepare to extend a helping hand, that am sure would be quite appreciated by the recipients.

Now on really securing the financial aspect of your life, that may seem more difficult that it really is, one of the best thing that one may consider is to find a project or business that you know quite a lot about, and explore it as much as you can, study it very well, and follow the direction that leads to it's destiny.

What I have done was to stay focus on building my financial dream, and with every thing considered I moved forward until I was very sure that I was making the kind of progress that I felt happy about, there were many a time that all of my efforts seemed impossible simply because there were just so many things to do, by my self, and it's not like I didn't want the help of others, some things just has to be done by you.

As I said before unless you are the dreamer the dream seems dim, so the best thing that I would advise you to do is to understand the dream, this is one of the very best way to bring dreams to reality, the fact is that you are now aware of some things that is very needful, and necessary to fulfill your financial quest.

There are so many factors for us to consider, but at the end of the day, it's all about reaching to the place that you are most happy with.

I have had my struggles, despite all of the preparations that I had do go through earlier, what I knew for sure was that they would come in handy at some point in time, nothing beats experience, as they say hard work pays off, that is why we should try and take hold of every opportunity to not only look on, but to get involve, in every thing that would enrich you life in every way possible.

As we recall pitfalls are places that puts us at the edge of despair, if the winds blow a little you can find your self dangling for dear life, now you imagine it's no way but down, as I write this I really felt sad, simply because there are so many people that are in this same situation with out a recovery plan that they can rely on, so let me ask you where is the progress? I don't see one do you? as a matter of fact I really don't like what I am seeing, but remember you are the one that put your self there, now may be only time you can change it, and I sure hope for your sake you can.

As they say we have only one chance to this, so lets do all that we can to make the very best of it, because there is a time coming that may find us very regretful of what ever mess we find our selves in only it might be almost too late, for pitfall or progress.

People with no progress in their lives are simply people that are stuck and are going no where, unfortunately there are too many of them to even start counting.

I only hope that all of those people will be able to see that it is people like me that's coming along to change all of that.

It is my sincere hope that we can set in motion a plan that serve as a constant reminder to those that are really hurting whether they know it or not, so we can begin to see the sort of growth that will no doubt reverse that course, all for the good that we need so badly.

Now, as we that move along singing our songs like the little sparrows, we should also remind our selves of how lucky and blessed we are and the opportunity that we have to help change from being on the brink of pitfall to progress in the lives of so many. Some times I find it hard to imagine how fortunate I am, able to make good decisions to alter my course.

For that I feel indebted to the rest of humanity and with that kind of understanding I can assure that I will never fail you, just as God promised that he will never fail us all, that is why I am writing this book to you that you may know that there are people like me out there that are thinking about you constantly, part of that is because we were never expected to be all in the same place in our lives, after all some has to be teachers, and preachers, lawyers, and doctors, with all of the others in and between for we are all here to do what we are called to do.

One thing that I wish that we all would try to keep in mind is that we are to build our selves to the highest degrees so we can operate like connectors to the others, rather than swelling our heads with the feeling that we are better than all of the rest

What I tend to do is to just keep myself humble in order that I would be able to feel better of my self with the service that I am here to give, other than I can easily become like a sounding noise maker drawing all the attention to my self.

I am here to do all of the good that one can do, and I wouldn't change it for all of the tea in China as the saying goes.

You see not only am I here to inspire you but, also to motivate you to do all that you can with the life that has been given to you for the short time that it is, and while you are here be happy and enjoy every step that you take.

One thing for sure when you do good things in life, you automatically open the doors for much more good to happen, and that I know for sure, and not only that ,but it is a very personal experience, do you know how great it feels when you wake up in the morning ready to face the day knowing that no one is pointing fingers at you, all for the things that you have done that was far from being ethical? I don't know about you, but as for me I am a watchman to my self just to make sure that I stay true to my self and especially to others.

This whole story must put you face to face with pitfalls and progress simply, that we may make choices that are associated with our belief.

Don't allow your self to walk past some thing that may have an effect on you beneficially. The opportunity is yours to affect or change things for ever. This would be your pitfall. consider your progress.

It is funny isn't it? that there can never be too much good any time or any where in the world, the more you do is the more that is expected, in fact needed.

I check my self every now, and again simply because I want to keep my self feeling up to the challenge all of the time, not just some of the times, just take a good look some time, and you are sure to find that there are multiple of people waiting for some form of help or the other, there will never be a time when we can say that it is over now, that time will just never be a reality in our life time nor any other life time for that matter.

One of the reasons that I write is just to keep us all alert of the ever pressing need in this world, then one may say not just the world, what about the communities, in fact lets begin here, and may be fan our selves out like ripples in the water, one pebble at a time.

It is really not my intention to burden you with that weight, while at the same time if we do nothing the heavier it will become.

Look! it is simple, this all part of our imperfect world colliding with a whole lot of imperfect people.

Far too many times I bear witness to the blame factors, it's like some one is causing much of the unwanted problems, especially for lack of necessities of some sort, in my estimation there will always be a shortage of some thing that is very needful, and necessary to some one hoping for just what can be done to alleviate the stress that may be too heavy to bear.

Like there is a constant vigil to some thing that is monumentally precious, so is the same for suffering humanity, we must not go to sleep at night until we know for sure that we have done our part to bring rest to some one under the burden of some thing very heavy that they may need help with, we may not be able to reach the world ,but we can try to reach some one where ever they may be.

As we know the world can be very big, while at the very same time very small, so there are no more excuses for the distance between.

It was not too long ago when I got a call from this older woman being troubled by a swam of bees right over her front door, that just won't allow her to enter, when I arrived on the site, there were thousands of busy buzzing bees that came much too close for my comfort, good thing I was bold enough to get close enough to point the raid right in the cluster, that made them a little crazy but I was able to take down a good many, which settled them allowing her to at least open the door and made her way inside.

To me it was like mission accomplished, hope to have a much better day the next time around.

In life there's always a need, and the need doesn't come to the rich, or poor, black, nor white, and all shades between, in fact it covers all sorts of humanity.

What I was very happy for was to know that we were able to turn that pitfall into great progress, and the wonderful opportunity to get a whole lot of good from a little bit of bad.

I love pitfalls to progress.

Just be careful about what you allow to stop you from progressing in life, there are so many obstacles in our way, that if we are not careful we may just dop it all and head back home, believe me that is certainly not good enough, we are to face all of our obstacles with a renewed sense of hope that there must be a much better way ahead of me, and if that's the case I must find it .

A long time ago I decided that I would be entirely up to me to change things for me first then for the others, all this is based on passion and purpose, if we are going to succeed, we must be prepared to face the daunting task of working with both the difficulties that lies in our way.

I always believe that there arc no easy ways out , but there are ways in, what ever the circumstances I am fully prepared to do the very best with what I have been given, and some times it is just the willingness to step out and into the thick of things despite what it looks like.

What ever it is that stands in our way may be in it's place we just have to decide just how to work with it, even moving beyond it leaving it to stand there like the monument that it may be every thing is in it's place just where it ought to be because the same can be said of us, we just have to do what it is that we have to do which succeeding, despite of it.

When coming to think of it quite a lot of the obstacles that we face daily are very good for us in more ways than one, they can help us to understand that there are opportunities that comes on account of them, take a good look and you may see for yourself.

By now most of us have heard the old saying, that if it didn't kill you it will make you stronger, or better which ever comes first.

There are good and bad in every thing, simply because they are here in the world with us, and part of our lives.

In order that we may have progress we must also have the recognition that there will be pitfalls in the midst of it all.

Some times it appears to me that we are still like strangers to this place call earth, I learned a long time ago that what is here was meant to be just like I was meant to here to do what I have to do.

I am full of determination to be successful in this world, not just for me alone, but to be able to do the very best that I can to the benefit of others.

I invite you to join with me, and lets share our lives with that of others as we try to make meaningful contributions in what ever way that we can, there are simply no set ways for us to do that, just what ever it takes to see some one happier today than yesterday would be dandy for a little bit can go a very long way to those going from pitfall to progress.

Do you want to see progress in your life? Do you think you can make it if you try ? then what is holding you back from at least trying, do you know that trying is the very first step to success ? no one knows for sure but at least we should try to find out.

There might a big surprise, but only if you would try and continue to the end, there is a great saying that goes like this, (he that started a good thing is also faithful to finish it", then and only then can we expect to claim that prize.

One of the main reasons for this book is not because I know it all, in fact I know some, cause I am still learning, so as I learn more I will pass some on to you, not that you don't have , but every little bit helps.

Before I forget the reason for the book let me tell you now.

You see, earlier on I really struggled in every area of my life, but I counted it a real opportunity that the struggle brought, first, it made me think, which was one of the very best thing for me, the thinking caused me to set myself in a learning mode, so I took in every thing that I could, and stored it in the back of my mind hopefully to bring it forward when I needed it most.

Today I can dig up some of the almost incredible ideas that can be found any where, or in any one.

As I said before, in fact let me say it again when difficulties come just don't drop down and die face it boldly, for it is not that unusual there are millions who have faced the same or similar things in the past and survived to write all about.

I am one of those people that I write about some time, simply because I know more of me than any one else.

So bringing you this book is because I survived so that I can edify you, and inspire, and motivate you to stand strong, if you are going to fight to win.

I knew winning was my ultimate goal, and that nothing was going to sway be enough to stop me from moving way beyond my complacency, I always say to my self keep moving for with those strides you can only get closer to your goals.

despite what any one can say, I know for sure that I am much better than I was last year, and that's hood for starters.

As far as I am concern I am still at the beginning stages as I work towards the big one, this is my   next goal. Successful people are constantly planning for their next move, as they say we got to keep moving on.

What I would love to see is that I inspire you enough that to make you jump up from where you are seating and rise with power, power that not even you knew you had, I have done it before I like to disturb the nest, just to see people get restless, and start doing what ever they can do, to move them from the brink of the pitfalls to unprecedented progress, yes, there is such a thing, and you will know it as soon as it happens to you, because you are going to work full steam ahead without looking back until you really move from pitfall to progress, it's like home at last.

Just what is pitfalls and progress any way? well if that is the question you are asking, here is part of the answer.

We all know that a pitfall is like standing on the brink of a cliff, I was there at one time in my life, until I to decide just what the heck I'm I doing there first, there are times in life when through no fault of our own we just find our selves being there, what we have to decide is how long are we going to stay there.

The fact of the matter is this a place of dangerous existence, unless we become careful enough to realize that we can end up in quite dire need for the rest of our lives, not a pretty picture.

But wait, this may be one of the very best thing that has come along in quite some time, simply because from here on you must make the decision that will change all of that, first you should have a willing mind to go beyond that position, so as you can tell it is going to be entirely up to you, to seize the opportunity to change your life.

I think what many of us fail to realize is that this is the place that rich people has come from, make no mistake about it that they are rich because they were born that way, for most of them, the reality of standing at the pitfall was part of what it took to go beyond where they were.

Now I hope that you can get a clearer picture of just what you might have to do in order to change things from pitfall to progress.

As some one said there must be a happier ending, but that will not come without a happy beginning.

Take a glance back a little and you are sure to find that, just what I mentioned earlier about liking things first may even produce that better finish, why put lots of time into some thing that has no real meaning to you, just call that a waste of time and, money too.

Please don't get me wrong, that has happened too many time over, even in some prominent places , now, that may never mean that it is right, for lack of judgment along with poor planning will undoubtedly bring about that out come.

What we must do is to always keep in mind that we owe ourselves the right and responsibility to take care of things far better than have done, to avoid at any cost falling into the pit for that will only do one thing, and that is to erode all possibilities.

In essence what I really wish to say to you is that you should spend enough time thinking, that is the little word that has a very big implication.

This is when I think, hope has brought this one is just for you, and that you may take it very serious, if you are going to get off the pitfalls in order that you may move on to progress.

Progress is quite admirable to me especially where I came from, I even said laughing that I only wish I was born on the right side of the track, but that was simply not the case. Any way, it really doesn't matter I am here, and I promised myself that I was going to be very determined to do the very best with what was my opportunity, to demonstrate what it all meant to change what was the status quo.

look! may be this may be your only opportunity to read a book like this one, that delve into things so deeply yet so simple, the fact is I just want you to see from a much clearer looking glass, so that you my get what is the real picture that I am trying to bring to you.

You can rest assure that my message to you is for real, may be that is why I call this a non fiction.

This gives me so much pleasure just to know that I have accumulated this sort of experience from my life's involvement in just about every thing that I can recall, and I am even happier now to know that some one some where will benefit from this, and for that I am so grateful.

A few years ago as I stood at the pitfall pondering what was going to be my next move from there, all sorts of things flashed before my eyes, for a while there my mind became a little cloudy at first, but as I began to think deep inside of me it became quite evident that I had what it took to move me from there to just where I am today.

From a personal point of view some how I think I know just what you can do if you dare to try at least, so as I listen to people say that they can and will never be able to do some thing I wonder how long have you tried, the thing is for all of these people none of them have even bother to attempt, so some how they bare not quite fair to them selves.

So what do want me to call you lazy? or unwilling does two and two make four.

Part of my blunt ness is you have not simply because you tried not, I could of been like you instead I decided to get involve, and get this wheel in motion for this is the only way to get any where.

My father once said to me son keep your self waiting for any one what if they didn't show up would you still be waiting and for how long, the answer is no one knows, so you do the best that you can mean while, and just in case they didn't show up you are still way ahead, and better off.

It really saddens me to see some people not making any investment in their personal life.

There is a time when we must take not part but full responsibility for self well being, it's our right, no one should not have to tell you what you are going to eat or wear tomorrow, that should be your choice, but that will be your choice if you made preparation for that.

Pitfall is like living dangerously on the brink, while progress is being just where you expected to be in life based on just what you have done to enrich your life with the many amenities that you have put in place that you are now so happy for.

It's simply amazing to see what happens to the many people that have struggled in earlier years, and now seating at the dock of the bay watching the ships roll in, to many it became an almost enviable place to be, but just keep in mind that it could be you at some point in time, all based on the preparations that you have made in your earlier days.

Each and every passing day I feel I should tell my self that yesterday was only yesterday, and that what ever I will do today should better than yesterdays accomplishments, you see, every day should be able to account for it's self, in that I am very satisfied with every bit of what I expected, all because I feel that I will put all that I have in me in order that may have that expectation.

What ever the case try not your day to sink into the sunset without you feeling satisfied with all of the many things that you planned, and have accomplished.

In order that you may feel better at the end of the day make sure that you just don't over stocked your self in the hope that you are trying to do too many in order that you may have much, the idea is set limits to yourself to the things that you can really accomplish in a given time, other than that it would be like all of your efforts are in vain, and living you sort of down trodden to say the least.

A day is a day which means that no matter what you do this day will come to an end at some point in time, so what we my do is to expect that tomorrow will come, and we will pick up from where we left off, so please try not to overwhelm our selves, for that can only help to set us back, and may be too far if we are not careful.

We must keep our selves in check all of the time making sure that we are staying in focus, God knows it is so easy to miss the mark side stepping our selves in nothing but the wrong direction, then you might find that may take away much of much needed energy to get back to where you were.

Really there nothing really wrong about that simply because it has happened too many times to count, living you may feeling like it is starting all over each time

We have to allow the human side of us to exist for the greater part, because that is who we are, while at the same time realizing that it is a constant reminder that we are to try to stay in contention at all times.

At the end of the day as we take inventory we should, and for that matter that it was all in a days work , and that you more than satisfied with all of your accomplishments, that's what it is all about, as long as you know for sure that you have done your very best that should be good enough.

What I try to do is to measure my successes with all of my efforts just to make sure that there will not be any disappointments lay in waiting for me in the dark corners of my trials, after all how else can I move from pitfalls to progress.

Lets face it some how we all came into this world almost individually, at we were born as they say with all of our faculties and that if we use them there is simply nothing that we cannot do. That goes to each and, every one of us, so why then there are so many of us waiting for some one else to take care of us, like we are all little babies, just take a close look at your self and you are sure to realize that the baby stages are gone a long time since and it wont be back not even you were the king of the universe, so please don't wait.

There is no time like the now, I realized that when I was a little boy, so by now it is very hard to pretend that I can ignore the now which is may be the very best time of my life.

My dad once read a passage in the bible to me, and up to now I still can remember it for all of the right reasons, that is why I keep saying to kids that you are young all but once in your life time, so it's wise to begin to lay the foundation now while you have all the time in the world that will serve you very well in some future time, after all I had to do the very same thing that I am saying to you right now.

The good thing is here I am giving you some of the valuable lessons that my father passed on to me, and one of the many reasons that I am passing some if it to you it has already been tried so we know that it is true, I happen to be a living proof of it.

The fact is I am quite a good listener, the first step to learning any thing from any one, any time, all of the great men and women today had to go to great length in their educational pursuit so I am very sure that they will quite agree with me that one of the reasons that they are some of the great leaders of today is because they kept their ears to the ground.

I am quite a giving person, my parents taught me well to give a little or as much as you can, there is so much more from where the first set came from.

The time that I spent listening and learning makes me very happy to be able to give some of these lessons to you, God knows that I am not the only one, there are many who realizes that what they have is not as a matter of hold and keep because we also learned that it is far better to give than to receive.

What I find my self giving to you now I hope you will use it fully so that you may move from pitfall to great progress.

I hope that you also take courage, and realize that all of the ones before you were like you or me with out much, but with willingness and determination came the enviable trophy that stands like a monumental bliss.

You will be happier when you move your self from pitfall to progress.

For any one trying hard to change his or her situation in life, just think that despite all of your intention to do well, there will be times when you may have to face the reality that yes, you can all of the things that you are wanting but it is not going to be easy as you would like it to be, so we use what we call hope to push us along to our expectations. One thing that you should always try to keep in mind and that is a quitter never wins, and a winner just never quits, those words almost all of the worlds inhabitants have heard before, so we should be quite aware of that by now.

Look, just face it may be you can tell where in this world things would be easier than right where we are, the fact is there are far too many people running mad trying to find what they think might be easier, one thing I can assure you there will always be like this mass exodus of people dissatisfied with where, and with what they have , and are looking for some thing better.

Although is very normal, some times we seems to forget to realize that what we are in hunt for might be right below our noses, so I think that we should an-a-lyses the present situation first before we start a brand new journey looking for what we already have, it's a very common mistake most people are making on a continuous basis.

In life we should try to get answers for most of the many questions that we may have, simply every answer holds a new clue to the things that you are trying to accomplish, the mistake that quite a lot of us make daily is that we become very reluctant when it comes to talking to the right people, try not to run around to every tom dick and Harry hoping to find answers, because they may need just as many as you.

There are a plethora of quite prepared, ready and able to go to for the right answers, after all that is what they are there for, there is a time in our lives that we must consider, as time to start helping those that are willing to at least try, also what's good about that is they after a while may be able to help those that were like them.

I also think that those that are prepared should also know that we all have a responsibility to share the burden of others, for this is just what life is all about, at the end of the day all of us can say that we have had a part to play in shifting you off the pitfall to great progress.

Unless you serve others, your life is not well lived, the reason why some one said so is because we are simply not here to take care of our selves only but also any one that you can help, in what ever way that it might be, the fact is as soon as you recognize some one is in trouble you should be right there to lend a helping hand.

My father once said to me, son, you have two hands one is for you and the other is for helping others, and both is really for giving good service.

I loved that so much that I now make it a great part of my life, to me it really doesn't matter how young, how old, how rich or how poor any one may be he / are still human in the full sense of the word.

One of the greatest things ever is for me to hear some one saying I love you, a little word that holds the greatest power that there is, but hear this, I remember one time I said that to a person, and a question came right back to me, like this, aren't you married, so I asked what does that has to do about it, any way I did not get a fair answer.

So I think I would love to take this time to clear some of that up, the word is just what is missing in our vocabulary, or for that matter may be misused which may be water down the real meaning of the word love causing us to misconstrue it's meaning. I love me very much that makes me a very caring person, so as for me I think I will be using the word love as often as I can, so we all may get familiar with this beautiful and powerful word.

I think we should all get back to some of the very basic things, just to get an idea of it's value and see if we can apply it to our lives today.

For instance the lessons that my father taught me I am still using simply because they formed part of my foundation, so even if I wanted to get rid of it I just can't, they are too much a big part of me by now.

What a real blessing, when I think of the times that we share with each other in the name of love, I can only say a big thank you, because that certainly helped me from standing at the pitfall to what is now known as the very best progress that I have ever made.

This page is for a picture of the cover of the book, and below the picture says

When you are tired, and feel like quitting remember these words.

I can do all things because He strengthened me. Please don't be afraid of the power of God, and just what it can help you accomplish if you believe.

I remember earlier there were pitfalls, and more of it , I was just standing on the brink all the time, it's like I just to hell and back.

The good of all of that was I was preparing for the event in my life as they unfold. You see, one must be prepared to do the walk before they can do the talk, it's like the gathering of information that you can turn into experience one day.

Along with that I spent a lot of my time listening to wise people as they related their experience to me, and today I bring my experience to you, but I am still listening, because I am still learning.

When I say that you can do almost any thing if you put your mind to it I really mean that, because I am the very proof of that.

When you come to think of it life is really too short for me not to have almost every thing that I can achieve, and have fun doing so , and liking it.

The fact is every thing as we know it is temporary including our selves, lets not keep on fooling ourselves that we are so special that we will be here for more than the allotted time that we are allowed, before you know it we will be long gone and forgotten.

Make the most of your time here, especially that of helping others which is part of the good work that we should be doing.

Some one helped you to move from the brink of despair while at the pitfall so we are to do the same for the rest.

That is why I spent the time to write this book, so I encourage you to read learn and, if at all just take what is in for you, that will help you to be a better person all around.

One day you may begin writing your life's story, that hopefully will help to inspire the world, and bring the type of change that will definitely make a difference in the life of almost every one.

If you can help to move people from what might be their pitfall to life's security, which mean self reliant and self supporting, then you have moved them to progress.

One thing that I love for sure is the opportunity to change my past, the present, and my future. I am grateful for my progress.

Some times you may really have to change the way that you think of things in general, that may mean finding better ways to do some of the things that you love to do, and then again you may find that the things that you love would be the very first thing that you should work on first, simply because every one will say to you if you love it half the battle is won when it comes to doing and finishing it.

Right on that note is where I say to people if you don't love please don't waste the time in even trying there must be a real reason why we all do things , and that is because we love it, then expect to excel at it.

There is some thing call fostering growth by involvement, simply put, don't think for one moment that you know it all, that is why we say listening is the first step to learning, then comes working together, adding what you have with that of others, and right away the project becomes bigger , and so are the rewards.

This is also a very good way to setting the stage for a life time of success. I knew this man who started a business from scratch doing every thing by himself, at the end of the day he became so exhausted that he was barely able to keep his eyes open, never mind having a balanced meal to up keep himself.

That was shear madness, every thing suffered to the point of him nearly having to close the doors for good. Luckily enough for him some one showed up just at the right tome, and saved the day, and the business.

What he thought was that he could own , manage, and do every thing by himself, little did he know that was not the way things work in the real world.

For a great portion of the time he found himself standing right at the pitfall, he could of lost his life, for saying it real.

You see, he thought that he would make a ton of money, and have all to himself, not realizing less could be more or better some times.

Now he can expect to get home at a reasonable time , have a good meal, and not only that, but now he is able to spend time with the family.

I don't know about, but I call that progress, and don't ever think that progress is only money, there are quit a lot of people that will agree with me on this, for instance I found a much better way forward that leads to a greater satisfaction.

I am so happy that I listened, learned, and I implement this is my progress, and I am sharing it with you.

It's right at this moment o feel compelled to share this little story with you, before I began this new career, things were rough, there were times I went up and down like a bouncing ball, one thing that I knew for sure was that this ball has to settle down at some time soon, so I became very serious, and start to pay particular attention more than ever more.

Let me keep it real with you, simply put I needed a job very badly, so I started by going through the classified as carefully as I could, until one day I came upon some thing that I liked, with any more hesitation I called up, and to speak with the manager, he literally interviewed me over the phone, and got hired at the end of the interview, simply because he felt that I was the perfect person for the job.

Before we concluded, he asked whether I could make it down to his office to sign the papers, and arrange for a starting date.

I entered his office, we did the kind of formal thing, like shaking hands, he offered me a coffee. It was right then he started to talk down the company, I was surprised, but I listened.

At the end he said to me, well, I wish I could take you on right now, but I am afraid I will have to wait till the boss comes back from vacation on Monday.

By then I became suspicious about some thing, he said to me call me on Monday, and I will be able to tell you better, so I did, that's when I knew that he was up to some thing, as we agreed to the Monday phone call, I did, that's when he broke the news that he changed his mind about the position. I did not get the job.

So here's what happens when life gets tough. As we all may know that life with out success can be a miserable life, it's like waiting simply nothing, so as I remembered that interview where I felt let down like a lead balloon, it's like I was now prepared to handle any thing that came my way.

From that time I have decided to really take matters in my own hands, as I began building one block at a time to take care of my self the best way that I could.

Today we have a building, and I am inside of it right where I belong, to me this is just one more time we are reminded that yes! we can weave a future from our tangled pass.

I came all the way from pitfall to progress. I landed safely with my two feet on the ground, some time I really think life is not for the weak knee, we ought to stay strong to fight if we are to win.

No matter how difficult things are , they can get better if you want them too, I have seen quite enough examples of situations that looked so dire and have changed to greatest, but that of course is only for the ones that are willing to write pages based on experience.

Don't forget that difficulties are only there to test you, as they say every thing is possible why would they say so if it they were not, the feeling that I get is that most things as we know them have been tried and tested long before, that is exactly why we can that every thing is possible, we want you to try, because it's in trying that we know for sure that we can.

While at the very same time we find ourselves preparing to compete in an all inclusive world, helping each other to get stronger, and better.

Competition brings with it true sense of willingness, as we show our abilities to accomplish more than expected, in fact if you want to have production to it's highest is to have every one demonstrating their ability to out done the other in a rather healthy way.

In the same instance I was quite amazed at just what I saw a little while ago, if you pay notice there are always some that are stronger, or faster that the others.

This guy couldn't be held down by any one, but you can rest assure that after finishing his task to find him willingly moving over to help those are struggling with theirs, the reason why I love this so much is because most of us have heard that there is no "I" in team, and that confirms it.

Those are the people that would say to you that they are strong, and that they are willing to help the others to get stronger, how unselfish I really love that, I am very inspired, you see, even though I am the one that is writing I can't help but to show my human side, and appreciate the greatness of others, that is exactly what is going to move you from pitfall to progress.

If that is the case I am with you all the way as I move to help this guy over there, progress a little faster.

I am really not expecting you run with break neck speed to get things done, but it is quite true there is an urgency in life that should be respected enough when it comes to getting things done, if it has to be done, then there should not be any discussion about it, instead let us take a hold of the time that we have and to the betterment of our own self, and that of the others.

Some times I feel like using the word consistency in my urgent quest of things,

the reason for that is one can build a sense of urgency in his/her need for consistency.

Simply put, I solemnly promise you that it will be done no matter all on my watch.

As a matter of fact I used urgency in all that I do, because I don't stop until I feel that is okay to stop now, why stop now, if it is good to be gin it is also good to finish.

Usually after starting any thing try to look way in the distance towards the finish, even though it might be no way in sight, what I find when I use that method every thing becomes easier, because it's like I am seeing the end long before I get there.

When it's your turn to see things that way, just know that it is a rather beautiful way to look at things, which for the most part stimulation your interest to go on.

Every thing in life becomes much more evident based on the choices that we make in life, every one says by all account try to make the right choices in the things that you are trying to do, the reason for that is because there so many options, one can easily get confused, then it's much harder to zero in on that choice, but what ever the case it is just the right thing to do, so we should leave little spaces in between.

Went it comes to doing things the better way which would you prefer, I am sure with out a shadow of any doubt that you would much rather know that what you do is to your expectation simply because it just better.

It is like the same with every thing else, we would much rather have the better of both worlds.

What we have to do is to keep it right up there when we are about to make the final decision, especially breaking away from where you are standing which is at the brink of the pitfall, in that case what ever you try not to look down, just keep your head looking up towards your prize, after all it is what you have worked for so why take your eyes off the progress that you have made.

Believe me nothing is better than finishing on the high note. Progress at last, and if that is the way you feel, celebrate it.

It is very true about celebrating every step forward that we make, it is a sign of success, which keeps on encouraging you to fulfill other important things that you are doing.

Every thing in life has degrees to them, it's like a tree it grows and grows into maturity, till that time of may be fruit production.

With us it's like the very same, we start and should not stop until our task is completed, and that we are satisfied with every thing thus far.

One thing to look out for is that as you tackle any thing, over a period of time we may find ourselves becoming sort of slow far from the way we were when we began, that is very normal over time tiredness can set in, and if you pay too much attention to it you may even find yourself stopping all together.

When ever that happens, in order that you may get back to the way you felt like when you began, is to start to think of the final product, I.e. the joy of finishing, the satisfaction that it would give you, and just simply knowing that you have had the pleasure of finishing high.

For that matter even our minds do have a way of playing tricks on us at some time, making us feel like lazy, if that feeling should persist for too long, your mind can become chronic, and every thing from there on becomes tedious.

One of the many ways to combat that is to take another good look at it, think of all of the planning that went into it, the anticipation that you once had about finishing celebrations.

Just remember that you were the one that went, and told all of your friends about, and just what you are going to say to them now.

With all of the above suggestions if some thing didn't work, drop it off your mind give it a week or two, allowing your thoughts to roam freely, thinking of the joys you once held of the way things were going to be, after that time period you will find your self bouncing back to that glorious beginning.

Now you are back to where you started it's time to go full steam ahead. It is very hard to produce with a shackled mind, once you are free you see all of the dangers of being at the pitfall, now you can prepare to celebrate in style with all of your friends for the progress that you have made.

Don't worry so much every one deserves a second chance, this is yours.

A great suggestion for you when it comes to doing any thing is when is to first free up your mind, so you are able to think well, remove any shadow of doubt, confirm to your self that this I just what I wish to do with the time that I have.

Once you have done that consider the source open and flowing well, nothing feels better and you are on your way to achieving what it is that you are hoping to succeed at.

I really like the part that start to think and start to taste the sweetness of the final product, that alone will give you all the courage that you need to go on.

Some people would say to you go on smell the sweetness of success, I couldn't help but agree more, because I have heard so many people say the very same thing, that it must be true.

After all what else would one do while building a house if not to expect to live in it when it is finished.

I have spoken to some people recently and about undertaking a good size project, and they said to me that they were feeling sort of jitters about it, although it is very normal it's like fears getting a hold of you, in order that you may find yourself sailing through smoothly is to look at fear straight in the face, grab a hold on it and toss it right in the window, and please don't forget to close the doors, and windows too.

The very last thing that you need is to be fearful about simple things. Fear is definitely an inhibitor, and will stop you in your tracks cold.

In every thing that you attempt, find a way to allow your freedom to guide you in the direction where you can explore all of your possibilities, so that you may find the assurance to get off the brink of the pitfall to a place where you know for sure that you are progressing in all of the areas that you would like.

Go ahead please your self with the decisions that you have made to bring real change to your life, then take it to the net level winning at every step, I know that it is hard to have it all at the same time, but that's okay, that is why we should be careful in the choices that we make, we are the ones that have to live with them, good or bad.

I will tell you this one thing, when some thing has to be done just go ahead and do it, you will feel so much better after, because you will find that the results are going to stare you right in the face, as if to ask you the question, so just what were you expecting? hopefully you will answer quite affirm with out a doubt, after all the out come is based on the choices and all of the planning that you have done that moved you from pitfall to progress.

Now let me ask you a question, are you afraid of success, if some one told you that you would be very successful after taking this special project, and it is some thing right up your ally would you say to them no thank you, after all this is some thing that you love and is quite able to do, what would possess you to say no, just think of the success that you will have.

The last time some one said so to me, was the last time they place eyes on me in a long time, simply because I made so much more than I expected, I just bought some property out of town and, relocated, and enjoying every bit of my accomplishments.

This is simply what life is all about working to change your life circumstance, and living to tell the story of it all.

What other way to get some bragging rights, but just putting your shoulder to the wheel, and going for it, take a glance back and you will find that this is the whole story of this book, it's all about not waiting for the lottery, instead creating your own.

You have to ask your self the question, do I have what it takes to move from pitfalls to progress? I hope you can do your self a good favor, and answer yes!, you will find that at that point of that moment would be all to start the ball rolling in the right direction.

I have personally noticed some one I knew, in fact when I was still a little boy, this kid was slightly older than me, but this is what he did. He had a bicycle which after riding for a while he would lend it to his friends, so one day he realized that he needed his bicycle while at the same time some one else wanted to use, so thinking cleaver enough, he went and bought another bicycle, now he has two, and since he couldn't ride more than at a time, he began to lend one out the other to his friend , but for a fee.

That of course started a whole new idea going, from one came two, then three, which climbed to as much of one hundred bicycles, but wait that did not stop there, he soon found himself moving from bicycles to cars, and then more business endeavors.

He became so successful that he was called one of the very best business operators in the area, and with that came all sorts of business awards. I knew him very well so it's safe to say I saw him move from pitfall to progress, not over night but in a fair succession of time. That certainly has inspired me to get off my back end, and find my self working to produce the things that I dreamt of.

From pitfall to progress, I love this.

As far as I can go back I remember always wanting to be self reliant, so I tried to all that I can to ensure that, no one forced me to do any thing, I knew that I was going to be up to me to get my act together and go for gold, and for that matter not only gold, but diamond too.

If you really want to make it in life you have to be prepared to face all of the obstacle head on, if in case you try to ignore them you are sure to find much more of them in your way, and that's when you may feel very stuck with little options.

One thing we should not do is to try to run away from our problems, because they will follow you every step that you take.

I can remember recording earlier that should know just what our problems are and get rid of them in order that we may have a much better time to focus on the goals that we set.

Whatever the case I prepared my self to work with the times, both the good and the bad times, simply because they always come together, we have to decide which one is going to take our full attention.

I know for sure is I am staying in the game as long as I possibly can, because their in lies all of my chances to succeed.

Whatever it is that you are hoping to find, stay true to the mission, you are the one in contention, and the one in need, find a way to excel at any cost, it is the right thing to do, if you are going to be able to see light on the other side of the tunnel.

You should also know for sure that in order for you to succeed you must be prepared to take chances, and there are no special set of chances to be taken just make sure that you are taking a chance on some thing that you have a likeness for, that of course will certainly take away some of the rough edges thereby making it easier for you to follow through.

What I try to see is the real beauty of every thing that I try to do, some time I may even paint a picture of things in my mine, so as to retain a good sense of it, some how to me it makes things work much better, it also helps to keep things in checks and balance, giving you a clearer imaginary picture, which really to stay on target.

Before you begin every thing is like a dream, so affirm your self that this the way every thing really began, no doubt we find our selves standing at the brink of the pitfalls, before we can work our selves to the progress that we are going to make.

If you take an honest look at life you will notice that there are really no progress with out pitfalls, because it seems like just about every thing has it's own sets of difficulties at the initial stage.

But please wait it can and will get better just if you continue.

Come on, get in the game, if you are going to make it to the top , you must begin the climb, there are way too many by standers, get involve, it is the only I know that to make things happen, some times we really waste too much time thinking about it, enough already.

How long is it going to take for you to realize your dream, remember that some times the dreamer may die, but does he care whether the dreams live on, get your piece of the pie, and enjoy it to the fullest, you have worked long and hard enough, this is your time have some fun.

One thing that I want you to understand is time will not wait for you nor any one else, time have simply nothing to loose only you do, for years you have been holding on to these precious healthy seeds in your hand, do you really want a tree at some point in time, then release some of them into the ground for only there they can grow into trees and even bear sweet fruits, worthy to share with family and friends.

Invest in your thoughts for they will soon become things, and multiplies into more things

you can even call that harvest.

You may think, that this is only a thought, but that is where the very best comes from, they simply just don't drop from the sky.

If you don't do some thing you will continuously be there waiting for some one to come along and give you, but be careful because what they are prepared to give you might not be enough, and just think of it for a while, by now you have demean your self to the lowest degree, I am sure that is not the life you intended for you, but as they say things happen.

Now if what ever happened was not good enough for you, the only thing to do is to fix it once and for all.

You have all the power within you to change what ever is not right in your life, other wise you will be for ever standing on the brink of the pitfalls looking down, but once you take charge of your part of the bargain you will find things begin to reflect more of the way you expect it to be.

I really like where I am standing at this time in my life, things could of been worse, but thank God they are not, and for that I am very happy.

The next best thing is to know that I took this opportunity to motivate, and inspire you, if at all to help you to seek that you may find what ever it is that you are looking for.

Can you see light on the other side of the tunnel as yet? keep looking, and keep moving towards it, and it won't be long till you will be there, don't give up now you are already too close to your goals, and in any case life is not about giving up, what if every one else did that, where would we all be today.

What ever you do please try and avoid falling into the pit because once you are there it will be very difficult to climb back up, so just avoid it at all cost, as you nurture your progressive mind to find a better way.

When I think of the things that I had to do to realize my dream, it's almost mind boggling, as most of us have heard the saying that if it didn't kill you it is sure to make you better, I can assure you that it has made me better.

You see, I knew that I really wanted to change things in my life for the better, and for that I would have to make some of the greatest sacrifices that any one can make, but when you are desperate for change you have to do any thing to bring it about.

There is no need for any one to sit in his/her comfort, and yet think expect that every thing is going to be okay, that's simply not the way it works, you must first know that you and only you are responsible for taking care of you , but you, there are times I have seen that people got helped because some one saw that they were willing to go beyond their comfort to do things for themselves.

That reminds me of the woman, who for years worked in several factories, and recalled that she's gotten fired way too many times, which made things very difficult for her.

One day she made a decision to go back to school and take a course in sewing, she graduated, and the first thing that she did was to make preparation to be self employed, she did not have a lot of money, so she decided to take a bite off her grocery money, to purchase some material, and that she did for several weeks till she had enough to make a good stock of pillow cases, and other pillow things, and then found a little space in the hall way of the mall, and there she sold her special made things.

One day one of her ex boss was walking through, and saw her , went up to her and said hello, and great amazement to see her there, he shook her hand and congratulated her on her bold move, but not only that, he right there offered his help to her, in the way that he felt would be most appropriate, she in turn said thank you very much.

The conversation ended, and he went his way, only to return later with some office equipment that he thought would do her just fine, she was very blown away, yet extremely thankful, and grateful, for such an action on his part, part of the goodness about this story, which I thought was worth bringing to you is that, if you are willing to help your self, there are people that's willing to help you.

This is just a heart warming story about moving from the brink of pitfalls to the height of progress.

It is my sincere hope that you never live in constant worry about not doing what you can do to secure a place in the future your self, we all have the very same opportunities, to do the very best for our selves and that of our families, waiting for too long will only serve to hinder your progress in life.

For starters this is all about sustaining life, your personal life that is, so why wont you want to take the greatest interest in making sure that you are really on top of things.

This world calls for a take charge mentally, if you want to be self reliant you just have to grab the bull by the hand, and wrestle it to the ground.

The time for gaining control is now, don't wait till your back is on the ground, by then it is already much too late, once you lost control, it's just like it is over for you.

If you care to know there are thousands like those people every where in the world, that's why there is so much struggling going around, like there are entrees , but no exist, that is what one might call being stuck on the tread mill, and just can't get off, before you know it you are down for the count, and laying flat out.

All of this is only pitfalls, where is the progress, can you see any? if you are not careful there will be no progress, and the only thing left to do is to join the well fare state, with quite a lot of people like you.

There is a picture here that I would like you to get a hold off, that is the perfect of what is commonly known as slums, you can even call it the place where wait to die.

I beg you please try and don't ever allow your self to be in that situation, it's not a pretty one to be in, as far as I am concern if you allow be in I can surely help you to avoid that situation by all account.

Now the way that you may do that is by stopping, and secure a copy of this book , read it from start to finish and you will sure to find the kind of motivation, and inspiration that will help greatly in moving you form pitfalls to the type of progress that you can now boast of to all of your family and friends, and be happy that you ever did.

I am very happy that I am here to bring you this book called, pitfalls and progress, we all can do better if we choose to do so.

Just know that this world is full of discouraging factors any way that you turn, but it is also fill with encouraging ones too, it all depends on who you spend your time speaking with, the ones that says do or the ones that says don't, any way that you look at it they both do have their valid interest, all you must ask your self is which ones are for me.

At one time in my life I had to ask my self the very same question, simply because I had a rather good idea about what I wanted for my self, I was able me to answer in a definitive way.

We have spent a lot of time in preparing us to able to make choices based on decision, know what you want, and go for it full throttle, you are sure to get it.

Zero in on your inner thoughts, that is exactly what is going to be the thing that you are looking for, that is why they say it's all up to you no one can do that for you but you.

Every one has to think for him/her self, those are just not words it is very true to the core, other wise I could say to you here is my brain go think for me, while I lay around having a siesta, some people would call that a real luxury, I would call it lazy.

What I want and need in life should motivate me enough to go find it, when I do I accomplish my goal, for I was personally involved, you see just doing nothing is very dangerous to ones self, you are taking your self to the very brink of the pitfall, and standing there, wondering why you are there, just remember you did not fight the odds, so inevitably you arrived to a place that would prove to be your challenge from here on until you can become serous to realize that you have made some very poor choices that led up to that place.

Just remember there is still that chance that things can be change, you still have some thing monumental in your possession, you have life, every thing begins with it, and ends when it's not.

Here is what I want you to consider, when I stumble upon hard times as most of us do, is the very moment I begin thinking like never before, that type of thinking brings about a very good sense or reasoning, which automatically takes over to help me figure out how I have gotten here to begin with.

Now I am on my way to fix it once and for all, I am determined there must be a good resolution to this, I must come out better on the other side, unless you can say these things to your self, there might be very little hope to making things better in your life.

Right now progress is staring you in the face, but can you see it, all of the changes you have made must produces some thing, let's call it progress, because I think that is exactly what it is.

I took a glance back a few years, and I am very happy that I tried first of all, then continued. What I am seeing really thrill me, after going through what I have gone through, certainly gives me the reason to celebrate all of my achievements, now, mind you not all as I said before has been glorious, there were times I thought I would fall to pieces, and part of the reasons that I didn't was because I firmly believed in what I was trying to achieve.

I all of your trials just know that you are only human, and that any thing can happen at any time, some one said the only thing that we can do for sure is to try.

What I have to say about that is to make sure that any thing that you are trying be the first step in a long process because it is some thing that you are faithful to finish.

Remember that you are on your own, and would do just about any thing to make a bad situation a good one.

The richest man in the world would tell you that his riches did not come to him in fact he had to move towards it, just as is said about the mountain that stands in the distance, I guarantee that you can stand in one place and wait for any amount of time that you feel, unless you move to that mountain you will be standing the very same place for the one hundred years for sure.

How long do want to wait for the things that you want and need to take care of you and your family.

Just remember that time never ceases only we do, time has all of itself so use all the time that you need while you can, because time will always out last you.

The thing is that we have so short a time to spend here, and you we tend to so little with the time that we have, what we should do is to have a jolly good time despite it all.

There too many of us do so little preparation which leaves stranded for our future journey, it's always been said to trim our lamps and get ready for the night that cometh, simply because when that happens, you are sure to stumble in the dark, and the things are no one knows chow long the darkness will last.

That is why I say to you take charge of your destiny work like there is no one else there but you, it is always nice to have your independence, with that you can always lend a helping hand, what's better is if every one is preparing there will be no one left to lend a helping hand too, but that's okay because every one should be able to take care of him/her self, and we'll still be friends.

After being on the brink the of pitfalls for so long we can all have a grand celebration together for the progress that we have made.

My message to you is clear to the point that you will be able to make an informed decision when it come to taking care of your life, there are simply no magic bullets, you have to go step by step as you move your self to what is going to be your destination.

When I started my journey it was just as it is for you a little bit cloudy, what I had to do was to flash the light on it, so it remain clear before my eyes.

Every one has had to face some of the very same situations, and not bowing to difficulties enough to stop you in your tracks.

Deciding to do any thing is the first step to finishing, the very same energy that you started with, because you love what the out come was going to be is the vary same one that should take you to the finish product.

Most of us go to long thinking about uncertainty, that will only cause you to build a tremendous amount of fear in the process that discourage your willingness.

If you have ever heard of faith, which I think just about every one should of by now, faith is believing in some thing, even though you have not seen it as yet.

Through out the many centuries it's been this way, people allowed them selves to believe that after planting this half dead tree, if nurtured enough that same half dead tree can spring back to full life and bear a tremendous amount of fruits that you won't even have enough room to store them, which turns out to a very good problem to have, some thing I have mentioned before was at the start of most things chances it would look sort of deem, but after careful analysis you could find that it is going to be okay.

Every bit of emotion are in us to be experience because it is in us, so when we feel happy about the things that are happening to us, just remember the very same can be said for sadness.

We choose how we are going to feel on a day to day basis, so please don't ever think for one minute that some thing is drastically wrong with you otherwise, in life there are good moments as there are not so good moments, let it be a part of your existence it wouldn't hurt you more than any thing else.

As I pondered what I wanted to do in life, was the time I found myself that I realized that

I was like every one else standing at the very brink of despair as I set my gaze on the pitfall, and found my self looking down, I immediately said to my self this picture was not looking so good.

So I lifted my head as my eyes looked upwards, suddenly every thing took on d very different meaning, I right away began to think on a much higher level, then and only then I felt that I was by then making my way to the top, as they say I saw light at the end of the tunnel, there were progress now in sight.

This was where my emotions were changed, I began to feel like my self, every thing was working out as planned.

We were made to go through all the many layers of emotions, may the best one stays with us to the end.

Lets face it we are human, and things always will happen to us just to remind us that we are exposed to all the things that are out there, some times I even think that we should feel blessed to have to deal with some of the things that happens to us on a daily basis.

Unless we have courage enough to with stand against the rough currant no doubt we will be swept away, thank God this is not the case, because we happens to be tough enough with stand it.

Now if we are to go from challenge to triumph, we must learn the rules of the game, and play it to our advantage, but winning we must.

May be that is the reason why I admire all of those that climbed to the top of the mount Everest for the many time that they did.

What do you think it was that easy, and enjoyable, there is so much work and preparation that goes into endeavors like that, they made that one of the pivotal moment of their lives, it was some thing that they told themselves that they wanted to do, what they did was stuck to their guns and went on to make history.

Now I want you to try to define your pivotal moment.

Good things happens when we don't take no for an answer, life is much too short for all of this dickering around, just put your mind to it and get it done.

That project that you had in your mind last year that you really wanted to get done what are you doing about it, is it dead in the waters,, or you just taking a respite if that is the case just know when to start again, because if you let it lie for too long you will miss your pivotal moment.

Let your pivotal moment be the place where you make all of your plans to excel that you may call excelling all of the progress that you ever wanted.

It was day a fall day not too long ago I stood in the window of my writing room, just taking in some of the beauty of a very sunny fall day, one the things that I took notice to was the velocity of the wind as it streamed the yellow leaves down the street, making their way to where no one really knows.

Now that was the day that I thought that I would be doing some sweeping and bagging, instead the wind took care of that for me, not so lucky for those down the street whose lawns just gotten dotted with an abundance of unwanted leaves.

Some of the lessons that I took from that day was despite what I wanted to do on that day it really didn't matter for the gusting wind, the wind will do just what wind does, what I better do is to find a way to fill my precious time with the sort of things that would be quite worth the while.

I knew then that shouldn't be using this as an excuse not to do any thing, there are too much to be done in any given day that could be satisfactory and rewarding, to make you feel that the time just didn't get lost from me, and especially to be non productive.

Right there I thought of what I might be doing that would be contributive to your life, so I grabbed my manuscript and began to write what I thought you could use in especially in your down time.

We all have some down time that we could use in our creative ways, and that's what ever that may be, may be thinking of brand new things, or even finding new hidden talents, what ever the case time is time and can be used in which ever way that we chooses, the fact is that we have to learn to get some thing out of the time that we expend.

It really is like making a well informed decision before an investment, what is good here is that you have the time to do so. I keep hearing people say just about all of the time that they don't have the time to put into any thing, while that excuse might be okay, it is still not satisfactory, because what we have to learn to do is to prioritize accordingly just that we may give every thing a fair time in our lives.

I heard of this one person that had an appointment to do some thing importantly enough, but have decided not to go ahead with plans because of some thing that came up, so they went on to do it instead, to each his own, you do what makes you feel good, as long as it is going to move you from pitfalls to progress I am happy for you.

Every idea, every seed thought is worth taking seriously to be considered as an option, that may bring about a happy ending.

Ideas are like real seeds plant them and you can expect a tree, or real growth in many areas in your life, like both and many others have done. If take some time and look around you, you are sure to find many people that you can go up to and ask them questions about how they did what they did to be that successful.

They are sure to say to you, I really tried hard, and while at it decided not to ever give up, because that would mean that I would loose all of the time and money that I have already invested, now all that is gone and for sure I really cant afford to do this again for now any way.

Ideas are nuggets of interest, they are worth looking into, some people have found their pot of gold an account of it, so the next time you have a brilliant idea, just don't pass it up for nothing for that can help to change your life.

Every now and again I will try to take you back to that simple little seed called the mustard seed, that if planted will undoubtedly become a tree, and bear flowers, that produces much more seed than you that if was capable of.

Now this is for real, one day I asked my wife to buy some mustard seeds in the grocery I prepared my garden and I took a few pinches of seeds and sprinkled it in the garden and for sure I have had quite a beautiful section of the garden flourishing with a very nice little patch of mustard greens, it was just a little test for me to see for sure what happens when seeds do grow into trees.

Every seed becomes a tree.

Every thought becomes a thing, and if taken seriously can move you from rags to riches, and from pitfalls to progress.

I can well remember the time came and the economy went from high to low, every one was panicking wondering just what was going to happen.

The good thing was the world didn't get flat all at a certain, so we are still here and still trying to find out the real reasons behind all of the rise and fall.

All along I knew there were quite a bit of good in all of this, because every thing wrong ought to be made right.

For a while every one were wondering whether they should spend or save their money for a better time, not realizing that the best time is right now, holding back on spending would only make things go from good to bad.

You see, in life what we may consider is to keep that ball rolling, if its going to get any where, it was that very time I started to speak about staying focus, keeping your eyes on that ball, and look where it's heading too.

Fortunate enough it headed into the right direction, and all that was old became new again, now the whole world was happy again.

There are great lessons that we can learn in this situation, that will keep us on the right track for a life time.

I think if we can have a little faith, in our selves the whole world will inevitably will have faith in it's self so we can work harmoniously in order that we may avoid the pitfalls altogether and have all of the progress that we need and worked so hard for. The truth of the matter when we have all cylinders fired up and running like a well oiled machine, we are simply building a better economy, that will lead to a much better world, what a change that can be, because there is nothing better than people being able to take care of themselves ant that of their families, but the very best of all is that there will be less sick people, there will be more, and better productions, can this be the ideal world, and do we care to have one.

For right now I think we have every one and their brother working against each other, that is why we can hardly make the progress that we want, we are simply making things much too complicated, then try to un- complicate things all at the very same timer.

The lessons that we were supposed to have learned was how to build on our difficult past, every thing in life that was not a compliment becomes an opportunity to learn some thing new and may be better, nothing is really in vain, there is always a reason why things happen, what ever that may be.

One thing that helped me greatly was the knowledge of the power of God, He is so much bigger, than any thing that I can ever be, that made me humble enough to go to Him and ask for the ability to cope that I may be able to do all of the things that I wanted to do and accomplished.

Before I did that I tried to look at some people that were very successful and thought I would be able now, but I realized that they were like me far from being perfect so I decided not to waste any time, and do every thing Gods way, and I was sure to get there as planned.

What I have learnt too, was not to be greedy in my approach to anything, in fact I did every thing with a good level of consideration for that of others, a willingness to help in any way that I could, simply because I knew enough to understand that I was just a little part of the whole, so with all things considered I have become the person that I am, with the progress that I have made despite the pitfalls.

Page 67

What ever you do please don't wait around for some one to come from the fray to help you in fact it is like quite the opposite you may have to help them, if you keep your head on where it ought to be, and thinking, you can surpass that of the efforts of others, so don't be surprise.

One of the reasons that many people just don't succeed is because they simply think way too small, open your mind, and your eyes then look up in the sky and tell me the size of what you are seeing, this is the reason it is known as the limitless sky, there's no length, no breath, no depth, no man can tell it's size., and may be that a good thing.

So how then there are so many of us that can't imagine any thing further than where we are standing, it is quite evidential that we will never be able to think beyond the magnitude of the vast expanse, but be able to solve the real meaning of love in this world, or the lack of it thereof.

The love for what I like to accomplish in my time made me succeed to at least moving me from the pitfall, and set me on my way to a better and more secured place.

Today I am looking in amazement of the amount that I have accomplished in such a short space of time, the fact is when I get going it becomes very hard for me to stop, which is not really bad because it helps me go through to the very end.

There is simply nothing better that looking at where you have started, when just about every one gave up on you, saying he will never make it, especially coming from the back, to over take even some of the ones that were ahead of you, I don't know about you but it is a very nice position to be in.

What's also great about that is like setting a very good example to all those that are looking on, in fact that is the exact thing that will motivate and inspire others to work for the progress that they can have, I really like that sort of thing.

I know when I gotten started I can tell you for sure that there were too many to count of the people that doubted me and my efforts, even some of my good friends, and relatives, there were quite enough bad eyes looking at me that wished me failure, but gladly enough every thing worked out for good.

For those of us that are trying to help our selves, I say to you stay on track , for that is the only way that you will get any where in life, as long as you know what you want, and have the ability to accomplish it then put on blinders like horses and go straight to what you are looking at.

As I said before if you want to succeed first get rid of all of the negative influences in what ever way that they come, because they are called the distracters and will try at least to derail your efforts, look, I had to do the very same thing, now, guess what, all of the ones that thought I would fail are now giving me congratulations, and special attention.

Follow your gut feelings and motor on, you are the one, and only one that you have to concern your self with, when you feel tired take a rest , when you feel sick go to the doctor and get well.

Some times it's like we are the only ones in the world, because in order for us to succeed we must stay strong, fight hard, use determination as your key to success and go like there are wolves chasing after you, because you are seeing progress ahead.

Every step takes you closer to your goal, this is the kind of attitude that you must take if in case you want to succeed, give it all that you got with out holding back on any thing, have you seen any seeds growing mid air, it has to be planted into the soil if it expects to find nutrients to grow.

Time is of the essence when it comes to working for success, the single most important thing that you should think about is what you need to do in order that you may have the kind of success that is important to you.

When it comes to what some may call the right time to do any thing, we should ask our selves which is the right time after all we have time, and that time is none other that now, for all you know, this may be the only time that you may have in a long time to get this thing done.

Too many people has asked me, why now, why do you want to do this now, why not wait till the sun stops shinning or the rain stops coming out of the skies, and I said to them, I really don't know about tomorrow nor just what it might bring, all that I know is that I am here now, healthy , strong, and able to do this and so I feel that I should.

As we speak there are thousands of people believing that they should wait to go back to school, to get their education so as to be able to secure a good job, to be able to take care of things satisfactorily, what long wait will do is to entrenched you in that rut of a place, like being at the brink of the pitfall, and finding it very difficult to get going again.

It is but time long over due for some one to tell those folks that they are waiting for a train that hasn't been built as yet, so this wait may be forever, with nothing accomplished.

Being responsible means that you will the vision to see a long way ahead of you, in order for you to position to take hold of opportunities to progress in all of your efforts.

I often said to my self oh! how I wish I was twenty again the things I would do, and the places that I would go to just boggles my mind, so you that is in that age range should use it to your full advantage to capitalize on all of these wonderful opportunities, so when you become thirties and forties, you would look back with gratitude.

I am not saying that you age would be the only factor, but it certainly helps to have it on your side, lets face we are human, we all get concern when things aren't going as well as it should, just remember when you were fifteen, and sixteen? you had the iron will, the courage to tackle any thing, it might even be like as they say, you will run and never be tired, you may walk a mile, and it feels like you have just gotten started.

Think of all that you are now, and work it till you are satisfied that is how you may be able to help others, because after all that is what matters most, going beyond self, to see others do well, by so we are empowering the world to move in a steadfast direction, that others may follow, and thus being rescued from the pitfalls only to find progress.

Here is some thing quite funny, when I was a boy, and just didn't know the true value of things, some one would hand me a penny and I would look at them like if they were out of their minds, not realizing that pennies leads to pounds, now should some one do the very same thing you would find me saying a very big thank you.

What we are saying is every little bit adds up, so the next time you refuse a penny just call me I will take it with thanks.

I am hoping that a good few people would send all of the unwanted pennies to me, what I will do is collect them all and let it keep growing.

When I started my work there were people saying to me, why start with so little, they wanted me to rush, and I wanted to take my time and do it just right.

You see, the word chronology means a lot to me, I like to go to things step by step with out missing any thing, that way when I am through, I also know that all of the steps are accounted for, you may think I am perfect, in fact I am not, but I love to try at least.

One thing I know for sure is that I just don't give up easily, what ever I want I go till I find it, and as you can tell it wouldn't be an over night thing, I still think that every thing has a process to it, and if followed would have amazing results.

That is how I get things done around here, and if you were me you would do the very same, because at the end of the day all that matters are the progress that you have made.

I asked some one recently, do you want to have a lot of money, and I was amazed for the answer that they gave, some how I think there are lots of people that really do have aversions to money, it's either they are sick or they are smoking some thing quite funny.

I said to the person just in case some one should give you some, or for that matter lend you some just turn it over to me, I'll be very happy to take care of it for you, and avoid your self the headache of trying to spend it.

Since then I try to teach people that money is a very vital thing in our society, you don't have to look far, just go to the grocery store tomorrow and pick up some food that you really need to feed the children, then try walk out with out paying, and see how fast you will find your self in jail for all of the right reasons.

Now, I hope you have had a little lesson about the usefulness of money, so the next time when you get back to thinking of important things, think of money.

Look, for years I have been trying to have enough of the stuff, and up to now I still can't find what I am looking for, one thing I know for sure is that I will continue to work even smarter, to get it, but I know I will for sure, it is a promise that I have made to myself, that I must fulfill, there is no need to be going around wishing with out it

The reason why I know I will have what I am looking for is because I am doing all that I can do with the time that I have just to make it happen.

I learnt long ago that if you do nothing, you should also expect nothing, so let us all try and do some thing to move us from pitfalls to progress.

One of the things that helped me on my quest for accomplishment was when I recall those words of my mother, saying to me , son, from here on I want you to seek knowledge, wisdom, and understanding, they are like the three basic wisdom keys that every one should have to operate with in just about every area of their lives, with them you are to find your self on shake ground.

That is the very reason that I spend most of my time thinking, before do any thing, the idea is to first find out whether you have the knowledge, and not find it because you just cannot do any thing with out knowing how to, and that comes from knowledge.

You will also find your self feeling very empowered, and assertive to confidently carry your self all the way, there's simply nothing better than to have that sort of self confidence.

Can you be like that? I am s almost sure that you could if you really wanted too, some people don't because their lives is not dependent on it, while there are others that will do just about ant thing to have it, they are the very ones that will blow away the competition each and every time.

Whatever the case you must decide just what it is that you want to do, and not leave the decision to any one else, there is more than likely that you might quite appreciate the out come, but then again the fault is all yours, try not to let others decide your future, they may even send you to hell for all you, would you like to know that? while at the very same time suffer the defeat of a life time, no one I know would like that.

The criminality of moving from the pitfalls in life can be very heart breaking to say the least, when I think of that I know just whom I can trust, and that is me, because I am the only that really is interested in me like me, and frankly why should give some one else that responsibility, especially since I am the one expecting the good results, and that to me, is fair enough, for I am quite sure you will agree.

Look, no one is going to willingly give you his progress, after going through the grinding mill to find, you would do the very same if it were you, so take responsibility for what it is that you wish to accomplish, and I guarantee you will have the greatest appreciation for the things that comes on account of that.

No one can tell me by   now, how difficult it is to become self made in this world, first you would have to know where I came from, and under what condition. I really had to work very hard to get my expectation, it took me a rather long time and efforts, and for that I love the opportunity to bring this lesson of inspiration to you.

I think I have mentioned this to you before, but I think it is important enough to sat it again, t I have lived through the toughest time in my boyhood days. I endured all, for I had no better way, but to do all of the things that I had to do, although it was tough, I really have had the opportunity to prepare my self for what I have become.

There are so many lessons one can learn from doing all sorts of things that it is all worth it in the end, just like it's like saying thanks for that, it is said that if it didn't kill you it would certainly make you better, that was the situation in my case, for what better way to put to script the experience that you have an account of the exposure to all of the many things, that made you to be you today, if you ask me I am sure to tell you all that you have to is to live where you are, that simply means to make use to all of the things that surrounds you, learn all that you can to become the very best at some point in time.

If you are going to be successful you should also expect to have unexpected hurdles along the way, don't be alarm for that will only help to test your courage, and to see how much it will take to have you fail at your attempts.

Just remember ,if in case you quit, you stop things for happening for you, and there are no chance of moving your self from the very brink of the pitfalls, so therefore there should be no progress along the way.

I spoke with some folks recently, and I can remember one of them were saying that one of the reasons that they are afraid to start some thing is because they are really uncertain of the chances of them succeeding, that is very common, there are much more people thinking the same way, which accounts for the kind of failure in many business startups, and then again we can say thank to those who with stood the test and went on to be very successful.

When you can tell the rest of us why you should just breeze through life with out any obstacles, we are prepared to ask you how special are you, no one is that special, every one were made to endure some form of hardship, if you, do just get use to it, and the one that haven't yet experience it as yet brace your self, but don't be afraid, it's all part of life, and may be only a test, so just don't ever give up on your efforts, progress is coming.

Some times in life we should expect directions, because times demands it and we may have no choice in the matter, with that new direction, comes a renewing of the way every thing is done, the fact of the matter is what ever the case let it be considered to be the continuation of the journey, we simply don't stop because we change direction, in fact that should give us a brand new perspective going forward.

It may even brighten our vision, to give us much needed hope when we need cit the most.

There are good reasons why things change, some times it is really for the better, we just have to keep our eyes wide open to see the relevance of it.

I can remember there was a time when I was at the end of my planning for my new business endeavor, when all out of no where came a snag that forced me to abandon some of the plans just before I have gotten too far into it, what happens I just didn't see all of the four corners which caused me to missed some very important components.

Today I look back and give credits to the very change that I had to make, it saved the day, and believe me I feel so much better for that.

In just about every thing that comes our way, some may be good, some may be bad, what we ought to be doing is pay particularly attention, if we are to avoid the pitfalls, and remember, that the only easy thing, is the one that hasn't been done.

How else can we really know if some thing will work or not, but by first trying, that is the very reasons why we do conducts test in just about every absolute thing that ought be done, so the next time you hear some one talk about prototype one thing immediately would come to your mind.

There is always going to be bumpy rides ahead, nothing is straight cut, roads are never straight, nor is it always wide, some times it better be narrow, it's all about how you see it that matters.

Because there are so many ways of doing things, you just choose what might just work for you, as long as you know that you are like the rest, and would have to deal with all of the very same things that the others had too.

Here is some thing that struck me, and had to pay some attention too, it really didn't matter who were first, nor who were last, there were an equal chance for either spectrum we just have to keep this in mind.

Some times it is even better to be the last, for it is really not a factor for success, in fact your success is depending on how well you prepare your self for the things that you have to do.

I have seen people spend so much time on just what the other guys are doing that they seem to forget to take care of their own, because of that I'm afraid that it is not going to be successful for you, every one may make their own plans for the success they expects.

Success becomes the progress that one expects, just make quite sure that you are one of those that have been persistent enough, and know ,that well deserve the progress that you have made up to now.

Lets just stop beating around the bushes, do you want to be financial stabled? or not, just what are you planning to do in the meantime, all of the people in the world that have quite enough to take care of all of their financial needs, didn't just sit around, and count their fingers, they had to work and continue working until some thing that they put in place materialized into their financial gains.

How many times are we going to say the very same thing, that if you want it you have to go and get it for yourself , I did it and so is countless others who had to go through the rough and rugged to find it.

I really am the living proof of the kind of people that makes it in this world, all because I just don't waste my time going around the in a circle till I am giddy, of course that would really throw me in a loop, and if ever that were the case, with the kind of head that I have on my shoulders, I would of still found my way from the brink of the pitfalls to what I considered to be my progress.

What really have gotten me moving was when I started to think, of things as they were, I really didn't like it I just was not making the kind of progress that I thought was good enough, especially as I looked at the others, not with envy in my eyes, mind you, but simply as a human being that needs to pull his weight.

I literally made me sick to my stomach, when I realized that my needs were mounting up on me, and to see how far I was behind, if I didn't get excited, and start focusing on what I must do to get in the game, I would of been lost for sure.

Some time you just have to get that ball rolling and hope to see it picking up momentum, then stay with it, as long as it is in motion you know it's on the way to some where, follow it all the way for at the end of this journey there will be some thing much more that you thought.

This is when I say to people to get out the champagne invite the family, friends and all others that you know, then get out the bull horn and shout from the top of the mountain it's party time, but please make sure that you invite me, I hate missing a good party.

That's when we should all remember that life is not just about work only, as they say if you work hard, you should also play hard, some how it makes it better for the next days work, simply because you appreciate life with all of it's many wonders.

In life we should even expect the unexpected things happen not al would be good at every turn, but it is here, and some times quite necessary for our growth, if not we would just take every thing for granted, and would have no regards for some of the things in life.

Every now and again we need to have a good head shake, to help us to remember that we may be off track, right after that we find our selves feeling so much better.

You see, life is not perfect but, as I often say thank God for it for with out it we are no where, so wouldn't you rather be here with all of the many things that upset you every now and then? after all what they are doing is making you think, and that of course is what we need to help us to make progress in life.

Don't under estimate the power of your thoughts, for it is the very thing that has all of the power to make things happen in every area of your life, and as a matter of fact it is some thing that none of us can really do with out nor would we like to do with out, not even for one minute, because frankly it guides our lives, and has it's involvement in ever thing that we do, so when you hear some one say they won't be thinking about any more is really because they are thinking of it.

It is very hard for any thing to pass us by with out knowing that it has, the only way not to is may be you are sleep walking, or day dreaming of in which case you may want to focus your thoughts in a targeted direction.

To me I feel that the very best thing that I possess is my thoughts, every thing that I do I make sure that I put all of my thoughts into it , simply because I want the finishing product to reflect the way that I thought, it's like a sort of pre inspection you put good in , and you get nothing but good out, so when you a planning to do what ever it is that you are doing just remember that you are going to give all that you have got, in order that even your enemies are well pleased.

Keep this in mind , when you are planning your success, it is just as important to note that the there are several people watching and waiting for you to inspire them with the end product, so it is not that every thing is going to be for you and you only.

What ever it is that we do is done hopefully for the usage of others, no one can consume all that he produces, other wise there would simply no trade taking place any time soon, I'm sure you have heard people say, I have made this and it is not for me, I have quite enough of it already, that is some of the reasons that we put all of your thoughts into it taking care the it is as exactly as the way that we think.

What some of us do is to create a real picture of the things that we are doing in our minds to measure against the end products, this is where our satisfaction takes root, because we know that we have quite a lot of people to satisfy, especially our selves.

The real magic is, every time we take our product to the market, we indirectly take our selves to the market, because what ever it is that we do becomes a true replica of the we way that we think.

The idea is to give the very best, and receive the very best in return, I always say, when I buy any thing, it means that I pay for it, one thing that I know for sure is that money transferred for any product is always good money, but more times than one the products are questionable, and that is where I have major concerns.

For after all I stood on the brink of the pitfalls for so long, now finally I can see progress in the distance, from here on every thing that I do must be equitable, and well represented by me, because when you see my product, you should also be able to see my picture imbed therein.

To say it mildly I don't mess around with my progress, after making it over the pitfalls.

When it comes to doing well, every one should have an interest fully engaged, and stay with it what ever happens, it's like enjoying what you have chosen let no one do that for you, for only you know what you love and capable of doing, it is very difficult for any one to tell you, that they like some thing and you should do the same.

Every one is or should be capable of deciding what is right for them, that is simply not the way it works.

Part of taking charge of your future is knowing what you really want, and how to get, once we establish that I think we are now able to set our priority in order, and bring it on home.

When I was attending college I recall my teacher handing out a complete list of things that are available, what we had to do was to identify what we love, and would welcome the opportunity to get involve with it.

There was never a time he said to us I would like you to do this or the other, what we did in fact was to read the list to find some thing that interests us, then follow up on it the best way that we could, which means that our interest would reflect our choice.

In general I think that it would be a great advantage both for teaching, and learning, in that case we have gotten to learn what we love, and the teacher got to teach what he knew well.

At the end of the day every one wins, because of the even playing field, but most importantly to us it was a wonderful way to learn from the master.

As one prepares him self, or her self for the future, and really wants to move from the edge of the pitfalls it becomes very important that particular attention is paid to the source of knowledge in order have the necessary foundation for establishing one self to make progress in life.

We talked a lot about progress as if our life depends on it, well, indeed, who wants to be at the bottom of the ladder for ever, I really don't mind starting at the very bottom, because it is the one place that all things grows from, the fact of the matter is I must know just what I am doing there, and if you ask me I will be happy to tell you that I am planting , and nurturing for real growth.

That is quite true, it like sowing seeds with out watering it, yet we expects it to grow into that robust tree bearing it's abundant of fruits.

Unless we take care of things, there is no way that we will get what we expects of them, the same is true, when it comes to our future, it's like really storing away an empty bag, it was empty when you put it away, and it will be just the very same when you return to retrieve it.

Prepare to use all of those lessons that was taught, and you will make significant progress in every area of your life.

I have seen quite enough of what I am warning you of, there are times you will even notice that three time or more that it's you alone, the load is heavy and you are all alone to carry it, but it's okay stay strong and you will have all the strength to carry pass over the pitfalls to the progress that you long awaited.

Now more than ever, you may notice that you may have to do much more than before, if you really wanted to succeed, the time are changing very fast, even faster that is comforting for many of us, but at least we are here to change what we can, hopefully to right some of the wrongs.

This is a very clear indication that times has not stood still, I know at times it is very hard to see, all because we are so pre occupied, that some time it's hard to see the forest for the trees, and then again we will be able to see it before the day is over.

I am quite sure you have heard the saying, nothing happens before it's time, it is very true, it's like the clock on the wall, it keeps on beating, counting the seconds, and minutes as it goes around, which becomes hours after hours.

The very same can be true about us, all that we should do is to take care of the little things that eventually becomes big things.

Don't be like some who wants every thing to happen right now, take care and you will see that every thing does have a time in which it can manifest the results, that is why they say, time is of the essence, which can be applied to many situations.

Some people even find that the time of the day is just not enough to do any thing , so they basically do nothing, and as the say, nothing ventured is nothing gain.

I say it sort of differently, if you plant a tree don't look for fruits, a simple analogy but in fact true. we all have the same time of the day to any thing that we want, if we care.

If we happen to go way back we might discover that a commission came out asking to trim our lamps, which prepare it and fill it with oil, for the night is fast approaching, and we just won't be able to see to do some of the most important thing that we should be doing, if we are to avoid the pitfalls.

Up to now we are still living in the very same frame work of life, we are simply not ready, while time is fast closing in on us, I think this is one of the time we can say it may be too late, lets face it we have the time to do certain things, and if incase we didn't do it, it becomes too late.

But wait, you can still catch on, only you will have to double up on time, just forget there is a thing call the clock, with your days beginning early and finishing real late, this is what it has became. Can you se any progress in sight now/?, may be not, but it is there, just behind the corner, in fact if you keep pushing the clock like you are doing, you are almost certain to find it around the other corner. Ah! progress at last.

What an amazing thing, life is very different any where in the world that you may venture too, ever where has it's own customs, and habits, what it is, is just people in different places, but despite of all of this, the same is expected from each and every one of them, after all they have to work, play, and take care of kids just as you may find your self doing where ever you are.

I am very sure that most of them rises early in the morning just as I did when I was a little boy working with my dad, taking care of stuff, just like I did.

Some times I think we sort of fail to imagine that an day is still a day around the world, with people running left and center trying to grab a hold of what it is that they are look for, and if in fact they are in some remote area minding their own business, and care less about what happens I other places just live them alone for they may be quite happy with what they have, and have no need of ours.

To them they see no need to, nor do they have the desire to stock pile every thing like the world is going to end the next morning.

They have no urge for the amount of money that we seek daily, but they get bye quite well, as they will tell you.

Life is just different, and should remain different, may be it is good, in some way or the other.

Believe it or not most people change when they change places, and that is why some take a much a longer time to make adjustments than others, it is because the old habits lingers with them for a while longer.

All in all they never knew that they were standing on the brink of a pitfall where they were, for what they had was progress enough, they were force to be assimilated because of the many demands that they face on a daily basis.

It is rather comforting to know that I had so much time working it out with my dad, and the many chores that was mandatory for me to fulfill, some how I feel blessed in many ways, because I was very willing to learn, from my father, the master himself.

It was a wonderful opportunity for me, it was like hands on schooling, today I would find it difficult for me to teach all of the many things that I learnt in a life time, but I will try, all because some may be inspired by my wealth of experience, and as they see the progress that I have made.

No matter what any one may say, every thing starts small, including our selves, and even out thoughts, this is where I call the beginning of any thing that is possible, we were meant to have a lot of every thing, because all things that was made for us were here long before we got here, there should be no doubt about as to whether we have entitlement to all of these things.

What we ought to do is to seize every opportunity as they come other wise some one else will move in and claim it all right your very own eyes, it's the nature of the world, just like finders keepers, that is if no one claims it.

Look, all that I want you to do is to go out and claim yours by working hard for it, then it really belongs to you, with all of it's entitlement.

I feel that every baled body out there should take pride of just what they are if willing can accomplish for them selves, it is the way things should be, other wise you may be surprised to find out that there is nothing for he that did nothing.

The more you learn is the more that you will be able to do, so with that kind of knowledge we would almost expect you to be setting good examples to those that are still thinking about just what they may do with themselves, as for me I will awake the giant inside of you if you let me, all that you have to do is to open your eyes, and ears, with a very willing mind, and you will be very surprised at just what you can accomplish.

As for me I learnt how to say no lightly, and say yes when I know that I should, so far it's been working like a charm. You see, when some one say to me, come over let me teach you some thing I always say yes, while on the other hand, if you would say to me, lets go to the corner store and chug back a case of beers, you are sure to hear me say no, thank you, it's not I feel too good for having a beer or two, I must know when to draw the line, and may be do some thing that is far more important than just letting time sleep away with simply nothing in return.

I am quite sure you will agree with me a little, because our sees just about the very same things, especially if you are ambitious, and willing to get things done, just before the sun sets, why stand at the brink of the pitfalls just taking in the sun, when you can you can find all of the progress that you want by doing something that will bring it about for sure.

You see, there is only one thing called life as we know it, so appreciate it , and do all that you can to sustain, and enjoy it always to the fullest, some times it's what progress has made possible.

We have all heard that, life is too short, which is very true, but what do we do to embrace it, why do we waste it away, there are so much that can be done while we have it, which can be very meaningful to so many, just seem to think that life was meant to be shared with all others with out borders, and limitations.

The fact is when we say share there are many things that comes to mind, some times just asking some one ,how are you doing today would be quite enough to give you the knowledge of just how you may be able to help.

Some people just brave enough to tell any one of their urgent needs, so they will suffer under the pressure of their needs until some is able to notice, then spring to action.

This is an every day thing, some people rather go hungry than ask for food because of their all consuming pride.

One thing that I have heard my mother say time, and time again, was to swallow your pride, before it swallows you, actually it is Avery true saying, you don't have to look too far to see the results got that.

Come on, I know that it is very hard to tell some one that you need any thing from them, but you have to think, of what else would you do if your life depends on it. Go on tell some one, be brave, be honest to your self, you may even save your life for that matter, and you just cannot afford to loose that precious thing it's the only one there is.

Actually I planned for this time in my life, I knew that I wanted to help people how I could, what I really had to do was to acquire all of the necessary tools in order that I may be able to fulfill that mission, needless to say I am very happy to be able to do just that, it would be pointless to me to come in this world live out my life miserably, that means not having to accomplish any thing significantly, to me that would be a total loss of precious time.

What I really didn't want was that of depending on any one absolutely, because that is not fair ,nor equitable, it has been said before that it is far better to give, than to receive, so I prepared my self to be able to give, you've got to have some to give, what ever it may be, small or large.

And some times giving does not mean some thing tangible, it could also be spending valuable time with some one that's really in need of some sort of support, in other words be there for some one when they need you, it might be the very first step in moving them from the brink of a pitfall, and setting them on their way to progress that would even warm your heart.

I am here to help you pass the pitfalls to your progress.

Do you know what helped me greatly? I started with the very essence of inspiration, and that was the very results that I expected, nothing makes you feel better than knowing that you will really make it for sure, it's like holding it in your hand, and enjoying just what hard work can really do for all those that were standing at the pitfall wondering what is next in my quest for being that self supportable individual.

This becomes the place that makes you feel that it was well worth it, even though I have traveled a thousand miles, with thousands more to go, it's all a step in the right direction.

I always say to my self just as a reminder, I am not finish, in fact I am only beginning, no matter how much I achieve in my life I know for sure there is much more to be done, the reason for that is, I am self driven for a purpose, generally I keep being very observant with just about every thing around me.

The fact is in order for me to be able to help in any way, I must know what the basic needs are out there, that is why they say that knowledge is power, but you must use it for it to be effective, if you have knowledge and not use it, eventually it will become absolute, so it's very true, if you don't us it you loose it.

Now, I prepared my self for years, by learning quite a lot of every thing that I felt that I will be able to use at some time in my life, so what I tried to do was to keep an open mind, quick to see, and easy to hear, with those factors I felt that I had what it took to implement based on what I learnt.

Just a little while age I have had the opportunity to visit a school, while there I was introduced to this young student, we look at each other in the eyes, then I asked him, are you learning lots, he responded, yes sir, I am, I said to him, and again asked him, are you listening well? yes, he said, I concluded by saying to him, let me remind you that listening is the very first step to learning, simply because if you don't listen, you cannot hear, and if you cannot hear, you just cannot, nor, will not know.

That is why up to today I am a very great listener, simply because I am a constant learner, I just feel the more that I know, is the more that I can do.

In short, what it is it's really empowering my self to direct others to a better way forward that leads to their progress.

In this life, it really does not matter which part of the world that you are from, or residing at, you can be successful right where you are, for most people are usually get themselves running from what they have just to look for it some where else, I learnt that a few years ago, it was as a matter of fact, after going through all of the avenues of learning, I began to look at those before me wanting to be where they were hoping to find my treasure, not realizing that the treasure was right there below my nose.

Although I found some of what I was looking for, it could of come much earlier than now, but that is okay, because I now have the privilege of opening the eyes of so many, to try where they are first, to catch a glimpse of what they have which would allow you to place a good sense of value on it before you come to the conclusion that is not here, therefore it must be over there.

Today I take a look back on the area that I immersed from, and I am still seeing quite a lot of valuables there that I left behind, so I am like a commissioner trying to direct people to begin their gold rush now before it becomes too late.

Some of the things that I am seeing is that we have to try and do the best , and most for our selves before it is too late, the channels are all closing slowly, but it is for sure, we must pay close attention to all of the signals, what they are trying to say to us is, you better be able to take care of your self, because we are no longer able to take care of you.

My advise to all is that to recognize the writing on the wall, try to re energize all of the people to be fully engage in the process and preparation towards self supporting, and self reliant.

Then and only then we will be able to meet the challenge of the times, in order that we may be able to ride the waves from pitfalls to progress.

Please don't get me wrong, I am not talking about having billions of dollars hidden some where, in fact I am talking about being to take good care of your self despite all odds.

We have to be able to develop commodities, and store up just to meet the demands of the times ahead.

There are so many ways one can be successful, all that we have to do is to think, and some times alternative wise.

Some where in the world right now as we speak there are fishermen going to the seas, and making good catch of fish, but when they come ashore they just cannot sell it because the people just cannot afford to make the purchase so what they end up doing is throwing it all, and count it as waste, now alternative thinking would create a much better way forward, by freezing, or drying which will enable them to secure a rather good market, and avoid tough times.

We must be careful not to miss the way that leads to the progress that we expects, and that can only be ensured by thinking ahead of time.

I just want to serve as a conduit where we all benefit at the same time, after all I found my way from the pitfalls of life to the progress that I well expected.

Don't live life with out expecting some thing, it is totally waste of time to go n forever one same old day after the other, the only ones that stays the same place going no were are the one that just cannot walk to find their way, and even so they still try and find, and make vital contributions despite it.

One of the many things that made me feel that I can do any thing that I wanted was the time I was looking at television, I saw the most amazing thing that I have ever seen in all of my life, before that, I would , like just about every one else, thought I was unable to do certain things, but after that evening my whole attitude was changed, now I have adapted to a brand new attitude that tells me that if I would only try at least, I could do just about any thing that I put my mind too.

Now how would you like to change places with the gentle man with no arms, and no feet, yet does every thing that he wants to do, with out complaining.

He completely turned his pitfall into progress for the whole world to see, I was so amazed, first I cried, then I laugh, and from that day up to now, you will never hear me complain again.

It is just too easy to give up for not trying, when all hat we have to do is to try at least, and as they say if it didn't work out try again, it just might be the second chance that you ever wanted, so here it is just do what ever you want to do with it, but please just do some thing, it might well worth it in the end.

On that glorious day I really used the inspiration from this gentleman to help me propel to heights that I never thought I could, today o am on top looking down from whence I came, and never to go back again.

Some of the lessons that have I learnt was that, was that life gives us many breaks you just take yours, and make the very most out of it, with two legs, two arms attached to your body, just get your mind working, and if you only try, there is simply nothing that you cannot do.

I am thankful for a very fair advantage, and I am using it to it's fullest, and with thankfulness, and gratitude.

In life one thing that we must do is prepare to do any thing, especially those that we are very familiar with, after all we were born small and grew into adulthood, and with it comes the willingness, and my be strength to accomplish some of the things that could place us in the direction for progress.

Yes, indeed, I struggled at the very beginning, but now I know that all of the struggles were normal, and were all meant for my own good.

It is very important for me to reinforce that point to all those that may think that life owes them every thing, not so, we just have to work for every thing that we want, and need in this life, I just hope this is not a surprise to any one.

Every now, and again I would take a trip back in memory lane just to see the roads that I have traveled, it is a long and tedious one, but here I am, and feeling very happy for all that I have encountered along the way, which only served as a feather in my cap for all to see.

Just don't settle for nothing, instead comfort your self with all that you can accomplish, and that becomes you progress.

When we talk about accomplishing, we are not just talking about being greedy enough to gather all that is there for your self, and put a guard to watch it all day, instead, now we must understand that being in a position of affluence is the greatest thing, because you can definitely afford any thing that money can buy, so here is where it makes a difference, there are several people that just doesn't have quite enough to put a meal on the table, do you acre about that, enough to give what ever support that may help some one from going hungry for a day? I would do any thing that I can to help in such a need, and I think that every one should do the very same.

Part of the reason for my thinking of that is we were never meant to be in the same position at the same time, people on the brink of pitfalls are people that at times are confused as the word itself, so some one better be there and be able to render some sort of help, after all I think that is exactly what I prepared for all of my life, that is why I am reminding us all to think about others, especially in times of great need.

There are times that I think we seems to take advantage of the time that we have, but uses it unwisely, like blaming every thing that there are, to hide our selves behind the reasons why we just cannot give any help at all.

Some thing that shocked me greatly was, one day as I was walking along the city street, I saw a man with an attaché, I didn't know what he had in there, and frankly I really didn't care, simply because it was no business of mine, what I understood later was, this man was a c e o of a rather big company, which belonged to himself, but for what ever happened he fell out on the way side, with all of what he thought was worth it to him, to say it mildly, he just lost every thing, and had no where to go that he could call home, so the street became his home.

There was very little I could of done for him, all that I was hoping for was for some one to see him and to help this now poor man, my be to at least help him to right some of the wrongs.

What ever happened to him, I couldn't really say, but I hope he encountered some kindness along his way.

To some one that was able to help him, would certainly be the progress that they have made, while at the same time earning their wings just to help some one else, some where.

It's always been said that from whom much is given, much is also expected, life is much too short for us not to use our hearts to bless others.

let this be our progress, because we do have the upper hand, my be we can now stretch it towards an out stretch hand, to give a blessing to some one in great need, for we just never know just who will give a blessing to us, nor in what way.

I came all the way From pitfalls to progress.

Although some times it seems to be like a rat race out there, is because it really is, there are so many people running from north, south, east, and west, many of them with out any sense of direction what so ever, but at the same time are functioning sort of okay, at least every one seems to be finding their way home, which is just about the very best of it.

What I try to do is to stay focus on what I am all about, because am afraid in this mess it is about me this time, and as I made a promise to my self that I will stay true to the things that matters most to me for that is the only thing that I can do that is going to move me from what ever pitfall that lay in wait for all those that are trying to bring some sort of change to their lives.

When you are already on the lower scale of achievement through fault of your own, for it is the way things are, you know that you are going to have to work very hard to get going, but fear not, this is may be your time to show the world that you really have just what it takes to make it after all.

Think of the seed that becomes a tree, and the tree that bears fruits, that brings a harvest, well it is the very same like every thing else, when you are beginning every thing seems so hard, but as soon as it begin to register it self the reality sets in, and now you know that this is well worth it after all.

Just about every one that I know have had the very same experience, so you are really not alone, the fact is that what ever the case we must keep one thing in mind, and that is to over come the obstacles as you make your way to the progress that is ahead of you.

In all of the things that we may do some thing has to make us really appreciate our investment of time and some times money, we already know that there is simply no easy way to achieving any thing, as they say if we want it we will have to work very hard to get it, and don't think for a moment that any one should be sorry for you because you are going through difficult times just to make it in this world.

Even the very best amongst us will have some sort of story to tell, about being independent, and able to stand on your own two feet.

That is exactly what it is, the ability to give it all that you have got, in order that you may get the success that you want.

I know that there are several people who just got fed up, and give up long before that they were able too, I even know that some times it is very hard to stay strong, but I am afraid that if you are going to succeed you will have to muster up some strength to stay the course, if you are to make it ,and to be satisfied with your self.

What I am saying now is just what I have experienced, and today I am very proud to report you that my progress is fully in sight, and that I am getting ready to celebrate with all of my friends, and relatives, and you know what? you are invited.

With some of my time I have listened sources that encouraged us to develop a millionaire mind, I like that because it reminds me that I must try to be better that yesterday, on one day should be a carbon copy to the one before, ever thing should take on a new look living us with the understanding that we are indeed making some form of progress by our efforts.

Some people my say to you, why do you want to be a millionaire, because they really don't see significance of that, while to some it's only a stare of being.

Once you plant a tree there is no way what so ever of telling that tree just how many fruits you want it to yield, in fact you are just happy to see some fruit on that tree.

The very same can be said of the many people that make wise investments, and make great profits on account of that.

The fact is what ever it is that you do make sure that it is going to benefit you in the long run.

Earlier we talk about mass amount of people making rapid movements, with out an apparent sense of direction, but what I have discovered it is not quite so, it is just that the times demands it of us, but in fact as we noticed they have been taking care of them selves well.

What I think is when it comes to going we just simply have no choice, just as long as we return with some thing to show for it then it's all good.

And just in case you sense that this is the case, just join in, to where it all leads, you might be even be surprise to know that this is sort of the all new normal, that aren't all that bad after all, it is just the driving force that takes you in the directions that you go.

As for me I tell my self that I will get what ever it is that I am looking for, simply because I am always on the look out for what might be there, and it is up to me to find out.

That's what going all the way means to me, as I hope it's to you also, because as I look down between the pitfalls it keeps on telling me that, this I where you just would not like to be, for all that is starring you in the face is nothing but danger, and that is why we all should do all that we can to avoid this place.

Now one of the only ways that I know of to escape it is to all that we can to make the kind of progress that would shift us from the danger zone.

And for real there are just so many people hanging the balance of that mess, that is very hard to count.

I just want you to realize that I write this book just for you, in order that you may feel the energy to move pass over the pitfalls, that you may be able to enjoy all of the finer things in life, it is easier than you previously thought, so may be this could be your defining moments as you make your decision to wrestle with the giants, and with winning as your ultimate goal.

Now just that I may help you what I am saying when I mentioned giants, they are those big problems that you find very hard to get rid off, it is some thing that almost every one faces at one time or the other, so just don't go about thinking with the poor me mentality, and feeling hard done by.

I am very sure you can remember there was a time when you took a good look at the world, and wonder why it is that just about ever place, and people are seeing and talking about the very same thing, and the fact that it seems to be so difficult.

What we are now face with is just what we are going to do have every body, every where feeling the need for change, and with all of the efforts together, and my be with one voice stepping up to the plate, and try at least to solve some of the problems that causes what is.

Are we in the same boat all at the very same time? the answer is simply yes, simply because we are all connected just about in every place that you can imagine.

I spent years thinking about that who is better, and who is not, and for the very first time I can say that I have found the reasoning behind that way of thinking.

The fact is not single one of us is better than the other, just some my be better off than the other, when it comes to buying power, but other wise we are all in the very same boat, and some times hoping for the very same things.

So brace your self, get with it, and get going, if not you may be standing at the brink of the pitfalls for a very long time yet to come, and really that is far from comforting to say the very least.

Progress is simply doing better that the times before now, some thing I personally think every one should be aiming at, despite undulations, and obstacles, for they are just part of our landscapes, which we have no ability to get rid off.

Really, you are the only one standing in your way, and holding you back, as soon as you decide to make a move in the right direction, you begin to climb out of the hole that you are in, although you may be at the very bottom, you can be at the top if you persist.

There are just so many things that we can say to ourselves, but some times we say too little, you see, the way to affirm our selves is by telling our selves that there are simply nothing big enough to stop us from accomplishing the things that we desires in life.

It is not about other people saying that to us, it is us saying it to our selves, and frankly when it come from within us it feels much better that that of some one else, I am quite sure you have heard people say, there are just no one that care about you like you, it is very true, just think about it for a moment or two, it is like we know that the ice is very thin, so just why should we venture out onto it, if at all to prove a point, like oh! look, am sinking or it's because we just don't really care about our selves.

Believe me, there is no one that care about the progress that you make in life than you, People may complement you on you achievements, which is mostly appreciated, follow it up with a great a generous thank you in return.

Because it is one of the very best ways to have more flowing your way, you see, people like people that know how to show appreciation for kind gestures, that is the main reasons why some may be surprised to know that there are people who make it their mission in life to seek out those kind of people and sow seeds of kindness in them.

For all of the things that I have received, even that of what my parents gave me one thing is very common to me and that is to show thankfulness in return, because by so doing you are opening up a plethora of avenues that can only come as blessings.

To me it is one of the most incredible feeling to know that some one or people in general just love to see you, around them for the difference that you make to their lives all because of the person that you are.

No doubt people always look to me as the kind of person that they love to be seen with, it's because I just really love people, and it shows, frankly I really wouldn't like to have it any other way, after a man that has friends must have shown himself to be friendly that why he is able to attract so many people in his surrounding.

Put it to the test, one day you should go out being just like a real grump, just to how many people you would attract to your corner, may be only those that are as grumpy like you, which in itself is a very bad tale, simply because too many of those people in one place would be very dangerous indeed.

Now on the other hand, lets make it the reverse situation, and go out with a constant smile, and being you friendly self, and see how many people will automatically join you doing the very same thing.

This is only too real, one day I went to a place where I had to join a long line of people waiting for service, as I entered the area I made a very friendly comment, and smiling, well, before you know it I had all of the people in that line smiling, even laughing, I thought to my self, what a way to bring change to a situation, and brighten the perspective of so many, this is what you may call making a difference.

In life we have the opportunity to make things better, or make it worse, for that I encourage you to help me to create a bridge to every where, rather than a bridge to no where, to me making inroads to each other is very important, because by so doing is building inclusiveness, which is one of the best ways to bring healing to a some time sicken world.

You and I both have a part to play in helping others to find their way, what is very sad is to know there are those that would quite willingly stand in the way to prevent what may be considered to be game changers for the better.

The next time that you have the opportunity to influence in the way forward to any one, just feel confident that you are definitely a game changer, and deserves it's praise, for I am sure you have heard the saying that a man is not to be considered to be a man by the amount of things that he has accumulated, but by the content of his innermost self, which may be even call self worth.

I feel like I have it in me to give, for all of my life I have been walking the straight, and narrow, and I can never grow tired of it, simply because I found it to be the very best of ways, and there is simply nothing to change that, I put a great value in what I have found there, and I am not letting go in exchange for any thing that I am not sure about.

Before my mother left this earth she gave me a direction that no one else can give me, and I made her a promise that I will do all that I can to stay there, it is a promise that is like a bond between her and me that simply nothing can break.

I know that she is watching over me, how do I know? one night I dreamt of her, and she was holding my hand, she appeared very happy, and smiling, it was the very best time of my life, I can never forget that, and in fact I never will.

All that my parents gave in my earlier years cause me to have some thing much more valuable than of that diamond, and rubies.

I am very proud, and thankful to God that I have what is called an impeccable character, that didn't come by doing things with out thinking of it's consequences, for I always believe in alternative thinking for a better way forward.

Some time we must change for the better, and for the great rewards that it brings, if ever you find the time to stop and think just do that for it is in thinking that we find the true answers to so many questions.

When coming to thinking about it you have been changing for all of your life, only you were not paying attention to define whether it was for the better.

You see, change is seldom worth it's name unless it will move you from the pitfalls that you face, as soon as you can say to your self that, I am changing this because it is simply not working then you are beginning to progress, and you are on your way to self satisfaction, and there is no better place to be.

Value you first as a person, then all of the things that you are made up of, and that will take you to higher quality you that you can love.

Now we can ask our selves, can we change the world? I hope that from here on you can say quite emphatically "yes we can".

What a progress.

Come on, assert your self what you are seeing is all real stuff, the world like it is, with every thing that is good, and not so good, just choose what you would like for you, just remember that life allows us the opportunity to have many things to choose from, may be that is the reason for we can be what ever we wishes to be, it's all based on choices.

I think it is the united states army that says, be all that you can be in the army, now I say be all that you can be in the world, it is entirely up to you to recognize the pitfalls and to avoid it at any cost.

When you are going to choose make sure that it is not based on just making a choice, in fact make one that has a real value to you, by so doing you will be full of assurance and from here on it's like smooth sailing.

One of the reasons why we do that is just to avoid senseless start ups instead we should be making firm steps forward that leads to our goals, remember that our goals are based on the clear choices that we make, so it is best to say to your self, this time I just does not want to screw this up.

Look, we are subject to mistakes, because we are all human, and it comes with the territory, yet we must all efforts not to make too many of them, for that can, and if not careful will take us down the wrong path, living us the opportunity to make yet another mistake.

Every thing that we do can be corrected, so go on and make your correction now just before it becomes too late, in fact things may take a turn for the worse, living you confused, and make it much more difficult for your self.

Any thing that you can avoid before it takes place should be your first priority, I just think every thing becomes far less complicated, why cause your self a major headache when you can avoid it.

There are way too many of us going down the wrong pathway just to check it out, when we can just take the right one, and make much more sense, and save us so much time that we may now have to set us on our path that leads us to the progress that we really want to make.

To accomplish all, or may be some of the many things that you are looking for, think long and hard before a decision is make, that will sure help to keep us on track, and stay there, because it is the very best for you in the end.

I try to use this method as my guide to almost every thing that I do, and so far it has been working very well, as they say if you find some thing that is working, why not use it, after all life teaches us all of the lessons that we may use in almost every application that we my consider.

Just think of the outcome when ever you are attempting any thing, I am sure you really want every thing to be the very best just like you have thought it should be in the first place, lets not change the way that we feel about the things that we like most, because in the end we can be able to write our ticket for around the world.

Man! I love progress.

From here on I know that every thing that I do I will succeed, I am now condition to that, and I am very happy for that, look, I am trying to stay in that frame of being positive, for the most and best that I can, because I quite aware that will only help me in all of the efforts that I make.

It is no wonder that I turn out to be the person that I am now, remember that I was a little boy just like you are a young person, what I did was to listen very carefully to instructions, there is no better way to helping to find your direction in life.

Each and every time I get in a quiet mode, and thinking it's like I am hearing my parents all over again, this is my constant reminder to stay on track, simply because I am very determine to make great progress in life.

We are not saying that it is going to be easy one hundred of the times, but close, we have to leave space for human errors, which at times helps to correct things before we get too far.

The idea is to use every thing as an opportunity to further your cause, when you think about it carefully, every single thing has it's rightful place in our lives, lets face it they are here too, what we have to do is to take what we need to produce what we want things to become.

I am quite sure you have heard of the process of elimination as we, some of the things that we attempt to use may not be the right things for us at the moment, or more time we my just never need, but that does not mean that it won't be good for some thing else.

Just about every thing is good for some thing, we can always find usage for the things that we think is not good for project number one, but can be used use for project number two.

Here's a simply version of things the way it is versus the way they used to be. In the hotel and restaurant industry, as almost every purchaser would say to you that they went to their poultry supplier for chicken, but at the time the wings, were never used, all that we wanted was the breast, thighs, and legs, it was much later on we wake up to realize that we could us the wings as snack foods for bars, and parties, now this has become a multimillion dollar business.

That is just what we get for using the alternative thinking process for a much better way forward for all concern.

I can't help but to urge you to use your thoughts wisely for they becomes the things that will make you very proud, and more willing to us it more often.

You, see I think that people are thinking, but the question is just how are the thinking, and what are they thinking about, it really doesn't help to us our thoughts as a weapon to destroy each other, but it would be better to us it to help each other, that can make a very big difference on the out come possibilities.

In stead I will use mine to help to move you from the very brink of the pitfalls onto the podium of progress.

In order that you may get the most out of life, you must first ask your self, just what does most means to you. You must be able to place a value on the things that you are going after in life, and just how you may be able to utilize them.

Now in this complex world where for the most part we find our selves trying to weave our way through, it becomes very difficult at times, because there are so many avenues that you can take in order that you may be able to find your meaningful place in which to be.

I am quite sure that you will agree with me, when I say one shouldn't have to look too far to find places that they can use what they have so much off to enable that of others.

For me I always had this thing about me that if I can have it by working for it, why shouldn't I be able to have it, after all what I am doing is working for what I want, and that should be noble enough.

What I would love to see is that more of us join in, and utilize all of the talents that you have, and invest them in a place where the benefits are sure to follow, once you accomplish that, it then becomes evidential that you are now have the ability to challenge any situation that will help to point people to the pitfalls, and serve as a director, as the others try to find their way.

That is part of the greatness of life that I like to take pleasure in highlighting, simply to me this is simply one of the great blessings that we can bring to people every where, and any where in the world that we may be.

Just about every time I get to this point I get a brand new feeling that I am doing most of the right things, and that is helping others to find greater meaning to their lives, I know it has been said before that the quality of a man is not determined by the amount of things that he possesses, but in fact by the quality of the inner most person that he is.

You may say what does this have to do about any thing, and I will say to you, every thing. I pride my self in trying to be one of the nicest people on the face of the earth, that does not come with out a good level of trials, yet I persist because I also learnt that if you are going to be the best you must also expect that you will have to be tried like mosses. and still live to tell the tales.

Just so many complexities, yet we are strong enough to go on, that is because we were made to endure all of this and more.

I think is very well said that the human spirit is truly a mighty strong thing, what causes that is simply because we love life, we don't always enjoy it to the fullest, but with out it there is simply nothing, that is sort of the reason that I try on a daily basis to be good both to my self, and that of others.

I sincerely hope that we all do struggle just about in every area of our lives, nothing is straight cut, if we are to get there, we will have to go through all of the measures that it takes to get there, just as you just cannot go through the wilderness with out a road map, which is the single most important thing to finding your way to making progress.

In order that I may help bring you from pitfalls to progress I first had to struggle, because struggling is just what it takes.

All of my fears are far removed because of winning after the struggles, now I can do almost all things that I try, simply because I endured the pains in exchange for the gains. I am very happy to be on this platform because I get the opportunity to say to you, that the only way to win is to persistent in your fight.

It really will not help the least to just make bold attempts, just to drop it and begin to run   back wards, what expectations do you have by doing so, as they say stand up and fight, if you expect to win.

I recall some one saying, that the race is not for the very swift, but for the ones that make it to the end.

If you are going to have what you always wanted you will have to work for it despite all of your struggles, but what is far better than just the work is that fact that you will finish high, which is the satisfaction you received based on your dedication, and willingness to continue to the end.

Now here is some thing that my tickle you a little bit, I am sure you have heard the story about the tortoise and the hare, did the hare won the race, the tortoise won the race or both of them won their race, the fact of the matter is that they both had their level of strength that allowed them to do their very best that they could in a given time frame.

When it comes to us it is simply no different do just what you can with your strength, and ability to accomplish what ever it is that you have started.

What is better than any thing is that you have done your very best, as long as it made a difference in your life,enough to enable you to affect the others,then you have done you job,to do what you are incapable of would be quite enough to frustrate you,enough to have you standing behind the pitfalls,for God knows how long.

All that I wanted to do was to use all of the experience that I have accumulated over the years,and made it count for some thing,that had the power to power me to the top of my game,because I knew that just as soon as I have gotten there all of the progress that I ever wanted was waiting right there for me.

You see, nothing beats expectation,work for the things that you want to have in life,and you are sure to find it,all those that have

have had to the same thing to acquire theirs,follow their example,and see your expectation soar to the highest heights,but,wait expectations are a part of it ,are you ready to get what is supposed to be your share?if so continue to be inspired,and there can be on surprises,only reality.

Quit doubting your self,and second guessing your abilities,if you were prepared for it, then by no means should be having doubts about what is ever so possible.

I have told you time and time before that my progress was not handed to me,in fact it was very well earned,I had to go through quite difficult channels to get to where I am today,and I am still earning more.

Enough about me the main reason why I wrote this book was not for me,but for you,I would love to see you succeed me and all of the others,I know you can do it, if you try as long as you know the first step to having is by trying,nothing venture,nothing gain.

Don't even get your self caught up in the things that are to try to stop you,just know that you have all of the power in you to change what ever you can.

Really I didn't know what I was capable of doing until I got my self fully engaged,and moving full steam ahead,now that I am there I couldn't feel greater,what made things so sweet for those that succeeded was to know that they have tried.

Page 93

Just quit all of the doubting an get on with the business of the day,time is not waiting for you if you are to make progress in this life you must go forward,or you will be standing still, or going backwards.

Having life alone should demand from you some action, for this is what it is all about,then some.

Look, I was never like you,dreaming endlessly I knew at any time now I was going to start putting these dreams into motion, and that I did,and I am very happy that I did,some one asked me,what are you working for,the answer was,just what I want to have in my life,I knew enough that I could stand there for ever, with a million people going by me daily, and not one would ask me how they could help.

It was, and is very common for people give you less attention when you are still struggling,it is when you become successful that every one wants to pay you all of the attention in the world,you know you really don't need it, because by now you are okay,it's the ones that are suffering that needs the attention,simply because they are mostly in the dumps stuck, and not going any where.

One time I said to my self that I wanted to be filthy reach, not knowing that some one was listening to me in the back ground, because they came up to me and ask why I wanted to be that rich.

My response to them was very simple, who else was going to give me all that I need, you? How quickly they responded with oh,no not me,I don't have nearly enough for both of us.

This is exactly what I mean, when it comes to money, just don't waste any time depending that some one is going to bail you out, it's your baby,you deal with it the way that you can.

Now do you really want to know the truth about why I would like to have quite a lot of money, it's simply, no one gave me when I needed it the most, I had to scrap from all corners just to find enough for my needs. Even that was okay to me, that certainly helped me to be able to stand on my own two feet, then walking to greater possibilities.

When I made it to my first leg of my destination, there were hundreds of people waiting to cheer me for the greatest efforts in my life getting pass the pitfalls just to arrive at destination progress.

For most of the times we waste too much of our time thinking about what if,instead of saying that is if you notice there is much more power in the that is,because by this time you can see, feel,and taste the results,that your determination brought.

Now this is where we sow the seed that became the tree,and bore enough fruits that you can call a harvest. Progress is sweet.

If you really want to taste the sweetness of what you have done,just take a good look at the final product,as it came through just as you have planned it,I am always amazed by that, and it is simply because I know just how much work that I had to put in it.

At this point it is just where a lot of people say how tired they are,and have nothing left to do any thing else,it's either they were spinning in the mud,or they were just a whole lot of nothing.

If you put a lot of attention in any thing, means that you should be taking a lot more than you have put in.

Time investment is just as money investment,you do it for a reason,and that is to maximize your return,which makes it all worth the efforts.

Too many times I have heard people say,time is money,time is not money,but the opportunity to make money if used wisely,so the next time you hear any one saying that time is money ask them to go and spend it, and that's because you know it is just impossible to spend time in place of money.

Actually that is why I am working, using this portion of time with you,as an investment for both of us,my expectation is for me to see you doing much better than even you ever expected.

What I usually say is if you are alive then you must have time, especially for all of the things that matters much to you, because one of these days you are going to be in great need of them.

Just remember that you cannot bottle time, but you can bottle things, have you ever stop to take a good look when driving pass a farm? first thing that greets your eyes a silo pointing up to the sky,the first time that I saw it,I wondered what the heck is this thing standing there in the middle of the beautiful rolling hills? that was some one said to me this is a place for the farmers to store their grains when it comes in from the field.

I was very well satisfied with that answer,because I made perfect sense,I just hope you can take a look at it again,and see what lessons you can draw from that concept.

For sure as times go bye we should use all of that chunk of time that is alloted to us to get done some of the things that we have to do before night fall and thereby enables to store up some of the things that we produce.

Unless we take hold of all of the opportunities to do all that we can now,we would be preparing our selves to deal with that inevitable pitfall that is always there,like a monumental destructive machine. Every one has the opportunity to do some thing that would hopefully help them to make great progress that you will need some time down the road,so just don't kid your self make your plans now so you won't have to make it later.

Run with time on your side, at least you will be going places,because time is always moving along,do you remember the guy that he was not getting any where? that was simply because he was not doing any thing,or enough to take him places.

How many times have you heard your friends say the very same thing,I'm sure it's been one time too many,until you have gotten sick of hearing the same old thing again.We all got to remember that some times we just talk way too much,with out doing any thing.

Why put so many limits on your self,the more you tell your self that this is enough,is the very least that you will get done, simply because you are setting the limitation in place, just don't blame any one for the lack of progress in your life.

Be like the reservoir and let it flow,some one is waiting for some thing coming their way,it's like good fortune,or blessings,the thing that is so needful in the lives of so many.

Some times I wonder whether there are enough people going into the right direction, because it is there we may find all that is good,and some times not so good, but it is okay because by so doing we may find all of the many things that we may be able to change,for the good of every one, not just some and not the rest,you see, no one is that special, but only to themselves.

Instead we may be find special things to do that would that would even change our own lives.

It's been several time now I have heard some one saying that as they help their own life has been helped,it's so funny how things can be changed so quickly,I have a feeling that as we develop the willingness to do good things in any way that we could,we becomes like that reservoir whose generous giving from it's source only opens up for receiving more from whence it came from.

So many lessons has been taught to us about the benefits of having and giving that it should be like second nature to say the least,when ever I respond to any situation that will help out some one,I think of how bless I am to be able to do just that.

Some of the many reasons for that, and the way that I am is because I am always get the thrills to see some one thrive in all of their efforts,it feel like my own efforts,I just get a real good feeling as I share their joys.

I really thank God for the way that I am,I am real that way,and will keep real in just about every thing, I don't know about you hey,I hope that we all can make all of the necessary adjustments in our lives to reflect all of the good that is within us, then we can help to move any one that we could from pitfalls to progress.

You were born, yes you are here, have you ever asked your self what is the purpose for you being here? believe or not many of us had to ask our selves the very same question

and each and every time the very same answer came up, and that is to be meaningful to our selves, and dedicated to our quest in life, because after all it is the same quest that will take us from pitfalls to progress some day.

If you are not looking for some thing, may be you will just get nothing, and if having nothing is okay with you, then it might be also okay with all those that can potentially be of help to you.

No matter what you think we are here for each other in one way or the other, and it better to be of service to each other.

When I was growing up as a little boy, and following my dad around the many properties, little did know that today I would be writing about, that how important the time was,I really had no idea that it was so valuable at this point in my life.

To be in the middle of the event some times it could be very hard to know the true values of it, it is way after it is all over, and done with that you can really see the enormity of it, since then I try never to prejudge any thing until I have a real sense of it.

I am quite sure that there are several people that may have similar experiences, as it relates to their earlier life.

I guess that is may be why when people find things that had been stored away for a considerable length of time, one day they come to realize that they have treasures of great value that may be now worth millions, as a matter of fact as soon as I am through with this I think I will be heading to the attic one may never know just what their luck may turn up.

You see, this is where the very best of you means quite a lot both to you, and to all those that may concerns, if you take notice, you may even see that people, don't quite like to just give away things of great value that easily, and as a matter of fact why should they, when comes to selling it we may even wait fro the very best offer.

And so it is, we make the best of our selves so that we may give the very best to all those that are in need of us, it's just like giving what you don't want to keep for your self,but look,when ever you give of your knowledge,it is really no lost to you,in fact it becomes like a carbon copy,no matter you do it remains with you, for as long as you live.

So go on,and give so others can be better an account of your giving,it becomes progress to all.

As I was writing one day,an email came in from my dear wife fill with these amazing photos as crisp and clear as the sky itself simply a demonstration of the grandeur and splendor of God's creation,I only wish that I could share it with you,but I'm afraid not at his time.

I sat back,and took it all in,then tried to put it in perspective,but I really didn't have the ability at that time,so I decided to wave it off for another time.

Right after that monumental silent event I realized how small I am on the face of the earth,but particularly just what I am doing here to begin with.

When all you can see is such dramatic manifestations of power,you all at a sudden becomes speechless for a while,simply because it seem like you have no words left to add to this.

After that I became very silent,and start thinking, of things that most definitely had more substance,if you are not careful all that you can see are pitfalls,because it's like that is all there are,land,water,and sky,then there are human beings,who thinks that they have all of the power in the world.

Not so says these monumental bliss,catch a glimpse if you can some time,then you will rethink your own humanity,especially that you have had the opportunity to see real life ti a different way,you may even ask your self how do we exist here.

To be honest,that only help to make me more willing to look at people straight in the eyes,and at that very moment abandon all sources of dislike,hatred,and malice,and replenish my inner most self with love,thankfulness,and gratitude.

That is one of the reasons that I have decided to spend this time with you today,just to let you know that as I live my life doing the things that makes me feel the way that I feel,it's not all about precious money,for there are so much more value to some things than money.

I will still help to move you from pitfalls,simply it is dangerous there,and put you in a place where you can realize that you have the opportunity to make progress in life,what I know now is exactly what moves me to do the things that I love to do.

But make no mistake about it,I really respect life much more now than before I viewed that site,you know, it's all about being better as a person,then all of the other doors will spring wide open.

For the very first time you may see your vulnerability as nature presents it in His majesty   and power.

I think it is an eye opener,that will certainly make us think a little bit of our lives here on this earth,which puts us face to face to the reality that all of these wonders will outlast us,and that is for sure,never mind all of the pitfalls and the progress.

That really encourages me to want to share life,and things with others more each day.

Join me if you may,it's great,and we will have a blast at the same time.

I will wait for you.

Here is some thing that you may keep in mind,it has helped me,it may help you also

There are limitless possibilities at the beginning of every journey.

If you quit,you stop the results that could of been.

Just knowing that there are pitfalls prepares you to over come.

Life is too short make the very best of it.

Don't worry about time it will take care of itself.

If people doubts you they are the doubters not you.

When you feel like crying go ahead empty it all out,after that comes the laughter.

money is precious but not more precious than life.

People are people you are only a part of them

Don't stop thinking if your life depends on it.

With all of the above sentiments from the heart nothing can really go wrong in your life simply because now there are so much there are in life for you,for you place no limits on your self.

Quitting only makes harder for you in the end,so why even attempt it,especially as you already know that very same reason that caused to begin was based on what you expected in return.

We have all heard that knowledge is power,and even went further to tell us that is only if we used it,you see,once you have the knowledge of some thing it at the very same time prepares you to over come just about any obstacles that might be in your way.

The way that I look at things is we have just a short time on this planet to do and accomplish all that we may want to accomplish so why wast the time that you have to do them,not too many people wants to acknowledge that because it seems as though they just don't want to deal with that sort of reality,when in fact we just cannot walk with blinders all day long as we pretend the just doesn't exist.

In stead what I think we should be doing is to be fair and equitable in all areas of our lives,this may seem like I am telling you what to do,but I am not,do you remember what every one were saying a few months ago,it was lets change the world,do you still want to do that? after all that was quite a brilliant idea removing all of the pitfalls for our selves and that of others,I am liking it already.

I would be thrilled if you can tell me just where I may go in order for me to escape the pitfalls as I try to make my way to the progress that I am after,I would be so happy to follow you there, and enjoy all of the fruits of our labors, now won't that be progress.

Do you know that there are people that really worry about time? as if to say I wonder what time would do if I try to do this, well quit concerning your self about that, because what I experienced is that time has outlast many things, and even people.

Just keep on doing just what you are doing, and keep minding your own business, and let time take care for itself, the more we worry it is the very least that we get done, because it just wouldn't help any. imagine your self standing all of the many things that I have to get done, yet trying to concern our selves about some thing as big as time.

There are just way too many times I have heard people say that the day is just not long enough to get done all of the various things that they have to do, although there is a fair amount of truth to that, gives the reasons to move on with things, because if it is the daylight hours that you depends on, there may be the very same amount coming at you like yesterday.

Although there is so much truth to this, yet there are so many people that allow them selves to go on doubting every thing that the have the opportunity to doubt, in order that we may stop that trend, what we must do is to take a very thorough look at things just to avoid that.

There are some that become very hard on themselves that they ends up seeing a doctor for the problems that comes from that.

I really like when people doubts me, that is the very time that I become very determine to prove them wrong, and for most of the time I have proved them to be wrong, you see I pride my self in fighting very hard if I expect to win, so people that spending me, they are the doubters, and not me.

It was only too recently that I have had a conversation with a favorite friend about expectations, immediately they began to fuss, and doubt with me, to the point where they started crying, what I do with people that cry for any thing at all, it's okay empty it all out, hopefully the laughter will come later.

What can I say there are times we will cry all for the right reasons to our selves, and that's quite okay with me, even me at time cry, this time it's for the right reasons, I am so happy for my progress that I can't help to let all of the emotions flow in a good old cry, then I begin laughing, and believe me it feels so good, that when ever it happens again I will be okay with it.

That is exactly what life is for all of the various highs, and lows, it's not like if we inherit quite a large sum of money, although that would be beautiful as they say money is precious, but as precious as life, I can take life over money any day, and I even think it would be the very same with you.

Don't think that you it is for some people, and not you, because as they say people are people, and you are just a part of them, so always count your self in because when the time comes you will for the rewards you will have nothing to fear.

I hope you will think of all of these things, and enrich your self enough that you may reap all of the many benefits that life affords, and what ever the case, don't stop thinking if your life depends on it, if you are a thinker at all you will know just what I mean.

Some times what we take for granted was not really not granted at all it happens just about all of the time in fact we took it.

In order that it would be more valid, we must start thinking things thoroughly by our selves, get a clearer picture of every thing, so by the time we lay hold on it is really a fact, and not fiction.

Life doesn't need more of that fiction thing, we need to keep it real, because the thoughts that comes from within us are usually good thoughts so if we desire them to bear good fruits we must nurture them well that they may give us all of our expectations.

Here is a great place to start, and it is with the very best of what we have, and that is our thoughts which brings about our expectations, you see, as some one said if you can think it you can do it, I found that out as I began to think things through, and through until it becomes a real part of the way that I think on a daily basis.

I think that there are too many of us holding our selves back because we fail to us the intellect that is within us, we were all made to able to us it, and it also goes on to say, here is just what you will get if you do so.

I us this as the carrot, and allow it to swing one time closer, and I will grab it for sure with the opportunity that I have, this just where a whole lot of fail, because we allow each of this chance to pass us, then wonder why we are not making the progress that we really want to make for all of our efforts.

In order that I may be at the very fore front of the signs, and signals, I must try and keep all of senses working together as I think my way through.

We must remember that what makes things come about is really working towards them, if in case you remember what we mentioned about the carrot, just get closer, and it becomes more accessible, you may even call it opportunity, don't let sleep away, for that can happen when you are simply not thinking enough about it.

I can tell you that I always have had this thing for looking at what was possible for me to pursue, as soon as I felt satisfied with my self, it became like a train on the track, and going full steam ahead towards what I am going for, and just that you may make no mistake about it I was not going to come back with out it.

To me it was always mission possible, it's the way that I live my life, some thing just have to work out one or the other, just find that way, and focus on it, because as soon as you can realize that where you are is at the pitfall, it should then become very aware that it is one of the places that most likely will be the least choices of places for you to be.

Just about every one that I know is wanting some thing from life, the fact is they some times won't exercise what it take to acquire it some of us should know that it takes much more than wanting it, you pursue it simply because it's worth it.

I got mine because I had to first believe that I could have what it is that I wanted, then I make up my mind that I will have what I want, and so it became the reality to me.

Now this is no bull, you ought to see where I came from to know why I was so determine to have some thing to show for existence on the earth.

From that disastrous pitfall to monumental progress, I would not change this for the world.

Part 2

Life is so beautiful that I want to live it forever, and will do just about every thing that I can to prolong it indefinitely, and it is simply because I really don't have any certainty about the one that has been promised.

For years I have been hearing all sorts of great things that might be, but honestly no one really know fro sure so as to me, and all of the others that spend years thinking about it, so far it is the sort of thing that helps to have a sense of solace so to help us to wake up in the morning feeling that day is well worth it.

After all it is we really just don't have another choice of life to take when this one is over, this is why I just cannot stress the importance of nurturing this one to the fullest always.

What I like the very most is the opportunity that I have to help to make sure that just about every one that I know, and care about does have my support I any way that I can to a good life, I may not be able to provide you with all of the things that you need for that life, but if I can at least point you into the right direction, I hope that it would be a help to you.

Since just about every one in this world need some one at any given time, it becomes my quest to encourage you to find you purpose, and fulfill that which is almost an obligation of any descent human being to take on this noble task of reaching out to where you are needed the most.

There are some that are more pressing than others so guess what, we get the chance to prioritize accordingly.

This may be a new call for us to wake up to a brand new reality of our selves, and what we are really doing here, and that if it becomes a matter of question, I can only hope that you can answer it fairly, and together with me, lets get on the mission of starting to help mend a very broken world.

Look, it is very simple if your house is broken in any way the very first thing that we would think of is fixing it, especially as it being our primary dwelling place, no one wants to sleep in a house with broken doors and windows, for fear of the fact that strangers, and even robbers can come in, and just one that I know would like that one bit.

Well, the very same can be said about our world, I wouldn't ask every one to think like I do, but if I can get every one to at least think, it would certainly be a step in the right direction, and hopefully to make difference that we can definitely take pleasure in.

We all know that fixing any thing, is simply because it is broken, and may be not looking good at all, so just to show that we have it together, we would try to make a very bold statement by trying to make it look as good as new for all eyes to see.

I am real proud to say that I have been trying to this sort of thing for a very long time, what made me know that is by the way that I know that others have seen me, it's no doubt that I really love people, and as a matter of fact they are loving me for the person that I am, that's what I am most grateful for, because I am making a difference.

I think that if we all would try to change our selves first, it would certainly be much easier to help others change.

Mine is to inspire, and motivate you to do great things.

You see, as it is said every one of us was made for greatness, that is if we can find it within ourselves to recognize the abilities that we have to turn it into what we would be proud of, so as we share it with others they also can be proud of it, and use it as module for the things that we wish to accomplish.

What ever it is use your life wisely by bringing to bare all of the principles that guides you into the path way that leads to real change in the lives of you and all those around you.

You can be more influential that you think, if you would pay more attention to just what you are able to contribute to your world, and beyond, having fun doing so while at the very same time building better lives for those that depends on you, and your influence.

What is amazing is that there are so many people that is very equip with the abilities to make major shifts that so many would be happy for.

Do what ever it is that would serve to make monumental up grades that would of never happen other wise, I don't think for one minute any one should hold them selves from helping to make a better world in which they too would have to live in.

One thing that I had to realize was that from being a little boy with a drive to get things done, was because of the vision that I had within me, at that time I really didn't know to express it in the way that I should, but like every thing else like a little seed it grows in side of you, and at some point in time it would flow out of you into others.

It was at that time I felt like I was specially blessed for the mission that I to undertake in life, that really fed my emotions, making me stronger each day, with each passing day I got the feeling that I could do some more, so what I did was to find things that I was interested in, and make it a part of my list of things to get done.

Once you realize that you have accomplished the preliminaries I think it is the right time to set your agenda to reflect all of the ingredients that has been imbedded within you for the years of your preparation.

Little did know that I would here documenting that things that could have a profound impact on your lives, and I really mean that, after all I just didn't spend all of those years gathering all of the necessary information just to be used by self, and for myself, I really had you in my mind all this time, so you can imagine, just how happy I feel to be where I am, and be able to help in just about any where.

I really feel humble, when coming to think about it, it tells me that I didn't use my time foolishly, and with out accountability, that's not the person I know me to be, and I am not finished yet, as there is so much to learn, it's no time to stop now, I have quite a lot of work left to do, and I'm on a mission to take care of them all.

This is just me going forward, and getting places at the very same time.

Some times it may seems like I am boasting, when in fact I am not, the essence of this is that as often as I tell you about me and the things that I have accomplished I hope it is at that time you may be inspired to set goals, and accomplish them.

All that you have in side of you is worth looking into, there might be treasure troves to be found after all lets hope you are no longer ten, and as a matter of fact have done some living already, and have some good experience that may be good enough to invest.

What ever it is that you have learnt is worth putting a prize on, usually people really don't retain any thing that is not worth it to them, if I have had a sort of bed experience, bad becomes the word that I despise the most, so some how I find it very easy to put it behind me, and forget all about it, the reason for that I just won't know what to do with any that has a bad implication, to me it's gone for ever.

On the other hand I am going through life with passion for the things that I like to most, and with great value to me.

I really don't know what every one is waiting for to maximize all of their efforts to gain all of life's treasures, and have fun with them? just what are you waiting for, life is sure not waiting for you to make up your mind about any thing, quit holding your self back, don't you want to have more fun with life? the fact is the more you grow financial is the more satisfied you can become, and the more fun you can have.

Why go through life with a constant gripe, find a better way to make things better for your self, and that of others, don't waste time doing nothing, that only produces nothing, and that is like stripping your self of any thing of potential that you may possess.

There are strange circumstances, that is worth a mention, and spark a ray of hope in any one that is just there laying low.

There are many times over, and over again people say that they were just going through some house hold effects, when all at a sudden they came upon some thing that was out of sight for quite a long time, but when found, it was like a major discovery of some thing of great value.

The moral of this little note is that most of us who have done some living do have some experience that goes with the territory, if you can search you may just find that the experience that you gain over the years is quite worth doing some thing with, the fact of the matter is, why do you think you avail your self to learning some of the many things that you have learnt? Was it just for passing the time away or to put it to work I some way or the other that would be of great value to you.

This a path that we are all familiar with, we grew from little boys, and girls to men, and women, that alone should tell us that there must be reasons for us being still here, and to do some thing about that may help us to be grateful, and appreciative for every thing so far.

I feel very thankful and it is my desire to show it to the whole world, that others may look at them selves, and develop any passion that they may have for the things that means a lot to them.

Life is so great, there is nothing quite like it, find a way to enjoy it to the fullest, and please try and help others to do the very same.

Just to let you know, I have a life quest, and guess what it is, now if you are having a bit of a problem trying to find out, let me tell you what it is.

I am looking for all of those little things that makes any one special, you see, when we were growing up to become what ever we are now, our, in fact my parents started at a very early stage to teach me,as you may think every one by now would know just what is right and wrong,and it really didn't stop there, they went on as they kept on adding the pluses, just to make sure that we got what it was that they were trying to convey to us, it many of the principles that eventually would serve as the guide forming the foundation of our lives.

Today, like many other days I would take a glance back in time just to see all the roads that I have traveled, and the many things that have encountered that made the journey so beautiful, in fact if I had to, I would do it all again, just to tell it to you.

And that is the basic reason why I listened to my first mentors, simply because they had the greatest interest in me, how I knew, was because they spent all of the time in the world just to let me know how much they really cared for, and about me, I could of felt it in my soul that even made it so much more special.

Today it's like they are still close to me and, still teaching me in silence, and I am still listening to their voices in silence I just cannot let go, neither do I want to let go, I guess it is exactly what I need to cheer me along life's way.

Just in case you are like me, lucky to have these favorite of all people in your life, just know that they are very special, so please take good care of them, nurture them like no other, because when they are gone, they are gone forever, and there is no one that can take their places, this only a once in a life time experience, make the very most of it, and treat it like the very best thing that has ever happen to you.

I stored mine in a safe place, unspoiled, by all of the corruptions of this world, it's in a volt, and I am using it little by little each day, so that it may last for a life time, as I am quite sure it will, it is simply one of the things that no one can take it away from me, no matter how hard they may try.

Now it is up to you to make memories of yours, and I hope that it is also your guide as you make your way through life's rugged pathways.

The fact of the matter is you do have a way, despite how rugged it may be, what we may have to do is to try and smooth the way making it passable as we to get on with our day, we have life that we may change some of the things that we can, other wise it would be like worthless, if all that we do each day is sleep, wake and eat, that is by far not enough to even make our lives worth it.

Ever since we came into this world there were things that we made for us to do, no one should even think for a minute that there is just not enough for them to occupy them selves self with, although there are those that would beg to disagree with that, but that's okay too, but just remember that at the end of the day it's you and only you that must give account of you.

I realized that at a very young age that entering life was only the beginning of what may be a very long journey, and I was quite right, because here I am telling you my story, hoping that it would inspire you to take all of your challenges and make the very most of them.

You must accept that as they say that at the end of every rainbow there is a silver lining, every difficult situation can produce, good results, you see in the very middle of it, if you take a good look around you will see just what I am trying to say.

Just go through life with an open mind, and you are sure to see all that is there to be seen, and not just that you may see them, but in fact that you will come to a good understanding that every thing was as plain, and uninteresting until some willing mind was able to paint a picture in their mind, and then brought it to bare, for all of us to see.

I can recall very vividly when my wife, and I bought this house, what I noticed almost immediately was that the surrounding was not carefully taken care of, living things looking sort of, any way, not pleasant to the eyes.

I knew that very moment that I had my work cut out for me, so I made a plan based on the way things were, and just went to work.

I love gardening, so I knew that my plans were going to work wonders, and that it did, I scraped every blade of grass by hand from the entire back yard totally moisten the almost rock like surface brought in top soil, arranged the way that I wanted, and plant the garden with a great selection of flowers, and shrubs, staggering them so we would have plenty of flowers for the full season from spring to December.

Today I take a front row seat and admire it's beauty, it's like a little paradise, the place where you can wonder around, or you too can take a seat and let the time just go bye.

This a real lesson that, yes we can change what we don't like, into some thing magnificent that all the world can enjoy.

Satisfaction come by succeeding in the things that you do, open all of the doors for you to do more with the time that you have, some how I just feel life takes on a sort of different meaning as I pursue the channels that I found my self in, simply because I get to see the rainbow in a very different light, rather from just being the end.

Do what you must for the things that you want for your self, take a good look inside of you and I am sure you will find a plethora of things hidden way down there that you can use in just about what ever way that you want, when coming to think about it, why can one think that there is nothing available in this vast arena, there is only one reason for me to excuse any one for that, and that is if you are totally physically blind.

Excuse is just simply to say, I am just too lazy to find out, but just think for a moment, what if we were all too lazy, well, I just don't want to think of what might have been.

If I were like all of the others I would not of been able to climb to the height that I am in now, you see I was so involved from the time when I was a little boy, that by now it's built into my frame work, and I can never get rid of it, I am not complaining because I am very blessed to make it this far, it certainly was not as easy for me like some people may thing, one of the very best thing that I had then which I still have up to today is my willing mind, which allows me the opportunity to formulate the principles of accomplishment which I am forever grateful for.

One just cannot stay in the bad times forever, after all it's only you that's keeping you there, because we have the power both in our hands, and mind to accomplish just about any thing that we may put our minds too, so go ahead and count all of the many blessings that comes your way, and find a way to appreciate them to the fullest.

That is just what life is all about developing our minds to bring about great things, believe me, I can attest to that, for there were times when some people thought that I was crazy as I attempt the things that appeared to them as impossible, but that was not by me, I know just what my limitations are, I attempt what I knew that I was capable to handle, so the expected results reflected that.

The very best thing for me, and I hope for you too is to get a vision of what it is that you want to accomplish, letting it take a form in your mind like a photo memory, then set your self up, and before you know it, here comes a master piece, that even the angels in heaven can rejoice for.

Look, you are on your way to becoming great, keep moving forward to your goals.

Usually what we are looking for may never be found behind us, but in front of us it's like the very same, when you set your goals it's for any thing that lies ahead, this a very normal thing that every one by now should be accustom to, but wait, don't hold your breathe you might be taking for granted right at this point, we just cannot assume that because we is on the same page at the same time, so let us ask questions hopefully to get some answers.

What amazes me is to hear people say that life is not taking them any where, when in fact it is because they are standing still, with out any movements, and at the same time they should be much further ahead.

If you want some thing the best way to achieve it is simply not by doing nothing, as an individual you ought to figure out what you love and go after it with all of your strength, and not stopping until you have achieved it.

That is just what many of us have done, we realized that it was possible, and achievable with that in mind there's no need for doubting your self, in fact if you are going to succeed in any thing, you better be assertive enough, and make your moves confidently in order that success may come your way.

Is at this point I would like to see you realizing that dreams will come before money, and just in case you wonder why so, it's because thoughts comes before things, as you find your self thinking about any thing is at the very same time you are clearing the way fro a better journey.

I really like people that have a passion for making things happen, and they will never stop until it happens, to them it is a real confirmation that truly all thing are still possible, what do you have to loose simply nothing, in fact which ever way that you look at it you always win, simply because there is always lessons to be learnt in every situation of line.

As I sat in my study one day writing, next to a big glass window, I just couldn't help but noticed that it was the very beginning of winter, out side looked sort of grey, and windy, now just realize that fall was just over, and here we are facing winter again, what I didn't think was I better get use to it, for I should be by now, because for sure it will happen yet again.

You see, what goes around comes around, the time has no respect for us, only we must respect the times enough that we may do just what we must do in order that we may experience then again another round of nature's some times unforgiving realities of life.

I looked, and learnt by looking at some of the world in my own spectacle, there I was able to have a birds eye view at conditions that may seem to be much too harsh for those that are there, not realizing that it is some thing call accustom to that becomes an enabling factor for their existence, one of the lessons that we can learn from that is, to use what ever it is that we have to benefit us just where we are, and still be thankful for the amazing thing that we have call life.

In a very recent conversation with my dear sister, we both realizes great changes in our lives, since we last parted ways with our familiar, and even highly treasured place of birth, we like most others saw the need to get a fair glance at the world from another vantage point, it was so very nice to hear that she prepared well by taking full advantage of what first offered to her in the form of education.

We both recognized that we have had the opportunity of being raised by what we can say for sure was the very best parents, simply because the held nothing back from walking us through all of the many avenues of life so that we my be well edified, and ready for just about any thing that came our way.

I call it the first step program, because they were the very first people in our lives that cared enough to teach us all that was to prepare us for life.

It was like drawing straight from the source of the spring, tastefully done, and easily assimilated, to day we are singing the praises, especially for what we have become.

From that we were told that in the end there will be simply nothing that would be impossible for us to do, they were so right, after learning all of the tricks of the many trades, from gardening to fishing we were ready to tackle them, and also did a very good job at the very same time.

There was never a time that we said no to our parents, they were the leaders in our lives, and well worth to follow in any direction that they were going into.

As for me I was wise enough to know that with all of this type of leadership, I was sure to go very far, so I stayed in close contact, and try hard not to miss any thing that was coming down that pike, we both agreed that life then was not necessarily a bowl of cherries, but at least it was cherries, and worth having.

It is very true, that nothing really comes easy, and as a matter of fact by then I quite accepted that was the case, so for me it was to buckle my booths, and keep on moving, for where they were taking us was the very best that there was any where.

I am so happy that I paid respect to my master, even if the master was my own parents, number one we honored our leaders very much, simply because they had the right stuff, and we needed what the had, to make us leaders after they are gone, I am particularly proud to say that I have made my mark, I have answered to the call, to make my way to unprecedented height that would be very happy to know.

That is why I take great pleasure in bringing this book to you hoping that you may us it as a bench mark as you make your way, to what may be your goals to accomplish.

You may ask the question, what is the purpose of accomplishing any thing, why is every body running after this thing call success, what do they know that I don't know, in fact I think only you just don't get it, start thinking again, and not just for a second or so, give it roaming space around your head, to let sink in, then you will know for sure what they know that you does not know.

You see, there are people that a passionate about success in their lives, and nothing, simply nothing is going to stare them from that, it is a personal goal that does have quite a lot of meaning to them, so in case you find some one just running for their goals, it might be a jolly good thing to get fired up, and begin to run for yours also.

Because for all that you know, time may be closing out on certain options, instead be careful not to miss your opportunity, if you do, it is like the train that is passing this way every five years, and after that, you may, at least have a donkey standing by to see if you can catch a ride to destination unknown.

It becomes very crucial for us to prepare to go it alone, it is one way to show that we can have our own independency, for all of my life, as far as I can remember it's been my ambition to be able to show the world that I would at least try, before I would even say to any one that I couldn't, for all along there were some thing ringing in my head, remembering me, that I promised my self that I must make sure, by thinking it through, and through, because it was always my obligation to do it like there were no one else around, I'm sure you must have noticed the very same thing your self, some how in think it may be the very reason that some people much rather to work alone, and it is because of self dependency.

I have seen this happen before, when you have too many people all in one place, you just increase the chances for very little to get done, simply because every one is looking for the other to do what ever it is, and if you are not careful nothing simply nothing will ever get done.

As I was growing up I can remember that our parents had to make quite sure that this was not going to be the case.

Coming from a very large family, there were always the potential for that to happen, so what they did was to give every one their own chore to get done, and should some one finishes before the other we would give a good helping hand.

You see, some how I have a sense that the world is trying to follow on, it was the we generation especially in my own family long before now, we did just about every thing in unison, we were a family, and for darn sure we loved each other enough to help make way for success, not failure.

One thing that I know for sure it is a very different world today, but some times I think it would be a rather good idea to bring back all of the old principles that guided us so well, and it helped us to arrived to destination assured.

Whether you are in a similar situation or not, it really doesn't matter, as long as you keep things in perspective, say to your self that there is plenty of opportunities in the world, and for sure there is quite enough there for me too, as soon as you can acknowledge that your quest is on.

Now it is entirely up to you to follow through to the very end, simply because the beginning sure has an end, and at the end is just where you may call your destination, but that is not all, expectation tells you that there are things waiting you when you get there, as some one said a very long time ago, follow your rainbow, for at the end there may be your pot of gold.

Don't ever go through life with out hoping to have some thing for your self, especially some thing that you have made, because some one just may ask you the question, did you make this all by your self? if you can answer yes, then and only then you will have a real sense of full entitlement, that will have you floating on the wind to cloud nine.

We are entities in your selves, every person were place here with the abilities to do extraordinary things, and so you can, you just have to show that you are able to, just remember the very first thing is to try, and continue, you will know when you are in the groove, and going places, as they say listen to your gut, it will never stare you wrong, believe me, the benefits are all yours.

Just know this, before I started my career as an author, it was not some thing that automatically dropped from the sky, as a matter of fact, I am a deep thinker, that alone gave me the edge to look for the answer where ever it may be, so just as I fight hard, and fight to win, the same is very true I always dig deep to find all of the answers that I am looking for, and as a bit of good news to you I find them ninety five percent of the times.

But what really made a vast difference was my up bringing, what you see in me today is a true reflection of my parents as my first mentors, I just feel as though I was very blessed to have good caring parents.

I always boast when it comes to my character, I always say to people, that I have some thing that money just cannot buy, immediately they would ask, and what's that, and I would say, it's my impeccable character, and I can tell you, I owe all to my parents, my first mentors.

Now you may understand why I became a motivational speaker, and author, frankly there were just way too much pent up inside of me, so this is the release that I chose.

Some one asked me some time ago, so why do you want to become a motivational speaker, and author, and I couldn't help by saying, I have had a long, and tedious journey, and I also knew that there was a destination, one that I would be quite satisfied that I had accomplished.

In all of your endeavors try and stay true to form, commit your self to find what ever it is you are in search of, and be careful not to stop till you have accomplished your list of things to do.

From my Motivational series, here are some things that I would like you to keep in mind.

This is based on, an evening with Paul, his rise through struggle.

In the natural realm of things, nothing is impossible

Don't allow a little difficulty stops you from pursuing for the very best results

I struggled with all of my goals in sight

I just couldn't find any one to help, so I went alone with God

Some times I have gotten tired, I rested and continued

I asked my self, what is life for, and I answered, to do things

Just know that you can accomplish almost any thing, if you put your mind to it

Every thing that you see around you, were difficult for the ones that made it possible

There's no easy way out, but there is a possible way in

If you are not sure, I am here to point you to the way forward

Nothing is netter standing on your own two feet.

We were all born into this messed up world, even though it was made perfect for us to inhabit, and enjoy, but as we well know by now, that it takes the unscrupulous way of thinking by that those that always seem to know how to make things better, while at the very same time has done nothing but to make every thing wrong.

I think that is usually cause by those that feels the need to have more than their share of that thing call destructive power, you see, that type of power in the one that says I am right despite the opinions of others.

Some times I think that no one is really right, instead we agree on some things that it is okay, and that makes it right for the time, but you wait, a few months down the road, you are sure to that there is some thing is wrong with.

Now it is not that it was not okay, some times things can out grow them selves, just to be replaced by some thing else, and hopefully better this time, so what we may have to do is to make sure that there are more collaboration when it comes to deciding on factors that has to do with the well being of plentiful.

In general I do think that as we spend much of our time enriching our selves first before we can enrich the lives of others, that should be our primary goal, for lets face it, we were not created to be all things to our selves, and even then no one person has it all when it comes to knowledge, wisdom, and understanding, thank God we even have some, let us not be too cocky about it.

For we may be special, but not that special, we are still human beings, and will always be subject to all sorts of misunderstandings, some times we can't even trust our own selves for making all of the very best decisions, how then will we be able to make it with out some of the others stepping in, and adding their two cents worth, just to see if it could help to make things more palatable, which we can only hope would make every thing work better for the good of all.

I am almost sure that you too gets the feeling some times that you wish you would be considered as part of the forum that involves your own life, but no, you are just not important enough for that circle of ill influence.

Don't even think for a minute that you would have to remain silent for ever, there are several ways, and things that you can do in order that you may have a vastly different experience, as it relates to you.

At one time I have had the very same opinion, so what I did was to tackle it from a different angle, and that is by writing, and speaking, that gave me a real advantage, now I can help people through writing, so you too can, learn a thing or two, that would help to redefine your life.

Look, what we must come to terms with is no matter what we may do nothing will make us perfect, and that's a given.

So what we can do now is to come to terms with, all of these things in life, and be thankful for being alive to do some of the things that we do, so lets try to make it good that it may last for a life time.

Yes, life can be hard at time, but would not have to deal with a tough world, than not having life to deal with it at all, some times I like some other count it all joy when I have to do things that are not so easy to accomplish, this is the tough part, the easy part is the finish, I am sure you know what I mean, when you have to give some thing all of your efforts, despite how you feel, because you also know that when the final product emerges, and the feeling of jubilation comes due, and the hands thrown up to the sky, that is when you know for sure that it was well worth it after all.

Some times may be we should just think pass the tediousness of any thing in order that we may have some fun getting to what's much better.

Every one is subject to the very same rules, so why then should some make it better than others, simple enough, the ones that make it, usually are the very ones that follows the rules, so don't west any more time if you know what to do why not do it, and avoid all of the other things that will haunt you in the end.

I have seen some one day built a whole house, while trying to go against the rules, and do you know what happens after? they had to start from scratch, and rebuild the house back again, only at that time following all of the guide lines, and building this time all for the last time.

Make no mistake about it in any way, shape or form what ever it is that is not done right does has it's consequences, what that means is that some how you are going to pay, and some times harsh ways.

Just remember that it was a very famous icon that once said, we did not go to the moon because it was easy, but because it was hard, don' be afraid to tackle difficult things, because they can be the life savers for tomorrow.

Just as I said before the only thing that I will never be afraid of is challenges, it was here from the beginning, and will be here in the end, you can count on it for sure.

You see every thing can be done some times we just have to put a little more effort, and that's what life is all about, and some time more, the fact of the matter is we well know that giving up is a lost case, and since every one loves being winners, I think it would do good to see more of us being winners, while at the very same time bringing out more of what is, and that is love.

It's amazing just what a little four letter word can really do in the big scheme of things, despite the messed up world, that too can be fixed, simply by injecting some love, or appreciation where it matters much.

With all of this I hope you can already see your challenge comes before progress, so don't give up yet, you are still working towards your goal, at the mean time don't forget to say thanks for life that causes all good things to happen.

As we go through life just about every thing will appear to be more impossible, but that's only a misunderstanding of the real truth, I am sure you have noticed that there are time we all have bought a bit of furniture as a kit in a box, at first glance this thing looks like the impossible thing to put together, but after you take a closer look at the template, grab your favorite drink, what ever that may be, and set your mind to it you realize that it is not that difficult after all.

It is just typical in our way of thinking, every thing that seems to be, doesn't have to be, the idea is we will find out by setting our minds to, and just make a start at least, before tossing it to the corner, and giving up all together.

Remember that when things gets tough, take a deep breathe, and rethink the process until it becomes a part of you mind set, and I can assure you that your life will be much easier, people will love to be around you once again.

Things that seems to be that difficult for the most time is only a figment of our imagination, some time it is only because we are just not quite prepared to accept things right way, and as a matter of fact it is not a bad way after all, and I am in total agreement with that, there are just too many people that has done just that, and are still crying today.

Like just about most things, I feel much more secure to teach a subject if I know what it is all about, so I spend a lot of time researching carefully so that I may have things set in my mind, and ready to deliver.

Part of the reasoning behind that is, for me at least I know that life can be ten times harder, and that is not what I need by no means at all.

Personally I have been through way too many turns, and twists in my earlier years, all in preparation for my life today.

I can safely say that those were the days that I treasure the very most, because it was responsible for my life's foundation, all that I am today is because of my yesteryear.

That is why I can encourage you to be successful in every area of your life. it may not come easy, but so what, mine did not come easy, up till now I will say to you that nothing is that easy but it is achievable, just prepare, set your mind to it and go for it.

Take all that you can today, tomorrow is not promised to any one, that is why it is said try not to put off what you can do today for tomorrow, for tomorrow may just never come.

I am very happy that I went through the many obstacles that I had to, now I am better able to help you to over come yours, the many years of preparing has done some good to me, if in fact you are not prepared like me try and make sure that you are, it would make things work much better than if you were not.

What made me successful was because I had to be very determined, I wanted to be successful so bad that I would literally do just about any thing to make it, just living and dying was just not good enough for me, not me I wanted much more than that, so I work as hard as I possible could with great expectations in my mind, to me it was a goal that I set for myself that I just had to attain to, and did not until I make it, now I am happier.

Go ahead satisfy your self, because no one can give you that sort of satisfaction, it would be you and you alone.

There are great rewards in all of the good things that we may do, the ones that will live us feeling that as though we are floating on cloud nine, some how I love that feeling, after al you have worked so hard foe years, and now it is just the time to celebrate your achievement.

What I advocate is that after going through life under what can be described as adverse conditions just about any one would love to have this time to look back, and see all of the roads that you have traveled, some times high, and some times low you have gone through it all, as you explored all of what were the possibilities which is now the results of it all.

There are reasons why I stand behind what are the trials before success, it's the reasoning behind it, it is great to see the ones that believe in themselves that much, to dare to try, just to realize that their trials were not in vain.

I too have learnt quite a lesson in that willingness to go through where some may never wish to but because you know what you were going for you went relentlessly to bring back that enviable prize that is now the trophy in the window.

You may give up all of your options, which is a way of relinquishing all of your opportunities to be successful, it is always better to come back with the bottle half full than empty at least you have entitlement to some thing.

I have met many people in my travels that willingly accepted 25% over 100% one of the reasons for that was not knowing their true value, or that the first part was all that they ever needed, until they went to use the first part, and realizes that it was not nearly sufficient, now they wish that had the second part, which already went to the one that knew the use of it, I'm afraid that about that time it was a little late to recover even belaboring the thought to do better, lessons has to be learnt at some time or the other, this was one occasion that would make you think, and learn.

If you age going to succeed in this life, just don't just stand there, move forward and move all of the things that is standing in your path impeding your steps as you try to make a way forward for your self, that is not quite easy as many may think, but it is the nature of the beast, and it's very movable.

I also learnt that as I try to accomplish on the goals that I set for my self, I would have to contend with that of the others, just remember that you are not alone in this space, so you will have to count all those factors in when trying to find your way up the ladder.

Step by step, just as it is demonstrated on the ladder, there is simply no need to try to make it up there before you are ready for the next move, other wise you can cause your whole effort to suffer a major set back, although set backs are part of the reality of many things, it is not a necessary thing in any one's desire to move forward.

While you are considering clearing your path of the debris that's hindering you, just know that's only a very small part of what you may have to deal with, as far as I I'm concern the human elements are far ,more dangerous when it comes to things in your way.

There are so many negative people that you may have to deal with, some of them will be jealous, some will envy you, and some just won't have any thing to do with your growth, it is just not for them, I have experienced those sort of people, but non the less they are not hard to push aside, you have to realize that you a work to get done, and nothing is going to stand in your way, and rob you from achieving you goals.

Pay particular attention, and you will notice that the people that has little interest in making it in this world would try to seek you out to engage you in trivial matters, that will live you with little time it get any thing done for your self.

Be stead fast in your mind, stand firm on your mandates, and be like the un shift able rock, because you just have to be real strong, because there are quite a bit of influences out there, to shift you off your base which will only live you feeling sad, and despondent, by that time you may have to make up a lot of ground just to get back to where you were at first, so take control of every thing that you care about if you are going to succeed after all.

As you removes the doubts, and negativity from your way, replace them with possibility expectations, and results, every thing that you do should be, like expectations based on your planning, if you make good plans, they will work for you, every thing will show that you are quite prepared for your celebration later, and at that time make darn sure that you will invite me, I love a good party.

Here's a reminder, that if you spend all of your time worrying about what people may think about you, you may never do any thing at all, don't give any one that amount of power over you, instead submit your self to the ultimate power of God, and every thing will be taken care of just the way it should.

Today is a very dark, and dreary day and there is no doubt in my mind that I just won't be doing too much out there, so I have decided to stay in for a while and continue writing.

It is one of the many things that I know that I feel that I must do, and frankly I think I like it very much, it a very good way to document the way that you feel about things in general, only at this time I have decided to narrow it down to specifically to an inspiring writing event.

Although it is not Monday, but it is raining, and if I'm not careful it can attempt to get me down, but not this time I will stay alert, keep my set on this computer, and get things done, because I do have many other things that I must get done.

With days like today, I remember when I was a wee little Todd I would get together with my other brothers, and play some good games to keep us from getting bored, although out there there were lots to be done, but when it was raining like today we would get a well deserved break from it all till all of this rain was over.

Because there are so many things for done to do in any given day, there would be very little time to complain about things to do, what we had to do was to prioritize on the list of things that we should get done and set our minds in order, and get going.

I can assure you that, there were times that I didn't feel quite up to it, but that would be only a figment of my imagination, when there is no one else to do it, I'm afraid it was going to be me, or the others, but made no mistake about it for it was going to be done.

The fact is when you have animals waiting to be fed, and cared for how can you say no to them.

Ti was a very good way to learn how to take your responsibilities seriously, so although it was chores, it was also a time to learn quite a lot of things, that would in some way or the other affect our lives,directly,or indirectly.

You know, as I was doing all of the many things that I had to do, I really didn't stop to figure out how to escape from getting things done, not that I wanted to, because as far as I'm concerned it also was a wonderful time in my life, because I was preparing to much with what was given to me in the form of hands on applications.

I knew that after that I would be able to quite a lot with what I have learnt,it is only now that I can really see the true value of my involvement in the things that made me the man that I am today, when you know that you are at the front line all of the skills that will guide your life, and transform you mind setting you on a higher plain of thinking, there is no price one can pay for that, I treasured it then, and I treasure it now.

So it is a wonderful way to give some of what I have become to you, simply because I feel that I have it in me to give, how else would you have known about me, my life, and how I have become noticeable in the eyes of so many.

To become better in life, one must be able to go through the darkened channels in life, with hope imbedded deep in their souls, because it is because of strong commitment, and determination that we become what ever it is that we are.

On this journey through life if you want to have right type of questions, don't be afraid to ask all of the necessary questions for the answers that will help you to make those necessary adjustments, that will put you on the right target for you to reach your goal.

Many times we doubt our selves because we may be struggling for answers that will help us, so please don't be afraid go on and ask, one can only say no to you, and as a matter of fact, I just don't think any one would say no for the opportunity to teach you some thing that will help to go forward.

I asked all sorts of questions because I wanted to know, as they say knowledge is power, but one has to use it to experience it's power, so if you think you have what it takes to accomplish great things, just go ahead and make your day, in fact you will be making much more than your day, you may be setting your self for a life time, for all you know.

In a recent research that have conducted, what I have discovered was that the ones that, was curious enough, and wanted to know was the one that became the experts at the long run, some times I think it is quite okay to be like curious George, we make much better decisions when we have the answers to most of the questions, in fact that really boost your confidence too.

Feeling set back in life is based on ones own lack of ambition will, and drive, you got to feel a need for urgency at all times that will help you to pursue, and in fact achieve your goals.

I really don't quite know how any one can live with themselves after doing so little, or simply nothing at all, yet expects to live a productive life like those that have done every thing that they could to live the sort of live that will compliment their efforts, I just have to do some thing, after all I have a little pride within me too, and further more I wouldn't like any one to think that they are contributing to my life more than I am contributing to me, some how it just doesn't fit the bill.

I am thankful for the life that is within me enough that I have made a promise to my self that I will do just about all that I can to affect other lives in the very best positive way that I would be happy for, and when I last checked I was very happy to see every thing working as planned.

Here is some things from my workshops that may be of help to you.

Ask a lot of questions, to get all of the answers that you need.

Defeat self doubts.

Don't use any set backs as a reason not to do any thing.

Keep going forward, your goal is ahead of you.

When some one says no take it lightly, this is not your no, it's theirs.

Develop a millionaire mindset, make things happen the way you wants it to be.

Always stay positive, it's the best thing to work with.

Keep all of your options wide open.

Live nothing to chance, make your plans, and work your plans.

Finally let your achievements be based on the goals that you set.

Despite all that I have to say to you, I'm sure you know by now that climbing that ladder is far more difficult that you thought, but I can assure you that this should not the reason for you to stop pursuing if it happens to be your life long dream, why would you not want to turn your dreams into a reality, after all it should be the very best thing that you possess that can really change every thing for you.

Believe me it was double time harder for me, simply because I had to start from the very beginning following my dad step by step, and learning every thing that he threw at me, being the well intentioned father that I had, he just would not have given me any thing that he knew was not going to do me some good.

Yes, I really had good on my side, I was very blessed to have that, because when you think of it, any thing that is given with that amount of genuine love, also would be very well received, it becomes the mutual way of the two benefits.

Some times I just cant seem to grab the notion that we want some thing, yet we are being held back by a little turn and twist in our path, make no mistake about it there were meant to be there, and not only that, but they also serves us good, one that helps us to stay focus on the mission on hand.

What I loved most as I started my journey, was the unexpected bends in the roads, some how that gave me determination to be more steadfast, and relentless as got my self for the next one ahead, I knew enough to help me realized that I was more important that all of the bends in my path had to have the power to move them as I tried to make my way forward.

I took courage as my main partner each step of the way, that helped me greatly with the purpose that I had in mind, you see goals are make for many reasons, one of them is to demonstrate that you are able to choose from quite a plethora of options and bring it to a successful ending, it's like just finishing what you have started.

In quite simple terms we say should be just as good as the beginning, because it is the very same thing that you have started for what it is that would be the end product that you have created, now I can say that I have prepared to compete in quite a competitive world, and we are talking about good, healthy competitions, not taking away from any one or thing, in fact adding to what ever is there.

I quite love gardening, so when I plan to do my garden, I first make a plan that I expect is going to give great satisfaction, that means choosing carefully all of the plants and shrubs that I think would bring me joy, and with no mistake it to be the case, little did I know that after it was said and done that I was going to be a model for other gardeners but little did they know that we were all learning from each other, one sees a beautiful flowering plant some where, and behold that it is going to be found in your garden at some point in time, you see every one loves a beautiful thing.

Go for just what makes you feel good, then share that good thing that you have found, some how, whether you know it or not, that creates a better mind set in people. I experienced it.

It is always a rather good thing to spend time to know people better, I find the better I know you is the better I can enjoy you as a person, and then I use it as an opening to see how I may be an inspiration to you in any way, may be I can uncover an opportunity for you to help you move forward, which to me is a real pleasure for me to do.

For over a year now, every one and their brother were found riding their wave of opportunity to at least attempt to change the world, it seems like no one liked it the way it was so the best thing was to change it, although this is not an easy thing to accomplish, it was a step in the right direction.

Did they accomplished any thing? I don't know, I an still looking to see the effects of their efforts.

In this world, we can say, yes, we need to do some thing that can bring about the change that has long been over due.

This is for sure the right time to grab hold of every opportunity that you can, and ride that wave for the change that would make things better.

First of all one must come to realize that in order to change any thing, you must first change your self, by the way that you think.

real change can certainly bring about all of our expectations, but we must be realistic of what it is that we want, not just for our selves, but for all of the people every where, then and only then can we see all the effects of the change that we appreciates so much.

Use every opportunity to bring lasting change, so we may have a better world, it's funny in a conversation I had only too recently, this person asked me just what I thought was wrong with the world, I quickly answered with what I thought was my best answer at the time, I said nothing is really wrong with the world, but quite a lot is seriously wrong with the people, and that is where the change in very necessary.

My goal is to help people to make all of the necessary adjustments in their own lives, and that is the wave that I would love to see them ride, because every wave is like a brand new opportunity towards making it happen for real.

Life as we know it could be tough, but that's okay because it takes tough people to make it in this life, so if you are not that type of person, prepare to be simply because it really tough times to prepare you for the good times.

Look just don't stand there and wonder why you can't make it, you and I both were looking on the TV when saw what happens to toughness, we all saw what tough men do to benefit us all.

Do you remember the Chilean miners? how tough do you think that was to endure, what was a very painful wait to be rescued, some times faith is all that make things happen, I don't know about you, but that was a turning point in my life, all because I also saw the rescuers doing what they were called to do, and what they knew just what to do.

If we are going to succeed at any thing we will have to prepare to succeed, that means seizing the opportunity to fight, and win at any cost. Some one may be waiting for you.

The opportunity is all yours to change ,things, change the way think, and change your life forever. The way I change mine was exactly as I say to you so many times, think alternative wise, that may lead to a much better way forward.

Here is a conversation that I once had about changing a situation. This business owner was running a business, but it was not doing too well at the time, so I asked him the question about changing his concept, he said to meow! no, I have been doing this for at least fifty years, so I said to him, look at all the time you have been here it must be time to make a change if you are going to last another five years doing this, well, as stubborn as he was he still insisted against it, he was just stuck in warp, and just couldn't see the necessity for the change, despite all of the other business's around him were doing just that, and as a matter were prospering.

The sad story of this business man was shortly after that he lost the fight to keep business going, ultimately the business folded, and what ever happened to him I really don't know and frankly I really don't care, it's not because I am hard hearted, but rather letting it be an example for others to follow, may be it is one of the best way to help people to see the necessity for change, not only in their business, but also in their own lives.

Wave of change: Those of us who loves going to the cottage, and have had the opportunity to walk along the shores, can surely testify of the rolling waves as they beat along the shores, as you make your way under the moonlit skies, and like me, who's tried on several occasions to count them, would tell you that it was very difficult, yet fascinating.

Then there were others who's been to Hawaii to really ride waves who will tell you that was an experience all in it self.

Then we ride the waves of opportunity to change things. It's all about the necessity of change, and just what can happen an account of it.

Just take a good look around you, and you are sure to see, the times are changing, we are changing, even with out our input, no matter what we do it is all a part of our existence, so when we get the opportunity to make them, it seems as though we are having problems doing so, look don't do it if is not necessary, only if it is.

We were all placed on this earth to do all of the good that we can do, and especially to obliterate all of the bad with the good, I know that this is just not going to be easy as it is said, because words has a way of flowing out of our mouths very easily, that is why we ought to be careful about what we are saying allowing our words to have the most positive effects as they can.

I can remember well when Obama ran for the position of president of the united states of America, I also remember all of his most powerful words that was filled with positivist, that even created some hope to the almost hopeless.

This to me was the single most interesting time in the history of the united states, one because an African man became for the very first time the leader of the free world, that was monumental in my estimation, and that of millions besides me.

That was not easy both for bema and the American people, and some times the whole world, never the less it was very good to see that history can be rewritten in that manner, it was a very big time in the life of every black person any where in the world that they may be, and that was literally from one corner of the globe to the other.

Up to now I am still feeling the effects of that moment, that was as he really became the president of the u s a, although he made it to the pinnacle of that mountain, and to set himself in a position to see all that needs to be seen by him in order that he may be able to do all that he could do for those that helped him to get to that point which was nothing but good, that was ever so needful, and necessary for the well being of the entire nation.

Just soon after that period I saw what looked like erosion by just about every one that had to do with the situation, it became very apparent that he was going to have a very tedious journey ahead of him, and that he would have to be very strong in every area of his life other wise he could of have a major set back in all that he may try to do and say.

After seeing what I may call abuse, I became troubled in my spirit because the jabs were coming from all sides at the very same time, I began to question my self saying, how can any one get any thing done under such conditions, there were fighting every where from the right side, and the left side, and back again.

What I thought I would experience was to see what one might call educated people behaving the way they were, believe me it was very troubling, I couldn't help but to feel very sorry for the president.

What I think kept him from going insane was because there were literally millions of people praying for him all at the very same time, I knew there is power in prayer, and that no weapon formed against him would prosper, with that sort of realization, I soon came to the understanding that he was going to be alright after all.

I know that I am a real thinker, one who thought that may be the best thing to do was for all to come together and put this train back on the rails, let it get to it's destination for the good of all of the people.

One thing that I know for sure is that we should try and make things much easier for ourselves rather than making it so complicated, just to un- complicate it again, I don't know about you, but some how I get the feeling that we may cost our selves millions in the process, that could of been used to do much better things for those that were waiting for the expected relief.

Today, there is a sort of relief in my mind, simply because every thing has settled down, some what, but up till now I am just not seeing the real change that I expected, hopefully we will get to that place at some point in time, because God knows it is long over due, and it is no fault of the president, but just about all of the others, that are not getting his vision.

I just happen to think that America the great has to demonstrate to the world that greatness begins here, and ends up in unlimited places around the world.

I personally love America like it is my own country, but all that I would ask for is that we try, and find it in our hearts to get along much better that we are presently such as finding a way to love more, and hate much less, thereby bridging the divides creating better inroads to each other.

Look! we are now living in the twenty first century, only we forget to live all of the first century stuff there in exchange for some thing so much better.

When I look at just where you have taken technology, to the moon and back, and every where in between, you are done some of the most difficult things that the human minds is able to comprehend, yet we cannot be more reasonable with each other, after all you, me, and all of the rest only has a very short time here on this earth, lets help each other to at least have a peaceful, and enjoyable time till then.

Just know that we came here with simply nothing, and we will also go out with simply nothing, and may be that is a rather good thing after all, for it could of been worse.

As we now make our way to on this journey it is my hope that I would see the type of change that we are all capable of be the manifested in our day, to day living, because of our new reality.

In all of the many things that you do just find a way to think, and make it good things, in order that you may get great results in the end.

Just an account of the state of the world, I have decided to set a new mission, and that is to show lots more love to every one that I may come into contact with, but one of my main goal is to win those that considers me an enemy, for as I make my way forward I hope to make friends, and to influence people every where.

I am determined to see the change that I expected, and I am hoping you may join mean this quest to help make a much better world, lets find answers together to make things better for all.

Mr. president you are amazing, I don't know you do it, but I really do admire you for your courage, your persistency, and your ability to stay calm in the midst of the storm, you for sure, taught me valuable lessons that could never forget, thank you, and may God continue to bless you.

Little did know that as was growing up following my dad around that it would ever lead to this, I feel specially blessed in many ways, because as I said one time before, I am very grateful that I made it to this point under the given circumstances that prevailed at that time, because to me that was a very peculiar time in my life.

Following the leader, but especially when the leader is your father, or in general terms, when he is worth following, any one that can get you where you wants to go safely, and securely that's the one that I am willing to follow.

After you lead for a good long time if you have mastered the course, I think it's your time to lead, because you have proved that you are quite capable of doing so, what happened for me was, I really didn't know that there were eyes looking at my every move, but in fact they were, and that was the exact time that I have gotten called from off the crowd, because of many reasons, one for being a good adherent, listening well, obedient when asked to do things, and maintaining a flawless character, now with that kind of characteristics who wouldn't to follow a person like that.

As it is said many are called, but few are chosen, and that is because you have risen to the occasion ,and demonstrated what the very best ahead of you were proud of.

The things for me is I just don't quite know how to say I have had enough, not that I really want to say that, because I just think the best thing is to keep taking it all in until you can't help but to start to release some of what has been stored up, and there is no better way than to make your self available to those that are really in serious need for your help.

You see, it is never that difficult to find places to sow seeds into other places, such as mentoring some one in preparation to take their rightful place in society in general, there is always a place to be filled by some one that is waiting.

Even as prepared as I was I can still recall there was a time that I really struggled to find my place to take care of my self, but when I did, I realized that just about every one will have some struggling to do, it doesn't mean that you are no good, it is because every one has to go through that passage on their way in, so I don't you are that special enough to miss it.

There are reasons why we are just who we are, I spent much of my time building up to this time, now I am able to say kudos to you Paul, you have earned the rights to brag, we all know that it was not easy, but you have made it through, and we are particularly happy to share your moments of joy.

I really don't know much about you, but as for me I just don't like the thing call failure, and that is why I always try hard to win as often as I can, and at every thing that I do.

What I have noticed is that it doesn't matter which way you go, or what you do there will always be your share of challenges, what I do now is never waste any time trying to avoid it, instead what I do is to work like it's not been there it makes much easier for me do what it is that I am doing, otherwise you will never have any thing to show for all of the time that you have used up trying.

It is much like just about every thing else, the very best thing that I can advise you on that is always recognize what you are up against, and make your plans to defeat it, I know that by then you may be working on two things at the very same time, but that's okay, this is the way things are at times, you are not alone in this, just about every one that I know of would have say the very same thing to you.

Life is life just about the same rules are there for, not just me, but for you, and every one else, so as I said before lets get use to it, and just to remind you that you can go ahead and change what ever you can, and the things that you just cannot change, you work with, for as long as you really can.

No one is really bound to any thing, we make choices to benefit us in the very best way that we could.

This is called taking care of our selves, and not only that but we have an obligation to our selves, it's like a promise that we have made to our selves that we just cannot relinquish to any one else, should you choose to do that, you just may not get what it is that would satisfy you in the end, and that is why we must take control where we can simply because there should be no other way.

Now let us take a good look at the things that would help us to redefine our goals to reflect the goodness of our selves to others, and that is why we are here to inspire, and motivate each other to do great things so that we may have much more success than we are seeing currently.

I can assure you that what I really know is that the more we help the others to be successful, is the less we would have to give to them of our own, so the burden would not be on you as a dependent, it is also a very good thing that will help to reduce the level of petty crimes that so often be the case.

Simply put, I find that if people have food they just go about stealing food unfortunately they may steal some thing else, and that is just where the law comes in to do what it does best just before it gets to that level of escalation, instead we should try to help people to be able to find all that they need, by being able to acquire it in the very best possible way, and that can be a very good step towards self satisfaction.

In preparation for life's events we may have some terrible falls, but lets hope that it is just before the rise, which is so much better that the fall, and then again it is also good for some people to have a fall once in a while, that's to show us that they are human too.

When it comes to falling from a position from your company, it is very hard to take, especially while still employed by that company, for what ever the cause, just find the strength to pick up from here and move, like never before, at least by now you know just how hard you can fall, next time you may want to avoid it at any cost.

Look, it the same as they say, kingdom rise, and fall, if for some strange reason you happen to have a fall, and it's not because you are just no good, don't worry about it, because the rise is by far greater that the fall, every one falls every once in a while, may be this time is your turn, so what is the big deal.

Really some times it takes a fall to help us on our way to be better,stronger,and wiser, so that we don't fall again.

A good friend of mine had a terrible fall, he lost just about lost all of his business, because of carelessness that could of been avoided, but it was also good, simply no one that I know wants to loose their business that, right after working so hard to put it together.

It is your life long dream you must realize that, because we all know just how much it hurts to see that happen, as a matter of fact it has happened to me, some where on my climb, so what I am telling you is based on personal life's experiences, just in case you are wondering, every thing that I write in this book is based on true life story.

I have spent a great deal of my time going back to where it was all started, just to find a good sense for all of the stories that I told to you, in retrospect I feel I really earn the rights to this stories, simply because they are all mine, not because I am proud of them, but it is because it is the kind of past that reshaped my life, and make life worth it all to me, that is why I am very happy for all of my achievements, they may not mean any thing to people, but it is monumental to me, after all I have experienced the fall, and then came the rise.

Truly speaking I have fallen many times, and each time I rose up and try again, only with a much better plan the next time, what I remind my self of was some thing has to work for me, so I kept on working till at last it happened.

In the madness of every thing I always tried to maintain my composure, and kept my head on at all times, you see, I made my plans, and worked the plans all to my advantage, every thing just had to go my way, or no way at all, because I always focus on success, it's not because I have succeeded in all of the many things that I have tried, but some how I am very satisfied with things so far.

Can you hear a sort of determination in my voice here? it's because it really is, I always walk with it every where I may go, as some once said, please don't leave home with out it, it is that good, and with that comes a sense of urgency, those things are part of just what I use to make things happen for me.

What it takes to succeed is not just wanting to do any thing, in fact quite the opposite, doing any thing that you can do to make things happen.

At one time when I was only beginning, I really didn't think that I had it together enough, but after careful analysis, knowing that I have had the all of the necessary upbringing that any one would be envious about, I took back that notion, and instead satisfied my self that I had more than enough to work with, and decided to get the work done.

A very big contributor to all things that I have done was that I was always quite wiling to do what I thought I was capable of doing, some times that is just what you have to do is to keep telling your self that you are well able, and nothing is going to tell you any different, because as soon as you begin to second your self, you are already in trouble.

Be very certain about all that concerns you, once you feel that way you will also see your confidence rising to heights that you never thought possible.

Here is a tree story that may excite you. Last spring I decided to try all manner of shrubs in my garden, but this time I got a flowering shrub that I really love to see grow in the garden, what happened I planted it in what I thought was a very good spot, hopefully to see it grow and give me quite a lot of blooms, what I did not do was to ensure that it would the case, you see, planting is only the very beginning, what we have to do is to nurture it in the way that you would do for a little baby if we would even expect a tree, and better yet tree laden with blooms.

Take good care of what going to be your pride, and joy some place down the road.

Recent I went to an office for the service that I expected, usually I always enter with a smile, and a very warm greeting as I did as always, the person that I have greeted was very impress, and responded in the very same manner, I then complemented the situation, here is just what came back to me, Paul, thank you, you are such a wonderful person, but what it is, you are just getting back what you gave out, so please have a wonderful day, believe me thanks was just not quite enough, but was well accepted.

As we do our best to take care of things, they always come back full circle.

In order for things to bounce back like we expects them too I really to have hope for a much better time than when we first thought it would be, and what could really make it happens is just to let it swing like the pendulum as you trust that just went will come again for sure, just like investing what ever it is in some one be it time ,or money to see things grow into monumental bliss in their lives, once that happens you will know that you have contributed some thing that is more tangle in their life, while at the other hand you get the opportunity to feel good for you have just done.

I think we should all be aware that our lives was meant to be shared with any, and every one who deserves of it, for real, it is just like the people who became heroes for their act of kindness, such as saving some one's life, or rescuing some one from some disastrous situation, you know what I mean? those things when thanks are seldom enough, but just can't help but to say it straight from the heart, just as it usually is.

Those are the kind of life's missions that you are seldom called to go on, but being there, is just what is going to change your own life.

Little did know that I would be looking through those lens, and seeing what I am seeing, really has helped me to zoom just a little closer in those lens, so I can be better ready when occasion arises, it's like just staying alert in a world that wants us all to be vigilant at all times.

And it's not because we too wants to be heros,but to be there for people under any circumstance that they may face, because God knows we can be the ones that others will be running to, to administer what help that we are capable of.

In this world where any thing can be the event of the day, it is only natural that we consider being our brothers keeper, and that simply means stepping right in the love, and care, some of the humanities that can be the main ingredients that we are made up of, I am quite sure that you know just what I am talking about.

One thing that we should always keep in mind is that we have every thing inside of us to give, and yet be not depleted, truly it's like a reservoir that keeps on pouring out from it's source, if not it may over flow it's banks, and causes more harm than good, but as you must have noticed there is always quite sufficient to go around many time over.

Now, are you still thinking of changing the world ? you alone just can't do it, but you can certainly contribute a great deal, lets keep moving along together.

There are just too many people trying to do every thing by them selves, as they say no man is an island, you just don't have every thing that is needed to get things done properly, don't crush the possibility by going it alone, when you know for sure that you are only kidding your self.

One thing that will happen for sure is that you will set your self back way too far just to realize that you really need the help of others, so that really happens just put a contingency in place, this not just for you only all of us had to do the very same thing, that enabled us to have the success that we sought to have.

When it's in the name of success just don't be afraid to get all of the help that is available to you.

Hear this two men went swimming in the ocean both of them thought that they were quite capable to swim adequately enough, so the set out, when the got half way to length that they wanted to go one asked the other, how are you doing ? are you going to make it the other said hoys I am okay, okay, the got to a fair distance, as the good swimmer looked back he noticed his partner on the swim falling back, so he called out again asking are you okay, yes he said but at the very same time has slowed down considerably, by the time he decided to turn around to go back to render some assistance his friend just could not of been found, by now you know just what had happened .

This is a lesson for just about all of us, don't wait till you are at wits end to expect the help that is no longer necessary, swallow your pride as it is said, but what ever you do just don't ever live things to caution ,.

This whole episode tell me that yes, there is a time that can come way too late, don't let that be you, we are here in this world to be a helping hand to each other, lets use it, and give thanks to the generous help of others.

I learnt all of these lessons just to know that as I succeed it becomes a mission to help others to succeed also, by so doing I am fulfilling my obligations to the rest of the population thereby creating a win, win situation for all concern.

I paid full price for the tickets to ride, I gave it my all so that I may win the prize, it's not that I did not get helps along the way, but first I had to take the initiative to do all that I possible can to make the difference that I expected, unless you make some efforts in life for any thing, no one will be encouragement to step in to help you,learnt all about that when I started years ago, after all I was still a little young man, and was still following my fathers foot steps as I try to learn all the lessons of life from the one that gave it with out bios.

Today it is well embed into the archives of my mind, not only being held in a safe place, but as a matter of fact just where else would you keep what you spend a life time learning, because frankly I make no apology for taking all that came my way to greatly enrich my life the way that it has.

I think that is the very reason that I draw any thing from within there, and use it to my full advantage, after all I am just the only one that does that ,in fact all those that took the initiatives to build their lives, so that they may depend on all of the things that they have learnt.

Just know that you too have all of the very same opportunities to do the very same things, all that does is to instill in us the confidence to do all of the things that we wants to do, and to appreciate it all at the very same time.

It is hard foe me to describe to you how I feel now that I can achieve some of the things that I always wanted to achieve.

Look, just open your eyes, and follow the right type of leadership if you have the desire to make it in this world. A blind eye wouldn't get you any where, because you just won't be able to see who is really leading the way to success.

But just remember that you, and only are responsible for making that ultimate decision to change your life, in fact if you are waiting for some one else to do that for you ,you may have to wait for a life time, and still have nothing accomplished.

That is one of the many reasons that I say be careful just who you put the blame on when it comes to blaming any one, because that one may just be you, and you know no one likes to take the blame to them selves, it is always some one but you.

So just before we get to that part, take a closer look at you, and while you are there, make a note of all of the things that you have accumulated from the time when you were a toddler growing up in, I am very sure that you will discover some hidden treasure in there that you never thought would be amounts to any thing.

Now that you know that what you have found would be like diamonds from the rough, it would be the perfect time to put some value on them, and start using what ever you have found like hidden treasures discovered.

The greater you think of what you have that is of value to you, is the more people would appreciate it too, you have to first validate it to them, and fro here on it's like you have just passed the exams bar and is now ready for the bigger picture.

Just a little while ago I was talking to a nurse, when she was made known of the work that I do, she said to me that she too has many abilities, but just does not know just how to go about it, then I stopped and think for a while about how many people are there like her, who has great things in store, but just does not have edge to make things happen for them selves.

So with people like her I would take on a journey through thinking alternative wise and try to bring value to their abilities first of all, then try to help them develop a plan of action of how to move from the first step and beyond.

You, see once I can help them to bring some true value to the way that they think at least I feel I can take them to the next level, which is actually just how to implement their own ideas to make thing work for them, usually people like that approach, because you are therefore helping with what is theirs to begin with.

I love high lighting possibilities, it's like creating what one may call a road map to destination assured, now the reason that it is destination assured, it's because I have helped them to give it a very good case study, as I back them up with the kind of support that would to make solid steps forward.

I really can remember when I have gotten started, after all I don't know it all, and from time to time would have the need to talk with some one else that simply knows just what I am all about, I find that to be a very good thing for me, simply because I really don't think it is all that necessary to have to go back and do things all over again.

This is what the world should be all about, not having to totally relying on your own self, because as far we know, that by opening up one's self to the opinions of others, we learn quite a lot that would help towards your over all success possibilities.

Some time the leader could be you, here is just what I had to first take into consideration.

First I had to established my self as a trust worthy person, which I knew I was.

That letting them know that I understood that being in front does not make one a leader.

Knowing when the facts are the truth.

By having a well defined, and demonstrated principles of leadership foundation.

Be affective in my leadership.

Be honest

Be humble

Have a good character

Have a good sense of direction

 Be Factual

Be understanding

Be consistent

Be considerate

Be kind

Be devoted

Be goal oriented

These are some of the attributes that will help you for sure, especially as you seek to lead others to their path to success.

You were born to be as rich as you can, but that will happen only if you have the desire to be rich, just be honest in your approach, and let it be noticeable to every one that is looking, most time when people are becoming well to do don't be amazed to know that there are all sorts of peering eyes looking right at you just to see if is for real or not, we call them nosey you know the ones that have this great appetite for talking about every thing that moves.

When I see that I feel good because I now have the opportunity to teach them a lesson or two, about getting their work done to enrich their lives.

The part that I play in life is to inspiring all those that I can to do what they can, because I know ,if you are like me having the will to do ,and be successful at what I do, then you will feel like the pleasure is all yours, and should also be willing even blessed to have had the opportunity to demonstrate your quality way of thinking. some one would feel, that this pleasure is all theirs to be able to learn from you, some of the things that will undoubtedly have a profound effect on some ones' life.

The passion that burns in side of me is not just for my gains, in fact it is the type of gains that will be very necessary to the people that are expecting from me, what I used for my self to change my life to what it is today.

Purpose, and passion in my life is always the order of the day, I feel like I must be doing some thing at all times to benefit the others, other wise I just don't feel like I have done my work as well as I should, and just in case it's true, meaning that I really did not do quite enough, then I will set back a little, take a deep breathe and reformulate my thinking to reflect what it is that I am trying to accomplish.

Here is what I discovered recently. There are two companies working for me both are doing the very same thing, or supposedly so, after having a lengthily conversation with the second one, I realized that I was getting a rather raw deal with the first, so now what I had to do was to set up my self with the last one because their honest deal was some thing that I couldn't afford to pass up.

I love dealing with honest people, and I literally hate doing business with dishonest ones, after all they both are getting paid for work done, but one is not giving you just what they should, it's a question that so few can answer, because just about every one stands behind his company as a very good representative you just have to find out that they are not.

May be that is the reason some one said never take any thing for granted, some times the people that talks the most have the worst stories to tell, what we have to do is to get an up tick

by listening very closely to what they are saying, and or be sure to talk to as many people as possible to help you to make a better decision, in order to get better results.

In just about every thing that we may do, the single most important thing that stands out is the results of what we have gained, which is like the benefits of working for what we expects.

And if that is not the case, then what, no one will ever have the nerve to tell you that they are doing this just to pass the time away, and really not hoping to find the real benefits to them selves, even the most accomplished person keeps on going for more of the very same that he/ already has so much off.

A l though there is really nothing wrong with this approach, the search for more should be coupled with the willingness to do more.

As it is said to whom much is given, much is also expected. I really think that some people are truly blessed to earn the amount that they have, and if that is the case, just know that it should be a real blessing to give, or help in abundant ways.

If you are simply afraid to give in ways that would definitely make a real big different in others, then you may be should consider your self a withholder of a blessing to some one.

It's amazing what can come from give freely, so much more will flow back to you, not only freely, but also abundantly, it becomes like that which we talked about earlier, and that is the reservoir, the giving never ceases, and the receiving just the same never ends, this is why it is there to bountifully supply our needs.

Now this is a very true story, there was a businessman that I know personally who owned a very successful high end restaurant in a very upscale part of the city, he was very proud of his business, for it was also the talk of the town, a place where all the big lawyers in the area would rest for a while to make agreements, and sign some real bags deals.

One day apparently things got to his head, and he just was not able to contain him self, after having a quarrel with a business partner, that ended up in some thing much more than it really should, what happened was, his partner was a Christian man, but he was not, the Christian man started talking about God in the heat of the quarrel, he immediately responded by saying that God had nothing to do with his business, God did not give him success, and that he should never talk about God to him again.

The very shamed Christian man, decided to live the business for the day, but came back the next day as usual.

To make a long story short, it was about three months later, the business gotten into serious trouble, which ended up in him loosing the business entirely.

He ended up roaming the streets in loneliness, and despair. Now the moral of this story has been documented to show that there are times in life when we must have reverence for God who made the heaven, and the earth, and that we ought to feel thankful to be in it, and also that we may know that we are much too small to wrestle with God.

On account of that experience I have become very humble, for I know it is that humility that will see me be exalted to be more appreciative for every thing that I have.

And may be that is the reason why I m not afraid to disperse with it at any time that I can for the good of some one else.

I was born with a real appreciation for life, and that is the reason that I would never hesitate to all of the good things that I can, and able to do for the good of humanity.

I prepared from boyhood to do some to of the things that I take pleasure in doing, what would you do if you had all of the necessary tools to do the job, the very first thing that you delight your self in is getting the job done, like a soldier I know that I have had all of the training that allows me to rise to any occasion, how then can I not do what I'm supposed to do.

What I am doing for my self is, has been just what I expect to be doing for you, I already learnt most of the lessons, by personal involvement, the more I do is the better I can be. It's like opportunity, don't let them pass you by, if so you may regret it later.

Recently I spoke with a group of individuals, about self development, and just what I really meant to them, some of them really didn't show any care for working to make them selves any better than they were, some of them even think that whether they work or not they should have all of the same rights, and privilege like those who did it all, because they just wanted to have it all.

It is quite simple, we must try to do all that we can do for our selves, and just in case we fall short, and needed some help, there is always some one there that would be quite willing to administer the kind of help that would be enough to help to get on our path that leads to victory at last.

Coming to think about really, this is why we do all of the things that we do, and that is to succeeding at doing it, it's a simple fact that just about every one that I know wants some thing from what they are doing, be it satisfaction, or that of monetary rewards.

What's interesting to note is that we must also have ethics, and principles in place too, which is the guiding formula for all good things.

I write about it because I believe in it to the very core, I even said at one time, it is part of the reason why it must have taken me longer than some others to get where I was heading too, but it really didn't matter, because I knew that I would get there for sure, thanks for the help.

If you are one of those that has been helped in any way by some one, and walk away with out say a simple thank you, it is not too late, you are still alive, and as far as we know in this case it is never too late.

It's like repaying a debt, until you do, you may be plague by it, so go ahead, and make your self feel better, by doing the right thing.

One of the thing that it can cause is to set you back way too far, that is because when other people learn about the kind of person that you are, no one else would like to render you any help at all.

I am so happy that I accepted being under the total guidance of my parents, the first mentors, I knew then that it would of been a very hard act to follow, and I still believe that to be the ultimate truth.

For that reason I often try to compare my self with what I am seeing out there, and some times it makes me feel very sad, to see what we call the product of today.

I never cease to call my self the diamond from the rough, that shines as bright as ever, and I can assure you that I will continue to shine, for all to see, with hopes that this light will serve as a beacon to all those that are struggling in the dark corners of their world.

I know this is very easily said, but it makes me feel rather happy to hear people say to me that I inspire them, and now they are changed, it makes me feel warm inside.

You may have heard me say before that I really don't like dealing with prehensile people, no one is perfect ,and God knows that I am not, so because of that I keep trying harder every day just to be the very best that I can be, because this I also part of my leadership, and I am not about to fail any one, so I'll be my self, I feel much better that way.

One has simply nothing to loose, when you are giving the very best, simply because some is going to receive it hopefully with thanks, and even if they didn't say thanks, it really doesn't matter to me the fact is I have done some thing good that will benefit some one, to me that's good enough.

What ever it is we must make a difference in this life with each other, simply because whether we wishes to acknowledge it or not some one has affected our lives in one way or the other, it's just the way the world is, we are all part of this giant spider web that connects us whether we like it or not.

Often you may hear some one say, how you did not help them to be at the height that they are in right now, it's only because they are just not thinking right, soon enough they will catch up to their senses and realize that it was just not true.

As long as you are alive you will have to do with the rest of the population in one way or the other, and you really don't have to like it, so just accept it, and all is well that ends well.

Let us enjoy this life together, because some where along the way it ends for all of us.

I am very happy to say that people like me just don't come a dime a dozen, yes, folks we are very hard to find, and that is why those that finds us really does not want to let go of us, and just in case you have the feeling that I am boasting, in fact yes, I am, and with absolutely with no apology.

I have worked very hard to make me, the me that I am, I had to go through some really rough channels and prove it to my self that I had what it took to make it.

So now I am at the pinnacle of the mountain looking down at you it's only because I made the climb, I have made it to where few men have ever dared to go.

When you can have the experience of trying as hard as I have tried, and loosing it all, when can loose you business, after working ever so hard to establish one, just to see it vanish right before your very eyes, it was very hard.

When you have lost your job, and have no money, no home ,no family, you are definitely in trouble, most people would call that hitting rock bottom, that was me.

When you are at the very bottom, and realize that you are down, you also know that the only place that you can look is up, that just where hopes begin.

If you can go through all of these, and not die you know that it would make you better, hang on, and make your way upward.

If you can imagine that there can, and will be a much better day ahead, keep hoping, keep believing, you are stronger now than you have ever been, hope springs eternal.

You are alive because you are very strong, just know that nothing can really stop you in any way shape or form, you are bound to make it through.

As I look back on this experience, I see nothing but blessings, I know now that the God that I serve would never fail me in any way, so I will keep trusting.

When some one can hire you over the telephone, and offer you a job, after a great conversation, and make you an offer that you just cannot refuse, you know you are blessed, hang on there is more coming, so just don't give up just yet.

When your now new boss can say to you I have two cars, please take this one it's free to you just as long as you want, you know that you are blessed, and wait God is not finished as yet, hang on.

When your rent is eleven hundred dollars a months, and be reduced to one hundred, and sixty eight a month, you know that you are blessed.

Now let go and let God have his way, he will really take good care of you, and will supply all of your needs from his abundance, there is just simply nothing to fear, because all things are possible as long as you believe.

I have been through it all, now if I have it all, is simply because I invested it all, and there is so much more on the way, from whence it came.

In all new reality, we must come to grips with a world that is not flat, there are mountains, and valleys, yet we are here, and if we are going to live here we will have to get use to the way that it is, what that done is make us very resilient to endure all of the various conditions.

Despite it all I am very grateful to be here, and I will all that I can to demonstrate that, in appreciation for being here.

Take a good look at things, and you are sure to find, that there are people that do have Angels habits, they are kind , they are patient, they are humble, they are gracious, they are loving, with many other fine qualities, that the general population just does not have, and that 's okay because angels are special people.

I just wish you were there to see the person that has affected my life when I was in my greatest need, and may be in my darkest hour,

I really have never experienced any thing quite like that in any one else.

That certainly helped me to confirm that there are angels all around us in disguise, and I am sure if you would take the time you might come to the same conclusion.

It's not that there are not nice, and well thinking people around, but when some one would go way beyond the call of duty it's hard not to see angelic ways in them.

Some how I think if you are right thinking, you too can change to reflect that type of very special qualities, but you may have to live your self wide open to a very different way of thinking for that to be a possibility.

If I only knew that I could rise to that level and be known for it, I would change in one wink of the eye, it would be rather hard for me to miss the opportunity to be this special, I say special, because it is a rather good way to begin to change this world, because we can, and that is for sure.

Why don't try it one day we might surprise to know that it was all that we ever needed to do to make a better world, I don't know about you, but I would be so thrilled to wake up to find that every one that I any thing to do with, seemed to be transformed all by the way that they were thinking, I really don't know just what I would do with my self.

First I may would be thinking that we went back in time while we were all asleep, or some thing.

Wouldn't you feel great to know that for the first time in a long time, you can walk late in the pitch black night, and have no fear for just what can happen, simply because nothing will happen, I don't know may be I am dreaming, and if that is the case I will just have to keep dreaming hopefully there may be a reality to this dream.

After all it was because I was raised with the insignia of hope written on my fore head, handed down by my parents, that I can feel free to pursue the dreams that I cherished, an account of the good tutorials that I have had just as I began my journey.

There is nothing like walking into the indelible foot prints of the ones that went ahead of you, that you may have a direction to go into.

For it is for that reason that we lay hopes for a better world, simply, because lessons learnt is just what will help us to implement all of the ideas that are found in them.

I we would only focus on the specific things that grabs our attention, we would certainly find a way to perfect them, for it is by paying more attention to the things that interests us the most, that good things emerges.

How can I ever forget, all of the pleasure that I had playing in the sweet rain falling from a warm sunny sky, although I was playing, it was also having fun finding ways to make things happen better.

I can remember practicing diverting water from the streams that was caused by the torrents of rain as it made it's way from down the slopes of the landscapes, into what is going to be a basin awaiting to be filled from it's new direction.

It was share fun while at the very same time inventing new ways that can be applied later on in life some where.

After all it was simply using what has given to us called the intellect, all that we are supposed to do is to develop them to their full capacities, thereby being able to solve many problems, that would other wise impede our ability to rise above them.

What really made things work well for me was, my acknowledgement of God in my life, where I developed my faith, in the things yet to be seen, but there was with no doubt that they would be.

Then comes the power of positive thinking that has done the rest, no one should go through life thinking long before they have begin that it cant, it wont, or what ever the other bunch of negatives are, if you want things to happen for sure, you must tell your self that it will, and that nothing is going to stop it from happening.

Some of the many things that really stops things for happens for us is really our mindset, so we may have to make some changes to our mindset, because it will make, or break it for us for sure.

So from here on lets try to change the way that we think, in order that we may have the success that we want.

After getting to this point, I have decided to go right back to where it all began, it is a back ward journey, but it is worth while, after all some times it is very important to see how you life took the shape that it took.

I know that at some point in this frame work of time, I will re encounter some of the most harshest of my up bringing, but that's okay, I am not a- shame of my past, because it is responsible for my present which I am very happy for.

In fact I am doing it just to validate just how much it takes to make it in this world, one should never wake up in the morning, just to find it all wrapped under a tree for them, even the ones the prepares it had some work to do before it arrived under the tree for you.

Now I know that is a vastly different time to when I was a little boy, things has changed tremendously , I just want to see some of the places that helped me to realize that good things can come from here, look at me I am a product of this place, there are so many people that would say, it was a place, so what, I had to come from some where.

That's all and well to say so, but it is so awesome to see your self as the once little person that you were, to just what you are now, like I said some time ago, that should some see me now they would never think that this could be me now, and it's all because of where I came from, and the many things that I had to do before I made it to be this person.

Every thing has to have a beginning, and mines were that place, that was very rough, but as they say if you look carefully you just might find that precious thing called diamond in the rough.

I am fortunate enough to say that diamond was me, what made it to be me, was because I was well groomed, prepared, and presented to the world as the one that they never expected, but don't under estimate any thing, for it's very true what they say, there is power in silence.

Not every thing that is as steel like the night, should be taken for granted, as I recall still waters runs deep, that is very true when it comes to me, I can recall when I was a little boy you just couldn't get two words out of my mouth, that was until I was brought to that place where I had to explain why I was so silent.

The very same can be said about that lake on the mountain top, I know it's hard to imagine, but is very true, I visited several times in my youth, each time I was more amazed, just like the very first time that I saw it. It is so peaceful, and steel, so un assuming, no one has found the bottom as yet, and I really don't even think that should try.

I only try things that I am familiar with, that is why I took a journey back in time just to discover the source of what was a possibility, now I am fully satisfied with just about every thing, but I am not finish as there is much more for me to do, such as a very different rout on that journey.

It is quite evident that by now all the things that are responsible for the reshaping of my life would be different yet again, and the reason for that is very simple, times have changed and so has just about every thing that has to do with it, after all that should be expected, nothing stays the same way for too long.

Also what I have noticed is that the attitudes of the people are vastly different, and not necessarily for the better, you can say it's just different, which lives me with great concern for their future.

No one has to be like me to be successful in the end, so I really hope that the different that I talked about could still help them on their journey.

No matter what, I am still happy to have had the opportunity to pretend that I was starting over again, I really wouldn't like too, am too far gone up this mountain, where I now have a clearer view from here.

I can still remember the time my dad and I spent some time on the property on the bay front, it is like the time has been printed in my memory for ever, and I am very glad that it has, not only was it very special to be with him doing things, and learning all at the same time.

I remember the time we went fishing, and caught some lovely small fishes, and he made a fire, and he cooked up some of the freshest fish that I have ever have had, I can still taste the genuine goodness of that fresh catch, there is just nothing quite like it.

Oh ! the memory of quality time in the very best of places, you would of love it too, so just in case you are so incline I am very tempted to invite you on the next trip of this journey.

Life is so beautiful, only it is much too short a time to spend here, that is primarily the reason that I try to just enjoy every little bit that I can at every time that I can, and you too should try to do the very same, we only have this short span of time here in which to do all the things that you love, and may be try to even love some of the things that you hate, the word hate alone is enough to stay away from, what good is it any way.

You know, right now I am feeling so good, especially capturing most of these memories, which to me is simply priceless, I'm so glad to have had the opportunity to share this time with you, it is not every day that some one would stop and share precious memories with any one, especially based on the life that they lived, so here's to you, I hope that you would make the very most of this time that we spent together.

One thing I know for sure is I will also continue to see all of the things that I saw then, but this time through a wider lens, I just want to capture it all, so I can share it all with you, as I bring you the stories of joyous times that I still find my self chuckling about ever now and then.

You see, it was not all so serious that I could not have found the time to have some fun, I just had to do it all, work, play, and learn, for in my world it was the order of the say.

There was never a dull moment where I came from, no chance to get bored there were just too many things to grab my attention at all time.

Like I said before it was the perfect time, and place to equip my self with quite enough knowledge that can last for a life time, which means that people there, and any where else now have the opportunity to experience the kind of life, that has produced such wonderful products, with so much more to come.

When the idea came into my head to re visit, what I now call the ground zero of my life, I really didn't think that would have to go back this far, but I keep on going, in hopes of finding some more buried treasures, that I can put on display.

Now this treasure is not really hidden some where, in fact it is there in the wide open for all to see, and learn from, even me at times were taking second take on some things, simply because they remind me so much of the old times.

I really understand more now about what they say about old times, for they remind us so much of the good times, they were the very best times, this time now is simply stress times, I wish all of us would try and take a few steps back wards, and get a glimpse of those un- forgettable monument of joy, and it is not a building, but all of the precious times, and places, that takes a grab of you and pull you back in it's surroundings wishing that you would for yet another time be part of it.

I can weave a very fine tapestry all from the memories of small things according to you , but very big things according to me, it's only simply because I do have a much better understanding of that world, where as for you it's only a figment of your imagination.

The fact that I am here to relate all of my stories to you, I only hope that you may stay for a while, and linger with me as we endeavor to re write my stories, that will help to change your perspective of similar things that would may be inspire me to live indelible marks on the path less traveled.

In order that you may have all of the things that you are looking for, you should also expect to go to many places, involve in many things as possible, any thing other to that would be considered a limitation on your self, and also your potentials.

Just do it like me take it and run with it as fast as you can, then secure it in the archive of your mind, where you can have access to it when ever you want, how convenient.

As the saying goes, we only live once, so just take every thing, have all the good times that you can have, but one thing I want you to do is to help others to do the same, you are not alone in this arena, try and make sure that just about every one has a fair chance, to access some of the things that you are now enjoying, because if it is good for you it is also good for them.

Before I arrived to this point, it was a real pleasure to share the find with the others, we look out for each other, whether we were related or not, in our mind it was only fair to hear others saying thank you, what that did was also was to create the oneness for humanity's sake, that every one belongs here too.

It may sound funny, but I have the feeling that if you help those that have none, through no fault of their own, or other wise, the one that you help usually don't try to take when you are not looking, so in a way you also help your self too.

That is why I spent time talking about those old values, that was so great, yes, the ones that we have left behind, and forget all about it, believe me it was good then, and it should be even better now.

What was once old, is now new again, and I can assure you that it will about some real change, that is needful, and necessary as we try to move forward to face the bold new frontier, are there any tracks on this sand, if we are not careful there may be noon, that means no module, think of how difficult it could be, if there is nothing to compare with.

So just when you thought I was not thinking of you, you better think again, because this is reason why I am sending these pages to you, so that you may find your way in this very dark world, come on, take some notes, that is just what I did, now I am able to recall them, and make good use of them both for my self, and for you going forward.

From child hood to man hood, boy ! what a journey, I am still fascinated by the whole experience, all of this good things I will never be able to use it all, and that is the reason, that I share with you, so that some day you may his experience reshaped mines, what I am saying is, that I am giving you more space so you can take in all that you can, after all life is quite a learning experience.

Really taking this trip back in time, was so good, what I tried to do was to recapture every moment in time that I could, ingest it all over again to the point where every thing has become new, that every author may say to you, is that we at times have to revisit to the place that the story began, there is no better place, than the place that literally started to be the driving force behind your life.

To me it has become the true essence of every thing that you accomplished, simply because of it you now have a story to tell, and , not only that, but in fact it's the one that you may use at some point in time as your yard stick, that is exactly what I did, with the accounts of those that were before me, I listened carefully, after all they had so much to say that was very important to as I adapt to the things that would make a very big difference in my life.

It's just as they say, nothing ventured, nothing gain, you are indebted to you self to do any and every thing that is possible to change you life for the better, no one should have to tell you that, but some times it is very for us to do so, we all need a little bit of reminder some time, may be it's as I am doing right now.

All that I want you to do is to realize that timing is moving along, and for that matter may be without you, unless you take a hold of the things that important to you now, you may find it very difficult in the long run, so why not do it now that time is on your side, because I am quite sure you are aware of the saying, that time waits for no one, you either move along, or stand alone, which inevitably could have a devastating effect on your life down the road.

If in fact you want to succeed in life, you must be prepared to sacrifice some thing in exchange for what it is that you want to achieve, success will not come to those that are wishing, and dreaming endlessly, just about every one that succeeded in life will tell you, that you may have to put a stop to the wishing, and dreaming, and put some action in place based on your expectations, other wise, there may simply may be nothing for you, simply put, your cupboard will be bared.

I am some what amazed to hear some people say to the ones that are working hard to accomplish on the goals that they set, oh ! you are doing way too much, don't you think? while they are standing there looking at you as you try to secure a place in the sun for your self, these are the people that you pay little attention too, because as the saying goes, misery loves company, be careful with that, because you already know that you are planning to take care of your self at some future time.

You are doing just fine, so keep on doing what you are doing, the others may follow your example.

As a matter of fact I look, and follow people, but am careful to follow only successful people, if you would ask me, why should any one follow the ones that are not going any where? it is pointless, for there I only one place to end up, and that is in the ditch, I can tell you how difficult it is to ride out of there, it takes much more than an effort to get out of there, so take care and just avoid that place at any cost.

So you think you would love to be successful? how then are you so afraid of a little pinch now and again, a little pinch never kill any one, as a matter fact it keeps you alert, and also helps you to recognize just when you are at the brink of the pitfalls, so that you may now move to a more comfortable place.

You think you are the only one that experience hard times in life, every one has in one way or the other, it is a guarantee, because life is not perfect, just as the world is not flat, just as much as I hope that you can see that too.

There are so many times I have lost all of my money, and other possessions but one thing I knew for sure was that I was alive, and really that was all that I ever needed to change things all for the better, better it is.

Don't ever think that you can have any thing in life with out going through some measures to get it, you have to work for what you want, I have had to do just that.

There are too many people with out, and it is all their own fault, every one should be prepared to use their brains, it is a master piece within you, and with it you can most definitely do just about any thing that you put your mind too.

When I tell you of my experience, and just what I had to do just to where I am today, it is very true, nothing, simply nothing came to me by flipping my fingers, as they say I had to work my fingers to the bone in order that could write you this manuscript, which I hope you will see as some real foot prints in the sand, just as I followed the ones that my father left.

Life is like that we should all expect to come with little, but leave a lot. for it is just no way of avoiding the things that you have accumulated in you time here.

Some time ago I had to give an account of life's journey to those that were listening, and it went some thing like that: We all were born as babies, and those of us that were blessed enough to go from baby to 45 years or beyond would say to you that they have no experience in just about any thing, can't do any thing, nor have any interest in any thing, all because they just don't have any experience.

At that time my question to them was, are you still a baby? or you forty five, are your eyes still closed up till now, strangely enough there are people like that.

There are some things that one may call taking initiative in stead of relinquishing it all to others so that they may use it to their own benefits, I am very sure that the recipients would say thank you, as I would too.

If you love to live, you should also love to live comfortable, that means have what you work for available to take advantage of at any time, and by the way don't feel that you should have a good paying job to enable that for you, there are a just too many things out there that you can count on to get you there.

I think the trouble with the world is that every body wants to have a nine-to- five job to be counted, may be it's the dressing up to go into an office that have people not thinking of other possibilities.

There are just enough of us using our head wisely enough, and staying as independent as they can, I know more now that you can stay right at home, and become a millionaire if that is what you desire, unfortunately there are those that rather have just enough for a day, and when the next day arrives they start all over again to look for what they need for this day.

What I will advocate here, and now is that you will live your self short all the time with that type of thinking.

Right now you are already rich in life's experience, simply because you are an adult, and that gives you the right to what ever it is that you have accumulated, now if you can just use it you just might realize that it was a very wise investment.

The great thing about this book is that it is written from knowledge, and experience gained by the things that I have gone through, and imp not talking about bad stuff, I have never done any thing bad in all my life, so I am writing from a source of purity caused by doing all of the right things, following wise consul and leadership from the first mentors,(my parents) and just that you may know God has been the true source of all things to me, and it's because of Him that I am who I am.

May be that is the reason why I so assertive, it's for sure not because I am the wises guy ever lived, in fact I might be just like you made many mistakes, and learnt from them, now I don't make the same mistakes, and I try to avoid similar ones as much as I can, but believe me I am only human, just like you, the thing is I keep trying daily, so although I will never be perfect, and would not even try to be, I will try to maintain me to the very best of my ability.

Some thing that I learnt in life no matter what I do, one thing is for sure, and that is I will try, and stay healthy to the very best that I can, simply because every thing begins with a good health, I have seen situations where people that were unwell, and trying to get things done, even at the very best of their ability, they still could not of done much because of the way that they were.

You know, becoming well to do takes some adjusting on our part, we now have to face the situation, and make some bold decisions in order that we may begin to consider doing what it takes to become that person.

But don't forget that determination plays a very key role in just about every thing, especially as you set your eyes on what you are driving to.

I remember some of the things that could of stopped me from beginning the journey of my life, but I am very happy that I did, because it's been a while now that I started to count all of the gains that I have made, which is enormous, there is no way that I can say that I am sorry that I did what I have done.

From time you may feel like I am coaching you, if ever you get that feeling, I can tell you that it is very true, and the reason for it is because I just don't want to write this book in vain, I would much rather you take this book as your good friend, and companion, because I know it will help you greatly as you prepare your self for the quest of your life.

I think that we are all very lucky to have some people go through all of the dark channels of life, just to find what they may call their treasure trove, the fact is it is some where out there, and I for one knew that I would do just about any thing to find my treasure, and I am very glad to say that I have found it, and I will keep it just to use it as a pointer for me to point you to the place where your treasure is kept.

Some one once said that if you found any thing it automatically becomes yours, just by the generousness of your heart you may relinquish it to the right full owner, and that the rightful owner may appreciate you for so doing.

In the case of learning all of the many things that are there to be learnt, take hold of that because no one can take that one away from you, for that is the kind of things, that you just did not find on the way side, and that is the reason you may not even want to keep what you have found, because you have your own.

In this book I promised to hold nothing back from you, just that you may know, just what I have gone through in the making of me.

Some times I use my very own standard for my self, just that I don't forget what was the beginning of this incredible journey.

I know that there are a tremendous amount of people, right now that is exactly like I was, but they don't have the very best mentors like I have had, they long went away, but I have what they left behind, and that's me, a true replica of them selves.

I really think that you are very blessed to have me at your disposal being your guiding light that will lighten every dark corner that you may travel.

Bon voyage, and grace be with you, but please don't come back with out your destiny's treasure.

I found exactly what I was in search of, and part of it is the ability to affect your life in some tangle way, and it is because some one has done it for me, and it's also a very good thing to be able to give some of what you have received into the lives of others.

One sure way to unlock the source to flow to you is by making way for receiving more, it is a sure thing, nature has shown us that for a life time, it is only that some times we are not paying any attention enough to see it.

I recall the time my dad and I went fishing as it was one of the many times that we did, he cast his net and caught quite an abundance of smaller fish along with some very large ones, that was only one of the times he taught me what replenishment means. all of the smaller one were thrown back into the water, allowing them the opportunity to become larger, all because the smaller the fish, the less meat to be fount, so throwing them back means the next time around if being caught again there would be more meat to be enjoyed, while at the very same time allowing the female ones to lay their eggs creating more of the abundance that we need.

This was a valuable lesson that was well worth sharing, after all it is part of those precious memories that I took away from spending the time with him, learning what I thought no one else could of taught me in honest.

The times that I spent with him was all part of the making of what is me today, and I am very proud that I able to bring it all with you.

As I look back to things in general, what I found out which is part of the root cause of society's break down, is because younger people are spending too little time with what could be their very first, and best mentors.

How then can the torch be passed from generation to generation, if you are not available to receive it.

Frankly in my opinion these young people are just spending way too much time with their pairs, who just does not have enough of life's experience to impact their lives, no doubt they become empty handed while thinking that can carry water in a basket.

Time has proven that, that theory in wrong, so the question remains what will the future be for this next generation.

How do you think that I can write this true stories, it's all because I spent my time with all of the right people, and frankly I am still saying thanks to them for taking me into their circle of influence that I was very thankful for, because now I am able to, I hope influence you to be the very best person that you know.

By the way this is not just the younger people's fault, the major problem is that the parents of today aren't doing a good job raising their children.

I say that with great authority because I am no longer a kid, but I am happy to tell you that up to today I still have an impeccable character which I am very proud of, and that is part of the reasons I am trying to show you a much better way for you to travel.

What I would love is that you, yes, you, and all of the rest to join me as we endeavor to influence the world I the most positive way.

Before you can do any thing, you must first make sure that you have it all together, because it true that you just cannot give what you don't have, we should all know that by now, even though I thought of writing this and other books, there was a time I just was not ready, simply because I just didn't have quite enough of what I wanted to say, so I waited till I felt ready, and really had much to say.

Although just one word can help to change things, the explanation of that word will help immensely, that is mostly because we are not all at the same place in our lives at the same time.

It is like some one giving you some thing with out telling you how to use it, that reminds me of the time my wife bought one of those small furniture, you know the one that usually comes with a template, in this case that one had no template, and guess what, I was the one that was supposed to put it all together, that was a time in my life,

Eventually I was able to put it together, but not till a few hours later, believe me I was sweating bullets, after it was finished, I went straight to bed, and I slept for eight hours straight, I just had to get this thing out of my system once and for all.

The next time that I had to do any thing similar I made quite sure that there was a template, and took time to study it in advance, that way when I am ready to build, it would also have fun doing it.

Like just about every thing else in life, if you would tell some one to go you may even hear them ask you just where too, and it's not at all rude it's just common sense to be shown, other you may have them going around in a circle, wasting their time, but getting no where.

The fact is after you have read this book you will for sure get an idea of just how every thing works, especially to your advantage.

I love to know that I am making a great difference in my life, and a very big difference in yours, you get the chance to keep what you have, plus what I am giving to you, you are in a win, win situation which ever way that you look at it.

I call that demonstrated fairness, you know, the kind of thing that have every one feeling that they were fairly treated.

I don't know about you, but I am very aware when I am getting what I think deserve, and if not, I can address the situation right away, it's better than fussing, and fretting about things, leaving it with a very unsettling feeling, which sort of ruin relationships, some times I also call that creating stumbling blocks to success.

I you would devote your time to enrich your self with all of the good things that would need it most definitely help you in your quest for the success that you are after, it is like most other things, that has beginnings, and endings.

First you go to school, but make no mistake about it, for sure you will begin at kindergarten, we call that foundation or other wise orientation it's nothing new just about every one had to begin there, you see, this is the very first step on the ladder, as you make your climb.

Our lives is just the same, we grow up, and get to adulthood, and inevitably we begin to make our way up into the work place, in what ever form it may take, what happens you were prepared from the very start of your life, so now that you are older and more responsible for the things that we do, that is when we start to value the things that we have gathered on our way up.

That is why we were encouraged to learn all that we can, especially in the earlier stages of our lives, really there is no better time, the more that we take in, is the more that we may have to work with, as we build the foundation that would last for a life time.

Just remember that pitfalls are all real things, and if not taken care early, can hinder our progress as we go forward, I have seen that happen way too many times, and it is just about every where that I go.

One of the many things that we got to take into consideration is that one day we may be called to answer for our lack of preparedness by then we may be deep into a terrible condition already that it would take many forces to delivery you out of it.

Every thing that I did with my first mentors, was well documented, and stored up in the archives of my mind, all because I knew how important what they were saying to was, take for instance my dad loved agriculture so mush that every thing that he touched became beautiful, I was simply amazed to see some of the things that we did together, one day he have me a seed and assisted me in planting it, that tree bored fruit before I was twelve, I began to pick from it my self, that was an amazing thing for a young boy to see, my whole body ignited with joy.

By then I really couldn't help my self I just wanted to help to do any thing that he was doing, lucky for him by then he had two very willing hands, that would do just about any thing to assist him, and mind you, he was very much appreciated for my help.

For me the willingness to help, was also the willingness to learn the kind of things that no one would be willing to teach me, you see, he left no stones un turned, he made quite sure that I would remain on the receiving side of every thing as far as he was concerned.

When you live your self open and willing, people in high places will take notice of you and reward you accordingly. I had mine, so I am helping to prepare you for yours.

Now please don't get me wrong, I am not saying that people will give you just what you want, because people can reward you by simply saying let me show you the way that might be much better for what you are looking for, as a matter of truth, this is the very same thing that has happened for me, I think it was because I was always willing to listen and learn.

I am quite sure that you may agree with me, in this one too. as we all have had conversations with people just about any where, as soon as you may make a suggestion to them, the very first thing that comes out of their mouth, is "I know" by all account I would strongly urge you to discontinue that if that is the case with you, it's like closing all options to learning, or being taught.

So if you want any one to help you to be better, you must first be humble enough to allow your self to be taught.

The way that I see it is like this, keep it very simple just in case some one wants to impact your life with knowledge you should consider your self lucky that this person is taking part of the time that they have to do so, that is why I recommend that you say a very big thank you to open that flow to you.

What I have done many times over is to put to use what I now learn with what I already have, now I really have more than I had to begin with, in this case more is always better.

It is very easy to leave your self short, and it is also one of the worse thing that you can do to your self, it is one way of being real to your self, and account of that you will always   thrive in life.

And remember that life is great, but you can sure make it better, and just tell me who wouldn't like it to be.

I have worked so hard to be better, believe me this energy flow didn't come by simply doing nothing, in fact it is the very opposite, I have learnt in an early age that I would have to work, not only very hard, but also very smart.

Some thing that did a lot of growing up, was to stand back a little, just to see how things were going to play out, and once I had a good understanding of that I knew then that I had it under control, from here on things will surely work the way that I want it too.

I always like to assess situations, and well in advance, so I know what I am going up against, some how it makes it easier for me, because it is not an ambition of mine to complicate things, too many people are doing enough of that already, I certainly won't like adding to that.

I also say to kids to start early, to finish early, and always try to be a step ahead of the competitions, this can an easy way to pace your self, and cruise to the finish line.

Like some of us who realized that very early, I would gladly say to you one of the most important thing that you may want to consider is to change, or make a good adjustment to your attitude, that will make every thing different for you.

There are quite a lot of people that has learnt the hard way as they make their way through life,.

One of the many things that will alter every thing, including all of the plans that you have made, is having a bad attitude, you know the ones that no one can ask a simply question of, or even say some thing to, with out them taking an offense to, some times just making a joke to.

I have personally witness people getting into serious trouble by having a bad attitude, what's wrong with being polite in just about any situation, you really have nothing to loose by being nice, I for one refuses to have a conversation with any that was not easy to talk with, and was ready to explore some new avenues, all by keeping a good conversation.

Some time it is just a matter of being way too cocky for our own good, that only serve us a no good portion, and not only that once people realizes how you are as a person, it better be good, or better thinking people just wont to come close to you, what a way to loose out on big benefits.

Lets not forget that I have traveled all of the places that you are thinking of now, and it's not by going places abroad in fact to all of the local areas, and things that you may have endeavored

So be sure to keep your eyes and ears open, if in case you really want to rise to the top, where every thing looks, and feels better.

It is very hard for me to tell you all that I want to at this time, so I will keep as un finish business, and hope that at some other time you may get the remainder of what I hope will inspire you to do great things.

As far as I am concern I feel that I have done a lot, but life is not over, and there is just so much work to get done, to feed society with all of the things that will ultimately help to make a much better world.

Now that you are ready to tackle things, that means that you feel good to know that you have the knowledge to get things done, that is only one part of the puzzle, are you excited to go through with things? the very moment you begin to feel good, or excited about things will be the very moment your energy begin to flow, and at that time it's like nothing could stop you now.

I think you are ready to roll, know that, feel it in you soul, let every thing become one big event, simply because you know that from here on this train is at last on track, and rolling to victory.

Once you find your self milling around, it's a signal that you are not too sure about any thing, and that means that you are not going any where too.

Be assertive, be sure, and start to things like you mean it, and your whole attitude about every thing will be different.

You know, it's like when we were young, and learning to ride our first bicycle, and as you know nothing goes right at the beginning, that is when you better have a double dose of patience, that will surely help you to get better, so just keep on practicing, for soon you will be on your own, and going places, all by your self.

When freedom comes you will be the very first one to know because you were the one that has been trying, and failing until you become so good at it that you are literally asking to join the racing team, and guess what you will because you want to, and others can see the excitement in you.

Right now I am feeling very excited, because I am doing just what I wanted to do, and not only that I am also succeeding at it all at the very same time, it really makes me feel good, especially as I know when I started there were many people that spent just about half of their day criticizing me for the efforts that I made to do some thing that I was fascinated about.

Needless to say I paid very little attention to them, simply because I knew what I wanted to achieve, after all it was based on the goals that I set for my self.

It is a very different situation now because I accomplished despite it all, and I am on my way to bigger, and better things, and they have front row seat to see it all come to pass.

Like I said before just stick to your plans, at least you made one.

I just couldn't imagine

 what would have happen to me if I didn't hid all of the signals that showed me to a better way forward, now you understand why I am so happy, there is nothing better than moving on despite the many odds that I face in the process.

Right at the very beginning it was like seating in a raft in the middle of the ocean, you know that feeling, when you find your self surrounded by water, and endless sky above, but some thing say to you wait, there must be some thing else in this mix, so just keep moving forward.

At the start you may doubt your self, thinking this is just crazy, but truly most things are like that, until you put every thing into perspective and you get the feeling that it is going to be okay, and usually it is.

There is a rough ride to just about every thing, nothing is simple enough that it wouldn't cause you to think again some times, so don't even think that it is going to be your piece of cake, take time you will have enough time to eat your cake later.

It's hard to say, may be it's because my life is one very big adventure, I really never like to wait for things to happen, in stead I get the feeling that I must make it happen the way that I want, it's just the story.

Despite that I am very happy that I am releasing this to you, because I really want this to help you, not just in business, but in every area of your life.

I think it must have been the very same wish that my father had for me, when he was passing the torch over to me, he loved me enough to want me succeeding at every thing that I did, other wise I guess he would not have bothered to spend all this time preparing, and grooming me for the roads ahead.

At that time in my life I didn't even know just how long my journey would be, now I have a much clearer vision, and I now know where I am on this journey.

One thing that I know for sure is that I am coming closer to the end, and I am seeing some light way over there, to the place where I will pick up my trophy, the mantle is ready and I am ready to accept it with great joy.

What are you working for? are you making any progress in your life, and if not, why not, if the road that you took didn't get you just where you wanted to go, just know that you have enough tome to seek an alternate road that may lead to a much better forward, but it is up to you, if you want to succeed.

In case you wanted to know the real truth why I went through those difficult channels that I went through, was simply because I wanted to make quite sure that I can depend on me and on the decisions that I make to have what I wanted in the end.

That's where most people make their decision as to whether will make it in life or not, because some times making decisions can be the hardest thing to do.

And frankly I think that is where you get to know who is going to make it or not, it is the real test, because from here expect that there will be ups, and downs, so if you can ride it out, you may be able to make it okay.

Look, in some situation life could be very harsh, but at least you are alive to experience the harshness of it, but don't be afraid, the whole world is exposed to the very same things, only some of us work it to suit our selves, and make significant gains.

What I am saying to you is this, as they say get out of your comfort zone, you have been taking it too easy for much too long, it is time we all wake up to the realities of life, and get things done for your self before things change against you plans.

Now is the time, not later, now, Look I really want to tell you about this, I always believe in small things that becomes big, when ever I get before a crowd it is not unusual to find me carrying a little plastic bottle of mustard seeds, some one asked me, where you going with these deeds, I said I will show you what I will do with it.

so I pull out the little bottle, stick my fingers in and grab a hold of one, and throw it to the audience, they thought that I was trying to fool them, that was not true.

One spring day I prepared my garden, and did all of my planting, then later I took some mustard seeds and sprinkled it in the garden, it grew to about two feet tall, now I have multiple amount of seeds all from that one seed.

Many of us have ideas, that we find are too small to be considered for implementation so they hold on to it for ever, where as that seed could of been the start of some thing big in the future, remember that small things grows into big things.

The lessons here for you, is seeds, and thoughts are always small, but take a good look at the size of the tree, or the size of business that came from a single thought.

In many ways I have the feeling that you would love to be successful, but what is holding back is nothing, but fear, and if that is the case, just remember what God says, I have not given you the spirit of fear but of knowledge, and of a sound mind, what else can we ask for, after all this comes straight from God to us, this is when we know that we can use it and be sure that we will be successful in just about every thing that we may do an account of it.

Now here is some thing funny, and it is a very true story, this man had this piece of attachment that he uses to make a connection to a small engine that he uses to do some of his work for his company.

I heard him fussing, and fretting, turning every thing up side down, until he has gotten tired with the whole thing, but with one more thought of searching again, and it was found right in his apron pocket along with every thing else.

Needless to say that at that time he became very happy, and was now able to do his work, and completed the task with absolutely no worries.

There are way too many times we find our selves in the very same way, looking for what we already have well secured right in the middle of our hands.

For all of us that have a belief in God, should know that with him we are on the right track, and need not worry quite as much as we do at times.

You see, we are the ones that convolute situations for our selves, and for the most time we blame just about every one, and the cat for not accomplishing our missions, as we expects too, some one once said we need to slow down some how, and start thinking of where we are, and just where we are heading to, once we do that we may find it much easier on our selves, and may be succeeding even at the very first try.

I use my success as a validation that I am here, and this is what I can accomplished if I would think, and focus on the goals that I set.

Firstly I used the clear, and concise direction that I have been given, and I knew that I could only follow on I would find my way for sure.

Now I am very happy that I did, because today I can see, and show the benefits that have gotten out of it, that enables me to extend it to you, just that you may find it easier for you to find your way to the path that leads to your destiny .

There is no doubt about the things that we think we can do will be done by us, it is some thing that we processed when we were planning to do what we want to do, if you remember well one of the very first things that we did was to plan from the start to what might the very end with a well finished product in hand.

Staying on track is absolutely important, once you begin to deviate at the very same time you loose focus, and now operates in a very different time zone, and you know just what that can do for you, confusion steps in, then comes, then a loss of interest, and just about every thing else, that's not worth while to be written.

As far as I know destination is a place where one may expect to be at the very end of the journey to collect the long awaited prize, if this is you keep moving along, you are no where close to the end, there is a tremendous stretch left to go, it's like ever thing else, just keep your mind right there, this way you are sure to make it to the very end.

I am not telling you some thing that I did not have to do my self, as a matter if fact I just happen to think that I have had a greater portion than any one else.

Any way knowing that made me so much more determined to reach my expected destiny, I just don't like going just half the way, if that is the case, then why did I begin, if it was just to fail.

Just the word fail is enough to of set me, and the way that I am used to thinking, in fact I really don't believe in that word, to me failure is based on a trial, but willingly refused to continue despite what is ever so possible.

look, stand strong, determine to succeed, know that there are odds, and you are going to overcome each and every one of them.

That is just what I had to do, I don't think that there were any one with more of a struggle than me, I really went through it all, and over came it all, if you know just who you are drawing your strength from you are sure to make it big.

In my case I have my faith planted in my God's ability with out fail, and I knew that if I can only hold on for yet a little time longer, I will see all of my hopes fulfill, and in fact they did.

Today as I seat in my study writing this to you, I am feeling very good starting this long journey, that I knew for sure would come to an end, and I was going to reap what I sow, now there is little room to contain it all, that is exactly what happens when you sow a seed, there must be a tree.

Yes there are struggles in life, but there are also success, on account of the many struggles that you may have gone through, they do come together, it's like fire and smoke, they come together too.

Look at me I am a prime subject of the thing we call struggle, the fact is if you are going to succeed you must come to terms with some times good, and some times not so good, the kind of thing that may make you feel like giving up, but, wait not so fast, you just cant measure success by a simple case of the way the tides may roll.

One thing that I always have troubles with is those that they should have it by the flip of the fingers, or else some one else should be doing it for them.

Like most of the people I own a house, and well as you already know when you are an owner, there are several things that you may have to do for your self, which is all to your benefit, so we advise people to learn as much you can from those that are willing to pass on some of their knowledge to you, and for free.

Here is how mine got started, one day my wife and I and the neighbor were having a very friendly conversation about house hold thing, including lighting fixtures, so he told us about how he had to change all of his light switch from toggles to sliders, but he didn't even wait for me to ask him it help me to do mine he offered him self, in which I said thank you ever so much.

The day arrived, and he came over to help me, I said look, I just don't like using your expertise to help me to do this all for free, I really don't mind, he replied, again I said thank you for doing this.

I said to him, why don't you show me how to do this and I will continue, and so he did.

It was so amazing to see how some thing that I was always afraid of became so easy to be done, especially in my case I learn very quickly.

After he did the second one I said to him, I think I get the hang of it let me take over from here, her agreed, so I took over and continued to retrofit the whole house, actually he was rather surprised to see that I was so willing to help my self.

You see, there are truly nice people in and around you and some time you may not even know.

Talking is good, so many things can come about on account of talking to people, even those that you don't even know so well, what a wonderful way to explore possibilities

They are truly unlimited, and can be found in you , me and just about every one else, it is for us to find out.

There is some thing called networking, which is very helpful in all sorts of ways, and it really doesn't only applies to business, getting, and sharing information that could lead to great things.

Some times even a very simple conversation can lead to discovering things that can help you to do better in all sorts of ways, after all this is the age of talking to every body, with out fear that you may get shut down.

The fact of the matter is we all should go through this life making as many stops as we can along life's high way, because as often as we do so is the opportunity that we may have to add to what we already have, just that it may things better.

Don't be afraid, this was the exact words of my mother as she coached me into becoming a minister, she knew that there would be a great amount of things to learn, that would help me in that possibility.

There were times that I thought that I really love it, and by all accounts I will, and there were other times when I thought that I'd better be an auto mechanic, either way neither came to be, instead I studied business, Hotel and restaurant business that was.

Despite the switch I enjoyed the choice that I made, simply because it served me very well, I have gotten the opportunity to do all manner of things which led me to a lucrative career over the years, that even mom would be pleased, it's too bad she didn't get the chance to see me in action, she would of been proud of me.

The very best of all was as I looked back to my many standing ovations that I have been given, by some very special people, that were clientele of mine, saying just how satisfied they were, and a job well done.

You see, amongst all of the many things that I have done, I was also a Chef De Cuisine, as a matter this is still my fascination, when it comes to cooking and entertaining I love it to my soul, there is nothing better than seeing people enjoy the foods that you have prepared, and cooked for all those that admires your dedication for the things that you love so dearly.

I found my passion, and they are many, all because I am one that thinks that one should not be too limiting in any way , do as much as you enjoy doing, that makes all the difference in your life.

Endeavor to make the head lines, stir people crazy, all in good fun, enjoy this life to it's fullest, because one of this days all good things will come to an end.

Don't allow any thing to hold you back, do as much as is humanly possible, and remember in all that you, live a lasting legacy to all those that you have met, let them enjoy the sweet memories of that which you have left behind.

In just about every walk of life, you will hear of people that have left memories behind them, but one may ask what kind of memories are they, unlike those that are prepared and won't live any thing behind but good news for the rest of us to en joy.

I for one, after spending all of this time trying to be the very best that I can be, and doing the things I enjoyed doing, not to make the news, but in fact doing just what I can, to help to make a better society, and a better world.

I recall some of the various things that I had to do, in order to change my life, and frankly some of the things, you may not even consider to do in this society, but I did it all with joy, and pleasure.

The moment you begin to fuss about, what might be responsible for making you the person that you would like to be, is the very first time you may want to stop for a while, and consider it's true value, once you have done that, and feel good about it it's time to move beyond it.

What I did, was first think of whether I was able by knowledge to do it, simply because way too many people just think that they can walk into things with out first knowing that they are capable of getting it done.

Before you attempt any thing make a case study of before you get too far, what the case study will do for you is to give you the assurance that you have done all of the research and development, and know for sure that you are onto it.

As we say try going through the forest with out a compass, the question is where are you going to, and just in case the answer is you really don't know, you are right, and should stop right now before you get too far, because you might end up in a place that you may not like for sure.

To put things simple, just know what you want in life, and make a good plan, and work towards it, you already know that you will never make it with out first having a plan to make things happen.

Once you have done that you can have just about any thing that you want, it becomes yours for the taking, so go right along make your day, it is that simple after all.

I am very sure you have heard people say in conversations, further more they ask the question, do you know what you really want, it is also observation that you may be just a little confuse, so think before you give the answer to that question.

Don't ever give the impression to any one that you know it all, simply because you just might miss the opportunity to learn it all before you begin to work for it all, leave your self open at all times to learn from whom the teacher may be, the fact of the matter is you must empower your self, so that you don't rely on any other person but you.

You may need some help, just ask for what you need, and nothing else, the rest is entirely up to you.

In this world you are free to ask for what you want, because we assume that you are missing in some thing, and that is why you are asking, the question is from whom are you asking, although I already have a very clear idea that you are asking from another person.

So why are you really asking, and I am sure you will say to me it is because I have a need, and that is fine, some one has to give to you, we understand, now what I would love for you to understand is that every one has some thing we call talents.

One thing that I learnt is that we were all born with the ability to use his, or her brains to think enough to be able to take care of them selves, ion what ever way that they chooses, that means that we can learn to do the things the ultimately would be responsible for getting all of the things that we need.

May be it's me I kind of like my independency, there is quite a lot to say about the persons that are willing to accomplish his, or goal, and be proud of that, some how you feel so much better, especially no one can say to you, can I have it back?

I love the sating, I rather have to give, than to ask for, or better yet, it's more blessed to give, than to receive, either way every one gives and receive, that is the way the world operates, but foe peace sakes, please don't wait to get it from any one else but you.

When I decided to change my career to writing, was because I felt that what better way to help you to know what happened back there, that causes me to want to reach you with what I knew all along would be just what you always wanted to help steer you into the right direction.

You see, I have been given quite a lot freely, and that was by the first mentors, after all they just wanted me to be well prepared, so they saw to it that I was, by passing on all of their trade secrets to me, what a gift! to this day I can hardly scratch the surface, it's like a treasure chest of goodies, am so thankful.

As they say it's like seating on a gold mine. that is just what it feels like, there is simply no way for me to finish using all of my knowledge, but I am going to try to make it available to you, but promise me that you will treasure it to the fullest, and let it show.

What I am giving to you is going to change your life, and I hope that it is going to be forever, I am quite sure that you can tell that mine has been changed, and that is for ever, or just what forever means.

What ever the case it has done me well, and I am very happy for that, especially putting it to the uses that I did, it's sure an investment that paid off at the end.

Quit stalling your self, instead you should follow the yellow brick because it leads to a place to discover some thing, there is no doubt that this some thing is well worth it's journey.

Usually I don't go any where unless I know that I am going for what ever it is that I am looking for.

There is a beginning, and an end to every thing that we may do, the fact is what are we hoping to find that we did not have, as I mentioned before there are some that are looking for they already have, if you continue to do that you may find your self tripping over your self, and I am quite sure this is not what you really want.

I had a sense that when I start, there were not going to be any stumbling around, because I had a very good idea about just what I was going to find, simply because I pre set the stage for my landing.

Take for instance if you are going to shoot at a target, you should take a good aim to ensure that you are going to hit your target, any thing short of that would be considered a total waste of your time.

I was fortunate to witness a base ball catcher making one of his very best catch one day, he made quite sure that in any case, that even though he would fall, this ball be caught by him, and that he did to the amazement to a cheering crowd.

For the greater part of the population, some times even though they knew that it was very possible, they still neglect the opportunity to make good at the moment that they could.

So whop is then responsible for you not having the success that could of been yours, the opportunity is all ways, and ever present for us to take at any time that we sees fit.

For me I was very hungry for my success, so I gave it al that I had to ensure that I would find it.

The thing is some times we seems to think that we must go around the world to find it, when in fact it is right in our back yard, all that we have to do is to stand and gaze for a while just to find your self fixated at what is now the treasure that you in search of.

I wanted to succeed so bad, that I could of taste it, even from the distant it were, at a time the light at the end of that tunnel seems more apparent, because I could see it better as I drew closer.

Some time just having a sense of life is good enough, simply because just about every thing that you can think about, begins with life, because it is so vital, and important to all those that still have it, one good way to show that you are appreciative of it is to do all that you can within this given time.

This is just where we create a sense of urgency in our liver, not the kind that get us running in all directions all the very same time, but knowing that unless we keep the charge to go after what we want with steadfastness and great hope, we might just be fooling our selves.

I have seen for quite some now, and may be this is one of the many reasons that I spend time to put my fingers to this keyboard so would get this message straight from me, because it is just one thing that I would love to get out of this, and is to move you to action.

After all in earlier times as I started this journey, was simply because I have been to all of those places of interest that I thought would yield the type of material to condense the true essence of what I have found, and make it great value to you.

I would love to see you take this book that I have written just for you, and make it your mirror to look into while taking all that is reflected back to you personal, because I know that is where you may find your greatest impetus, and from here on you are on your way to becoming the greatest you that you can ever imagine. This may be a little thing for you, but it is at this time I would love to see you take such a very small thing and balloon it to one of the biggest that you have ever seen, and experienced.

Successful people will tell you that if ever you are looking for the biggest of things to grab on to just to say that you are successful, you might be mistaking, it is the very small things that becomes the very biggest things that we have ever seen.

Here is a picture that I have painted before, and that is I great comparison to the little seed that was responsible for huge harvest.

How it works is like this, take a good look at a seed, then at the very same time turn your head, and take a look at the tree that is because of that seed, now you are sure to think, which is just what I wanted you to do.

Just to keep it real for a moment, take an apple seed, look at it while standing below an apple tree, for an instant a brand new reality presents it's self in a very sharp contrast.

It is no different to the thought that you have stored up inside your head, about the thing that you would love to do that my help to change your life forever.

Do you still wish to hesitate, or even procrastinate rather than bringing this thing to bear, just take a good look at the potentials. and stop wasting the valuable time that you have, right now that you are not using.

If you want to be successful, and be able to take charge of your life once, and for all, then, release that seed, or thoughts, and instead of worrying about what is not, think about what is, you have the time, and the opportunity to do just that and more.

What I have seen, when talking about things that multiply, I am thinking about the time when my dad and I went out and did some planting, in a newly prepared field, in about three months later we had so much yield that we didn't know just what to do with it, even though my mom took a great part of it to the market, the rest we gave away to the neighbors.

Now the very same can be said about that little thought that you have been cherishing for so long, why don't you do some thing about it before it vanishes away never to be seen again.

The problem with some of us, we have to start seeing things long before it happens, that may give us a little glimpse of things to come, urging us to take action while the time is good.

Just think for a moment, that what ever things that you start is, or should be considered a small part of the bigger picture, so when you seem to forget, just start to think of the reason that you have started.

Do you know that when I started to write, was because I felt that I have had experienced enough of some of the things that would simply amaze you, to find out that any one would even take on that responsibility.

You see, one thing that learnt was that every one loves a story, so you should tell yours, because those stories like mine was meant to show you that life can be tough at times, for it's at that time you are supposed to show that you have some of what it takes to win over such challenges.

Just about every day I hear people say, oh, I wish I had started some thing like that when I had the time, it's like if to say time has ran out, and that there is simply no more time left.

Don't kid your self there is quite enough time to go around the world on as many voyages as you choose, just think that if every one would say the very same thing, that there is no time, where would we be today, in regards to especially our health.

The fact is there are way too many people that keep putting off what they should do today for God knows when.

Just in case you are waiting to do some thing, make sure that you are also preparing so when the time comes to do, no time is wasted on account of waiting.

I waited for this time to begin this project, but if you should take a little trip back you will notice that I was fully engaged in other things that I know would help me to accomplish my goals.

Let us learn together that waiting is a form of patience that produces all of the results, for it is with it that we can run the race, and not get tired, you see when you think about that finish, it is worth the beginning.

Just to be sure, let me say this again, as I struggled, I quite accepted it, but was determined to win despite of it, so I struggled with winning on my mind, for I was darn sure that all of this hard work was going to do me well in the end.

Some how I feel like you really don't have to hear this from me, but in fact I will, all because I really want you to make note of all that I say, so you may learn a new way of taking care of things for your self better.

Winners fall, and rise again only to be much stronger the next time around, but wait, isn't that the way it should be? we all have difficulty in our lives at times, but it doesn't mean that we should fail on account of it.

As they say when you fall, you get up, dust your self and move on like nothing has ever happened.

Here is a silly thing that happened to me one day, which I am sure must have happened to you, or to some one that you know.

I was walking one day it was winter time, and there were ice every where on the roads, because I was really new to this sort of thing, I had simply no idea what really happens when you try to walk on ice, especially wearing running shoes.

I was walking very casually as any other time, not knowing that I should be tip toeing like a cat instead.

It happened so quickly that I had no time to recover, my legs just went up, and before you know it I was lying on my back flat out on the ice, I was so ashamed all that I could do was to get up as quickly as I could, so people just won't even think that I had fallen.

Some times learning does take some strange turns, but what ever the case it was a lesson that I learnt the hard way, but I learnt it well.

Be it falling, from a roof top, or falling from missing an opportunity, I made a promise to my self that I will find my way through the maze of this madness that some times drives every one crazy, I will triumph to the highest mountain, and while I am there I will shout from the top of my lungs, in amazement for where I worked my self to be.

After all of this I will have a party to celebrate the end of, and the beginning of every thing new, and guess what, you are invited, along with all of your friends.

It was only recently I received a note from a certain celebrity describing, just what led him to his celebrity status, many of us seldom stop to think that most of the people that we look at on television happens to be real people, with real life circumstances that reshapes their lives on a daily basis.

A person with great amount of wealth, happens to be a person that spent most of their time thinking, planning, and doing, just that they may have the what they want in this life.

As I read their note I paid particular attention to the message, there I was learning first hand that this individual was very poor, grew up in the slums, struggled in every area of his life, and like me, he says that he struggled with a goal in mind.

He realized that it was either he stayed there and wallow in tough times or while he is in his tough situation work out a plan to see him getting out of that place.

Good for him he dreamt a dream that spoke directly to his heart, after pondering over, and over again he decided to take action, and started to formulate the dream, so that he could bring that dream to a reality.

In that note he described how, after working so hard in life, some one tried to rob him, after being very generous to people any where including his community.

He took that attempt very serious, and then put all of the measures in place to protect him self and his family.

Fortunately every thing is okay now, but it was not until he doubled up on his security measures.

After spending a considerable amount of time on this, I realized that there is just so much work yet to be done to help our society to face up with their own situation, and like those of us who struggled found a way out of our tough situation.

Just about any one can be like the persons that lay it all on the line, some times going for broke, and that is quit okay as long as you are doing what it takes to change your life situation.

It's like just what I had to do, God knows just how many times that I had fallen, before I could shake off the dust, and determined that nothing was going to stop me from the life change that I want and expect.

I stood at the very brink of my pitfall, just to gaze at what was going to be my mansion in the distance, all that I had to say to my self was that there was the dream in a new reality.

Putting all pretense aside, because it is just what quite a lot of people do on a daily basis, deep down inside of you is a desire to have all that you are seeing in those that made it good for them selves, but at times you just don't know just where to begin, nor what to do.

I am really not a jealous person the least bit, but that doesn't mean that I won't end up having what some others have acquired, some times from great struggles.

What I would tell you is that as a person with great ambition I gave up quite a lot to have what I earned from investing in self.

Some times it seems like we forget that we should be the ultimate driving force behind our plans to succeed in the things that we love so dearly, and as a matter of fact it is at that time, that we should know that we are already standing right at the brink of what can be our greatest opportunity to succeed.

Look, some people must have already said to them selves, what's with all of that success thing, every time I listen a little more, that is all that I am hearing, and believe it or not, for it is entirely up to you, but these people really gets mad at you for just what you want to accomplish in your life.

I know that there were some that poked fun at me all for doing the things that have taken a delight in, but that was okay, because every one has a right to their opinion.

In your quest for the things that makes you happy, just know that it is based on personal interest, and you must do what ever it is that makes you happy, simply because at the end of the day, you know that you will be the one that is responsible for you.

The was a time, when I thought that some people really didn't want me to become any body, what I had to first understand was that I wanted to become just about any thing that I could, because right then it was me and simply no one else.

It was a very good kind of selfish, the one that is not with malice, or indifference, as they say selfishness can turn into nothing but greediness, although I have seen it in many places, doesn't mean that I would allow it to take a strong hold on me.

In fact what I really believe in is that as I prepare my self to be self reliant, it is just because I have it in me to give, and I wouldn't trade this opportunity for the world.

Yes, this is what I have became, I have watched my self grew to this level, from very humble beginnings, today I am only looking back at the foot prints that led up to this moment.

There are times that I really get lost in some of the places that is responsible for the way that I see things today, I still see palm trees, fruit trees of all sorts, including acres, and acres of cultivated, and uncultivated land that occupied the greater part of my child hood, but because it was all meant for good, it is still all good.

I tried not to allow my vision to get clouded by all that others may have to say, because as long as you benefited by the events that helped to reshape your entire life, then you cant count it all meaningful to your over all person.

There was a time when I was very young, and following my mom where ever she went, that we met a friend of hers, as usual they would stand to have a real good chat, and they did.

That morning this friend of hers came from tending to her property, and she had some of the yields that she was taking home, but just before she left, she gave my mother a portion of what she had, and asked mom to feed this to Paul for dinner that evening.

I really loved that lady, may be just as much as she loved me, which led me to think that is might of been that God was signaling that he is looking after me in ways that was quite mysterious, what ever the case it was great, because he made a promise that He will take care of his own.

I can never, neither will I ever forget that gentle act of kindness that will last for my entire life time.

She was able to give from what she had, from the preparations that she made, and today I am giving this experience to you, which I hope will be used to alter your course in some way or the other, she influenced me, I hope that experience will influence you.

Some how I think that is one of the many reasons that I am so happy to give of what I have found, and it is not from the street some where, it is of what I have worked all of my life for, the things that I hold very dear to my heart, so you can say what ever you wish it is very precious.

And I am very sure that if you would treat it like the way you should it would work very well for you too, and for that matter, may be even better, because the times have changed, including all of the circumstances that surrounding it.

To me this is a very unique way of giving things, some people gives money, some gives ideas, what I think of this sort of giving is that it would last a life time with you.

I am quite sure you have heard of rod, the line, and the fish, my kind of giving is that one that would stay with you, encourage, and inspire you towards great things.

You see, just in case I give you some money, for sure you will spend it in the way that you chooses, and unless you are very thrifty, and know just how to take care of your money, before you know it that gift will be gone forever, living you no better that when it was first given to you.

I told you earlier that when I started I struggled with my goal in sight, that was very true, when I started I really had only a few dollars.

So the very first thing that I had to do was to recognize that I had very little money to do any thing, so as I went out to buy some of the things that I definitely needed, I knew that I would have to watch my spending, and I did, that really gave a leg up on things.

It's amazing what can happen when you are know just how to take care of money, I remember when I started in the career that I have chosen, there were many asking the question, so where did he get the money to take on this project, and further more accomplishing it, this was a surprise to them, but not to me.

There is some thing that we call purpose, and passion, they are two of the most powerful words that you may find in life, because we are called to do a certain thing, you must know what you are called to do by how determine you are about it, as some one said if there is no passion you really don't have a lot going on for you.

What really helps in every thing is from the very moment you are about to begin, start to anticipate what the end would be like, by how sweet it taste right now, just keep that in mind, and that will give you all of the power you ever needed to drive you forward.

The power is in all of us to change things, so what we have to is to recognize just where it lies, and tap into it, you may be very surprised to see what the out come may be, but I think you have to first be doing things to find that out.

If you look carefully you are sure to notice that there that in the big scheme of things, that there are some who lifted them selves to that place call powerful just to push people around, but to me the real power is not domineering over any one, in fact is the opportunity to show them just how things can be if they do a certain thing.

I have seen enough people in power, and it a fact that quite a lot of them has gotten wrong for much too long, so all that I am proposing is that we re-examine what powerful means, for it is then we may find a much better response to what we now call leadership.

Just make me feel like a real human being, all by the way that you treat me, and for that alone you may see a whole world on the move to change for the better.

What I really think would make a very big difference in the lives of us all is when people start to lead by example, that is more powerful than any thing that you may try to do.

It is very important in this fast moving world that we put emphasis on who would be leading who to a better way forward, after all that is may be most of what we need, in order that the present situation would be better and more beneficial to the masses.

Looking back in order that I may go forward, I just couldn't help but to add a little to this thing call powerful, and that what I think that would be helpful is the ability to help people to move in the same direction agreeably.

That will undoubtedly act as a major encouragement, all because they do have a clear understanding about just where you are taking them.

There is no need to be led in a place that you may have questions of later, one must be sure to satisfied that the possible out come is just as is expected.

I know at times it can be very hard to predict, but some how you may know by your gut instinct as they say, so just stay tuned to you inner most self in order that you may get that feeling.

I know because it has happened to me, and in fact it is still happening, and may be for a very long time yet to come, some time I feel that it is far better listening to my self than listening to any one else, simply because I will always be true to my self.

And just that you may care to know, I write from the power from within.

My advise to all is to please get to know your self, and just what you are capable of, I call that first thing first, simply because it is very easy to prejudge situations which may hamper your efforts.

And now that you are aware of the power that is within you, you can literally lead the way to changing just about every thing that you are not happy with, but just make sure that the masses do feel the same way like you, in order that you my see the effectiveness of what ever you are all about.

There is a place that I know personally, called Grand Tang lake way up an top of a mountain in Grenada, this lake is very wide, extremely quiet, and very unassumingly deep.

It literally bears great significance to the saying, still waters runs deep, this lake supplies nearly all of the island with it's water supply, and has been doing so for as long as I can remember.

So when I talk about things that you are capable of, and able to deliver on that, I think it's fair to say that it is the very same that I am looking for in supplying the kind of leadership, and directions like this lake is doing, using the most gentle approach, while supplying a very big result

It is a gentle kind of thing that is saying to us all, that look at me I am here, and I am quite able to supply all of your needs, with out making a fuss, like the giver that keeps on giving to you no matter what.

It is ironical that I had to take you in that direction, but some time we have to use various scenarios to get our points across, so you are better able to assimilate what we are bringing to you.

My main objective here is to help you get a true feeling for what you are looking for, under any circumstance, it's a rather good way to mobilize you into the right direction that will eventually put you right on the cutting edge of things.

Well, I am quite sure you have seen the results in me, from my first mentors (my parents) and my professors at collage, I followed because I knew they were taking me to that place that I would be more than happy to be in, and that is with out question.

Just in case they did not tell you, I am telling you, because it's my desire to see you taking a brand new approach that will change your life forever.

I think we are now at the place where we can take hold of opportunity to champion the cause, and win at the game, or it may be like you have heard, the dreamer died, but the dreams will live for ever.

For all along I have been telling you, that if you want it you can have it, but you must work for it, other wise it may just never happen.

That to me is very sad, simply because you are positioning your self to fail, by doing simply nothing, as the saying goes, nothing venture nothing gain.

There are too many people waiting in their own little corner for some one to deliver some thing to them, because they think that they have nothing, not realizing that they really have to make great off.

For years I have been exposed to a tremendous amount of natural elements that if processed can be like wonders to the world, while at the very same time obliterating all of their dependency on others.

I want you to realize that every where in this world that you may happen to be has quite enough to take care of you, and all of the rest of the inhabitants.

This world was not made to fail us, but to enrich us, we have not because we ask not, but here, I want you to be careful about what, and from whom are you going to ask.

Some times we just have to ask our selves, for the answers are found within us.

Go ahead, and ask, self, how willing am I to find the answers that would lead me to the place where I may find just what I need to implement some of the things that I found towards the change that I am looking for.

I am quite sure you have heard several times over, people saying, don't depend on me, we all have heard so on quite a regular basis, that is why I say to you just ask self, because self does have the answers.

I could of sat where I was for as long as I wanted waiting, just to realize that I was waiting for simply noting, now tell me how much good would that do for me.

I woke up one morning, and I usually do I had my water followed by my morning coffee, then turn on the television to get the morning news, right after the news came a little documentary of a place, that has so much that they simply just don't know what to do with they have, so they remain in a very poor state, and suffering on account of that.

It took outsiders to come, and utilize what they thought was no good, and turned it into thriving commodity right before their very eyes.

Just what are you really waiting for? don't you know that from here on it's finders keepers? don't wait your self out of time.

When I was like you, I was awaiting for when the time was right to step into action, that time couldn't come quickly enough for me to show the world just what I was made up off.

I readied my self for almost any thing that could be thrown at me. today this is only a very small part of what I am capable of doing.

When talking about living by example, I hope you will find it here, because I know that I will only demonstrate what is right, so as you follow me in what ever direction that I am going you may find it worth the while to you.

I really don't have much time to waste it away, so I will use all the time that I have to accomplish just about all that I am expecting to accomplish, and a great part of that is helping to highlight a better way forward for you.

Mine has been highlighted some time ago, and I have used it to the greatest of my advantage, today although I am still on my journey I am seeing tracks on the journey way back there, my destination is fully in sight, and now I have a glimpse of my prize trophy that I stayed determined for.

Oh! what a journey it's been, but I love every bit of it, and if I had the choice to do it all again, I can assure you that I would have the very same amount of energy as when I first began, all because I am working for results.

I hope that you would take all that I have said to you seriously for I am sure it would do you good, in many ways.

In my travels one of the many things that I have noticed is that all of those that used their talents, and ideas to multiply their returns were very happy that they did, while on the other hand, those that did absolutely nothing, were very jealous for the accomplishments of those that did.

The fact of the matter is the very same things are happening today as we speak, we must find a way to show people a way to succeed, and having their own, shifting them from the path to self destruct to a place of self worth, and happiness.

Remember that as you try to make your way to the top, keep in mind that no one has promised an easy way out of your dilemma, at times you may feel like turning back, and giving up, but that is not going to be the best way of choice if you are going to succeed.

I truly endured all of the pains that came with every thing that I have tried to accomplish in my life, the doubts, the negativity, the set backs, it was difficult, but as I was reflecting on things that were very possible, my mind suddenly shifted on great men whom has gone before, but just how they happened to make it to the very top of their game.

It was J.F.K. who once said that as they went to the moon. quote: we did not go to the moon because it was easy, we went to the moon because it was hard, I really took that at heart, although I could not of been compared to the great J.F.K. yet I am a human being just like him.

The fact of the matter is one should almost expect to face some of the toughest time in their life ,simply because it is the toughest times that reshapes us to the men and women that we are.

Don't allow minor infractions, to derail your chance to succeed, because it is by the toughest situations that we are made strong.

Some times we may get close to the very top, and slide right back to the very bottom, that's okay because we are still alive to try again, and if even we did not succeed the second time, lets try again.

Some times it is very hard to say that I am talking about my self, when in fact I am, it was I who made that treacherous journey, and survived it perils to bring this story of hope, through patience, that you may know that any thing is very possible if you put your mind to it.

It is the very same perils that all great men, and women had to go through, side, by side as they took on the toughest task of all times, before they were able to sing the glory song, we have made it at last, we have made it.

All of that happened just that we may have the courage to pursue to where few man and women have gone before, it is with that courage that I managed to aspire to my height of glory in all humility.

It is my sincere hope that you may reach to the top of your game, so the others below may make you their greatest example.

What ever we do in life, though we are doing it for our selves, may also have a lot to do with the others, because they will have a thing, or two to say about what you have contribute to them in one way or the other.

We may not know just who is looking at us from across the way, and who is really taking note, of what they may apply to stimulate their growth, so I hope that you can take all the time to look for all of the things that may be of importance to you.

Here is some thing that I felt was very important to me. This comes from James Martinez, a leader in the entire marketing industry. Sorry James I will not quote word for word, but I will do the very best that I can, just to let the people how serious I took what you have sent to me, that really change my life may be for ever.

As you said, one of the prices of " leadership" in any industry is criticism. Now I did not know that, so I learnt some thing new today. I did not realized that, but when spectators are watching a race, on who do they focus their attention? on the front runner! and the main reason for that is, very few people pay any attention on those that are not in the lead, or "out of the running". Those who are viewed as being out of the running are often ignored, or dismissed.

But when you are "out in front" and ahead of the crowed, every thing that you do attracts attention. Plain and simple.

As you begin your climb there will be numerous eyes peering at you wondering just what you are doing, or how you are going to do it, some times it's because they are just jealous which happens to be very sad, but what ever you do, just keep doing what you are doing, the rewards belongs to no one else but you.

It is just the way that it is, when you are down and out, just no one pays any attention to you, you are just not important to them, I have experienced that my self, but I kept on going simply because I knew that my mind was made up, my compass was set, and I knew just where in was heading to, and that was to destination assured.

Do your thing, what ever it is that you are about, there is no need to get distracted by all of those peering eyes, they are there to see how far up you are going to get to.

That is just why I advocated that you, should aim higher, that you may see further there is nothing better that getting a full view of such beautiful landscape, it's a climb that you will never forget, it's the progress that you always wanted to make in life, and you should be proud of your self.

Now stay humble, and know that you have helped to carved out a way for all others to follow.

Every thing is hard, but any thing achievable.

Yesterday I spent a great portion of my time listening to the news, about all of those baby boomers retirements.

What ever the case the news was not good for those in question, there were no rosy pictures painted here, and in am very sure that after that news many of the boomers must have felt down right sick to their stomachs.

This I am sure must have been some of the worse news that has ever been in quite some time which left a lot of people under a real cloud of uncertainty, for no one knows just what is going to happen from here on.

It is very hard to swallow as one ponders what the out come of this may be, after all, not enough money saved, no jobs to be found, but despite all of that, there is one thing for certain that has to be taken care of and that is the mounting bills that you face on a daily basis.

Despite the doom and gloom, this is the right time to get really creative, and it is best to face the situation head on, for it's by doing so you may be able to see the scope of what is now your great concern.

Coming to the very end of the road will undoubtedly cause you to do some pondering, as to what the next move might be.

Through out life there has been similar situations, that some how managed to annul themselves all because more careful attention came into the focus, allowing them to make better choices that lead to better results.

This is one of the best times to make tough decisions that may alter the situation, may be for the better.

There are times when it may seem like your road has come to an end, and some times it really does, but what's good in all of this I that you are still alive, so there is still hope, that things can get better.

As I have been in a very similar situation before, what I had to do was to find an alternate road that would take me to my destination to avoid the pitfall that could of been.

What has changed every thing for me, was doing some thing that I have never done before, that gave me what I always wanted.

In situations like what you have recently experienced, it is very easy for just about any one to step right into the fear mode, so let me warn you that this can only help to make things worse.

This is by far not the time to start laying blame on any one, we have a great part to play in what has just happened, so it is time to start to put things into perspective.

What I encourage people to do in this circumstance, is to begin to take a good look at what you possess as workable skills, that you can apply, to help to change things.

Take a look at your life's experiences, all of the things that have accumulated through the years, while working for the many companies that you have worked for, and see if you can offer those up to others as a service that you may use as some form of self employment.

This is the time when every thing would take a different turn, hopefully for the better, the fact of the matter is, it may seem like a real start over, but that's okay some times life can be cruel, but that is the way things work some time.

remember it is not the end of the world, nor the end of your life, try to pick up the pieces, and make the very best of a bad situation, at the end every thing will work it self out, and the whole thing will be like a bad dream.

I have personally seen people who have lost it all, and bounce back as if nothing really happened, so take comfort, in that you are not alone in this.

I recall the time when I had my major set back, it was not easy, but what I had to do was, start looking at all of the mistakes that I have made that led up to this disastrous situation, one thing that I didn't wish to repeat was the very same mistakes again.

I took a good long look at every thing from a long way off, then I zoomed in as close as I could, that gave me an opportunity to see clearly enough, to enable me to make wise decisions that I knew would be worth while in the end.

I saw my circumstance as water under the bridge, no matter I did nothing would bring it back, that part of me was gone forever, so I focused on what could be, and later it all worked out to be.

In my estimation, it is very to see people fall, like I did, but as they say what ever goes up can come down, there is nothing good about that, so we may only now get the chance to come to grips with the cause of the fall.

at Some time a fall can also be a good thing, when we look at it on the positive side, it's a chance to grow stronger, more determine, than ever to do better as we make our way to our destination.

When I on fell I really didn't care to deal with the fall, instead I began to focus on the rise, some how I knew that where I was not comforting enough for me to stay there, it was dark, dingy, and unforgiving in it's nature, I felt miserable, to say the least.

I cried, I wiped my eyes, I prayed, then I laugh, because I knew crying would only served to weaken my self, and destroyed my strength to make the climb, this incline was very steep, and deserved my undivided attention, if I was going to make it.

Coming to think about it, it was quite a time in my life, I was found to be in a place that I never thought that I could be found in, but I guess I am human, and should of known that those things do happen to human being, so any way I took that and consoled my self.

Although unexpected we can get to very low places, when that happens it is determination that we need to at least help establish our position before we begin to build the next fortress of greater hope, it is within us, all that we must do is to realize that.

I recall to memory those words that, was said, things of great displeasure may happen to you, and that if it didn't kill you, hopefully it would make you stronger, and better.

That was the case with me, today as I take a look back I feel very happy to know that I am here, and I am feel very fulfilled, especially as I can give you a personal and ,eye witness account of the past, that reshaped my life in the present, as I look into the future.

It is at this point I must add this very reasonable verse of a song that asked the question, should Jesus bore the cross alone, and all of the world go free? that was exactly what helped me to be thankful, and appreciate His sacrifice for the whole world.

It is quite okay to fall, only to rise again.

This just where I have decided to change my focus, from the growth of you and I, to those that for the most part, think that they are forgotten, and they are the younger people.

I have made a promise to my self that I will never turn my back on you the younger ones, all because the people that happened to be my mentors stood side by side with me in the earlier part of my life, each and one of them helping to point me in the right direction that lead to just where I am today.

Thank you is not quite enough at times to say to them because the end result of what they have done is me, they passed on to me some of the most valuable attributes that they have learnt from those who generously gave to them what seems to be like template for life, and living.

Every experienced person who have lived life longer than you have, is quite willing to assist you, the younger ones with all of their accumulated wealth of knowledge, so that you may have some thing to bank on for sure as you mature for the road ahead.

Some thing that I would love, is for all those that are really young to open their eyes, and ears, and show willingness to get hungry for all of that knowledge that can be theirs

so as you grow into life, you can rest assure that you can use what has been given to you as tools that you can implement.

As young people in order that success to come your way, you must first want to work for the success to come, for sure it is not going to drop from the sky, nothing is that ready made, so you may abolish that mind set right now while you have the time to do so.

There is a sort of pride of ownership that comes to every one, who willingly give of their time and, resources to acquire what they have.

Every thing is hard until it is achieved, what ever you wish to accomplish as young people, will have an element of difficulty to it, simply because we may have to think of, the preparation that will have to take place in order that we may realize our expectations.

It may be difficult, but that should not be the reason for not to do it, I know because I have been there, that is why you may hear me say that I love challenges, because it gives me the opportunity to work harder, and smarter to win the fight.

I take a great interest in the young, because some one first loved me when I was young, but mind you, I was very obedient, and very willing to learn from any one that was ready, and able to teach what I needed know, I was always like the sponge, ready to absorb just about every thing good that fell from the mouths of all baled mentors.

It is entirely up to you, if you are to succeed, don't be afraid to ask any question from those that are older than you, simply because they have been here much longer than you and, they have just what you need, to be your game changer.

Now go on and succeed in every area of your life, you will never regret it, I am still thankful for the direction that I have taken.

Very seldom you would find a younger person that have a good sense of direction, it's not to say that they are clueless, it is simply because they are young and, have not lived long enough to have a good supply of cumulative experience.

That is exactly what happened to me when I was younger, I knew that under no circumstance I would have more experience than my parents, so I took every opportunity to grab a hold of every thing that would be advantageous to my life.

One of the many reasons that I wrote this book is with the hope that all younger persons who are serious about being the very best that they could be, would find it to be a real source of inspiration to them.

If we are to change the world for the better, we my have to sacrifice a little of our selves in order that we may achieve that change.

When we change any thing in life, we do it not only for our selves but for all of the rest, that is what I set out to do in life and, I am happy to know that I am making the progress that I am pleased with.

In my opinion It was all about people and, it is still all about people, that is not going to change, what we may do is to try and change our views on some things.

A square object has four sides to it, and all of them are very important to what is the whole, so it becomes very important to validate that object, as some thing that may hold real value to us and, that we may use all and, not part of it.

To get the real benefit of any thing, especially when some one is trying to transfer their knowledge to you is to listen very attentively, simply because it is the very first step in the learning process.

That is why I encourage younger people to lay aside the pretense and be true to your self, otherwise your future could be very hard to say the least.

What seems to be so important to you now, if you should stay on this current tread mill, will prove to be your greatest down fall, and just in case you don't care now, there is a time coming that may be very painful, and may be very hard to live through.

This is a rather good time for you to start considering all of your options now, and not later, because I have said before, you are only young once in your life time, after that comes the real awaking.

I have personally seen way too many of you being caught in this terrible web, with no hope of being untangled, if you remain on this train that goes nowhere.

Some mistakes are easier to take care of when you are young simply because you have that element of time on your side, as time goes on you should be checking your self to see just how well you are doing.

Don't take any thing for granted, it a simple mistake that many of have made, always try to make sure that what you see is making some sense to you, that you will know by the way that you feel in your gut.

Prepare to get the very best out of life, and that may come by doing your best to staying realistic in every thing that you do, that means that if it's green, call it green, not may be it's green.

Believe it or not, that will help greatly because you are facing the real truth instead of some thing that looks like the truth.

One of the very best thing that can take place is to see young and older working together, learning from each other, thereby creating a better fonder relationship, after all we are all people, only some are older than the other.

You will find that in order for a world to function well, we must first have some sort of appreciation for each other, all of us have some thing to add to each other's life, just a spend a little time to find just what that may be.

There is quite a resource out there to draw from, by pretending that it is not there is only one way to short change our selves from what can make us greater.

For me Growing up was nothing short of that, I made my self hungry and, thirsty for just about thing that would help me to become the person that I envision my self to be.

I had a plan in my mind, and in fact I kept it there, till I was ready to implement it fully.

Because I have seen so many things in my life, I feel that is very important for me to take this opportunity to keep being a constant reminder to you that you and you alone are going to be responsible for you end up.

I am happy that I am just where I always wanted to be, but what makes me feel even better is that I am in a place where I can lift up that ray of hope just that you may find your way in this dark and dingy world.

One important thing that I would love younger people to keep in mind is that, being younger is only steps to getting older, so all of those older people that you seeing out there were like you young men and, women that has become older.

I remember hearing my sister saying to her grand children, be careful, because the way that I am , so you may be, if you should live this long, to be good people, you should treat every one in the way you would like to be treated, especially when you become like me. older, so think.

There was a time that I really had to ask my self, why are there so many people willing to help me, I asked my self the question, but in fact I really knew the answer long before I asked it.

It was simply because I was always respectful, especially to those that were older than I, and that came directly from my parents, who taught me earlier that one should always show people that you were raised by generally good people.

That was not a joke, I think the best men and , women would tell you that they have had the very best parents, that of course was music to their ears, every parent loves to hear people say that their child, or children are the very best that have seen in a long time.

As kids we were particularly proud to show people who we were and, who our parents were, I beamed with joy to know that my parents would always hear good reports about me, after all I would not let them down, not even the slightest bit.

I lifted them up just about every where that I went, by the way that I lived my life, it was a sure thing like a match made under heaven, up to now I still keep my head up high, not because I am walking around with false pride, but that I am proud for the way that I turn out to be.

When you know that you come from good stock, it is a rather good feeling, in that you know I will be with you for ever not only that but your children too, it becomes a pleasure to pass it on to them and, see them shine like you are.

We always hear some people say that life is for sharing with every one no matter just who they may be, it is some thing that I fully believe in, and in fact I try to practice that in my daily living, and I found out that it is working out just fine.

The fact is one just cannot give what they don't have, some one gave it to me, and now I am able to give it to you, actually this is one of the most important things for me to do, the opportunity to enrich lives is one of the very best that any one can do.

As I take a look at all those that I am touching with my life, I really couldn't be happier to know that I am helping to heal this messed up world and, trust me I m not saying this because I hate the world, please don't get me wrong, I love every thing in this world, I dislike the way that we try to accomplish what many of us already know is going about it the wrong way.

That is why I am spending some of my time with every one that I can, to see if we can get on the same page, just for a little while at least to set a precedent for things going forward.

To be honest what I expected as I grow up, am still having troubles finding it, and that worries me some how

Some things that has troubled me for quite some time now is just to see how some people are raising their kids in this society, that is why I find it very hard to put all of the blame on the recipients of the raising up factors.

Some one has to remember that what they get from you is just what they will be taking with them every where that they may go, so be careful, because you in turn my feel the pinch when the calls start to come in and, may be at dinner time to boot.

I really don't know whether you read the Holy Bible, but if you do I am quite sure that you have came across that instructional piece that says, train up a child in the way that he/she should go, so that when they become old they won't depart from it.

Those words got drilled into me for all of my teen years, today they become a part of me, that some time I feel that I just cannot live with out and, frankly I don't see any reason to try to.

When the times got real tough I knew that I could dip in the back of my reserve and low and behold there came my guide, guaranteed to support me in all things.

All these came back to me in full supply, because some one has to form the basis to the younger people's life, we just cannot expect them to have all of the answers wrapped up in a single question.

I want you to catch my vision here, what I am doing is helping to prepare the next generation for the many tasks ahead, because what will eventually happen is that as they mature, and ready to give service, this is your time to guess to whom they will be servicing? if in case you say us, then you are very right.

What we are doing is preparing the next generation to take care of us, therefore if we train them well, we may get just what we expects.

Nothing thrilled me more than the time I was talking with a certain person, and as I am usually very friendly, positive and out going, the response was, Paul look, it's simple I am only giving you what you put out, because it is such a pleasure to speak with you.

What was important was that I made a positive dent in their day, as much as they did for me, because it didn't cost me any thing, in fact I had gotten a friend.

That day I really saw just how we may be able to change the world, one pleasant day after the other, together we can accomplish the greatest things, that will last for a life time, but wait, the world that you helped to change is the very world that you will live in.

Every thing that we do for our selves does not have to be selfishness on our part, in fact what I know for sure is as I build up my self to the degree that I feel comfortable with and, I also knew that I was preparing my self to impact other lives.

Every one knows that you cannot give what you don't have, so the very best thing is to make sure that you are well equip your with what it takes for you to do the sort of thing that you were preparing for.

My youth was nothing but the perfect time to foundation my self, by looking and learning some of the most important things that I could and, that is just why am able to demonstrate my self to you by all of the many things that I am trying to accomplish, all because I know that I can.

It was only too recently I met this young man who had big passion for plumbing, he lives, breathe every thing pipes and plumbing, I so amazed, because I have never known any one who wanted to some thing that badly, that they would do almost any thing to accomplish it.

For the very first time I have met some one like me, with a passion for doing things, that ultimately would lead to a life long dream, that is exactly what happened, it didn't matter what the condition of the weather was he was willing to get going, just to make an investment in him self.

I found him one day in one of the local building centers, while shopping around for some materials, we struck up a conversation, that led me to getting to know him just a little better, it was one of my lucky days, because nothing feels better that to have a younger person right under my nose that I can influence, if ever to stay on that path.

Some how I was convincing enough to see that take root, after all he was the one that was willing to be the Plummer and to me, it was my opportunity to help consolidate his desire, it was quite a win, win situation for both of us, because all that I had to benefit from that was just to know, that this is one that has well chosen his path and, that progress was a sure thing.

That was when I decided in my mind that mentoring was an awesome thing, there are people out there that just don't know just how to ask for our help, but that doesn't mean that they don't need our help, some time what we have to do is what they call breaking the ice.

Some one has to make the first step forward, just to know that you now have a crowd following after you, that is particularly good, because the reason why they are following after you is because you are the kind of person that is well worth following.

I am sure what I said earlier about following step, by step after my dad, literally walking in his foot steps, it was because he was leading me to a good destination, I knew that because I knew that he was my dad and, that he was not going to lead me down the path that would take me down into the pitfalls.

It was then that I really came to the understanding that, we can play a very important role in the lives of every one that we may come into contact with, if they are willing to be led and, if you are willing to teach them, in my case I was very willing to learn, so I was led easily.

That is exactly how we should go about helping people to change for the road ahead, because God knows that if not totally prepared we my find that there may be some real tough and, unexpected bumps in the way that would live you unable to move forward.

Every one knows by now that most of the things that we would love to acquire, could never happen unless we are know how to work to make it happen, what makes it better and , easier is because some one took the time to help us to get the knowledge that we needed to make it happen.

Want to make real change in the world and, in the lives of others? when you see some one going down the wrong road, step right in, especially if you love people, and have a caring, heart we are all here to make a difference and, that difference may never be realized by us turning a blind eye to our opportunity to impact some one in the right way.

One thing that I will never do is to stop looking for ways that I can use to help any one, no matter who they may be, simply because every one needs a fair chance in this world to succeed in what ever it is that they are involve with while at the very same time we are lightening the burden, making their load just a little bit lighter.

It is amazing just what the little word care, can accomplish when we apply it where it's most needed at times , and I am quite sure there are several situations that may come to mind, I am sure that if you would turn around twice, you may find your self feeling spell bound and, inundated with the opportunity that's there for you to get involved.

Look, it's all about changing situations, changing mind sets, helping to redirect people so that won't loose their way, which is some thing that you would like your self, that would definitely make a very big difference in your own life, or some one that you know and, love.

There is not a person in the world, no matter where they may be, that would say to you,

that they don't love the one precious thing that they have, that is very dear to them and, that is call life, my! it's a treasure.

I don't know why any one wouldn't want to do all that they can do when they have the time to do so, this is our time to take control of every thing and, make the very most out of it, I have seen too many people, that fail to do just that, and lived to regret it.

Believe me there is a time coming when you may wish you had done more with the time that you had, only this time is sort of late in the game, so you may have to toss that in the wind.

You may even hear some people saying, I could of, or should of, you can almost hear the regrets in the way that they speak, although it was one of the very mistakes that some people makes, some how it is still a good thing, although the results were bad for them.

What is great about is people like you me, and our friends listening to that should use their mistakes as to motivate us to press on harder to avoid the same mistakes that causes them to be in the position that they found them selves in.

When it comes to success and failure one should take mistakes seriously enough, because too many of them may have serious consequences, the kind that will live you crying the blues day in ,and day out with out end, not a good way to build one self.

I have traveled for miles just to avoid some of life's terrible pitfalls, instead I came face to face with it, which I called the time for decisions, and may be you would have done the very same thing too, one thing that I didn't do was run away from it.

This the very time I feel like asking you a question for the causes for some things as they happens, instead I continue to write, and I am sure you will get the answer as you read on simply because there are so many answers to be discovered that here.

As I said before I have gained quite a lot of experience in my involvement with the caliber of people that I associated my self with, those of the people that I called some of my mentors, those were some of the very best days of my life, because that was where I have gotten started on my road to success.

One regret that I have and, will be with me for quite some time is that most of those people that contributed in my life, helping me to over come every hurdle that I really had to deal with, they are gone to their rest, but will always be remembered by me as long as I live.

The life that I live now I am living because they helped to carved out this path way that I am on and, I am determine to be on it for as long as time allows me.

Here is some thing that I want you to remember and, that is when some one gives you some thing , the very best way to show them that you appreciate, it is by allowing them to see you using it, that happens to be some thing that quite a lot of us have already experienced at some point in time some where.

Giving does not have to be any thing tangible, any thing that goes out of your hand, or even words from your mouth, for instance, giving an idea, an advise, help to carry a load, as long as it comes from you, is giving, now it is entirely up to you to at first saying thanks in appreciation, then at some time later showing that you love it enough and is using it.

Some people take great offense to know what they have given is not being used and, it may even strain a relationships, simply because they are so hurt and feeling like it is a sort of insult to them, the same is in every situation.

I remember a time at school, when the teacher gave an assignment with an example, but some thing happened and I did not use what he gave me, well, that day in question, I got a very strong reprimand, all because I did not take into consideration what was to be the very best of ways to get things done, and right all at the very same time.

People usually gives you things to be used , and not to be destroyed, I learned my lessons, now I am far more sensitive to some one giving any thing.

Giving is giving and, we are to receive with respect to the giver. Last year my wife went out of her to buy me casual clothing at that very same time I was pumping up at the gym, so I had gotten a little to bulky so that was when I decided to take the scissors to them and, made a cut here and, a cut there well, don't ask how mad she became, I sure had to apologized many times over, I really had to promised her that it was the very last time I would do this.

Some times people will give you things simply because the really like you, so what would you do, destroy a nice relationship, by not showing appreciation? I'll say no.

Since giving and, receiving is based on mutual respect, we should treat it as such, for whether you agree or not it can certainly add to making this world a much better place.

In these times we can never do enough to show the world that we care and, will show that we do in every way that we can, after all that is truly the very best for spreading a positive message that will no doubt help to make people think of what they can do as contributing factors that may be responsible for inspiring every one every where.

Every morning as I wake up I get the feeling all over again, that today I should be doing some thing, what ever that it may be, to point some one in a better direction, the direction that I am pointing you to may be based on the way that I see things, it's up to you to choose your direction based on the way you think.

If I can at least awake your interest, about any thing, then I am not doing so bad after all, some how I try to get up to speed with most of the events as they unfold, so I too may be able to change direction as deem necessary.

This is all based on purpose, there are things that I feel passionate about enough to make me spring to action in a flash, that does not mean that I am not thinking, I already gave myself leeway so in won't find my self wondering what is it going to be.

It's always a plus when you have the advantage, based on your life's experiences, that was why I spent my time developing and growing so as to meet the challenges that lies ahead, there is no use pretending that the way is all clear, when in fact it is not, so may have to make a way for you to go through.

Don't be surprised to know that there are others waiting to follow in the way that you make for your self, that too is very normal, just stop and think for a moment, and you will see that where you are was created by some one who has past this way before you got there.

We are all a part of every thing that has been made, it is now ,and will be for ever. like what my first mentors did just that I would have a place to go to, knowingly that they gave it all that they could in order that I would have the pleasure of enjoying it.

If you are going to purpose in your life, and really want to make a big difference in your life and that of others, you must first develop passion, that means that you may have to love what it is that you wants to do, because wanting too and, doing just about any thing, may seem easy at first, but at second take, it would be a vastly different thing.

Any thing worth doing for the purpose of relieving some one from a difficult situation, should give any one a real joy, because by doing a noble act of kindness from the heart, in my estimation would be done from a sense of purpose, and will at that time have all sorts of passion just for the benefit it brings to some one waiting.

I have waiting for quite a long time to bring this experience to you with hopes that it would change some thing for you some one, in some way or the other and, that is why I do the things that I find my self doing and, I do have pleasure doing them.

When we take pleasure doing that many things that we do, it becomes as sowing whole some and, healthy seed, that if we nurture will bring us great harvests, the harvests that it yields then becomes an opportunity to share that with as many that are in their time of need, and support.

As I enter this career I did it to accomplish my way of bringing a different kind of knowledge to you that you may see just what some people had to experience as they made way to change their lives.

I did this for me first, because it was the thing to do, you see, it is very important for us to enrich our lives so that we may help to enrich yours, now that I am well able to stand strong, and able to fight, not a ruthless fight, but in fact this fight is more like a determination to go way beyond my potentials.

Some of the many things that keep ringing in my ears are things that learnt long before now and, that is, what ever it is please don't ever think that any thing can, or will happen by standing with time hoping that there will be some magic bullet, that will go off, and then comes the results that I really want.

One thing I like to do is to look at reality squarely in the face, for by doing so there will be no pretense to the obvious, I like to take a good look at what I am looking at, that gives me a much anticipated expectation, one that I am sure I am going to love.

It is unfortunate that for some people it is not that easy to recognize the pitfalls and do all that they could to not fall into the ditch, I really don't think that I am that special, it's just that try to keep a constant vigil, after all I really want to succeed the very best that I can.

As you may know by now, is that I am one of those people that believes in doing well that I may help to see others to do better, it is some thing that is within me, as I think about I will also try to do some thing about it.

It is certainly not worth it for me to hold any thing too close to my chest, like I am quite aware some have done, when ever that happens, we can rest assure that there will be the ugly thing call greediness that is sure to prevail, which can easily be our own down fall.

Fortunate for me the way that I think will always provide the kind of results that I am hoping for and, with that result comes benevolence, that is why I chose the path that leads to success, what I personally would love to se is that more people trying to do the very same things, rather than putting all of the attention, and the results to them selves.

We must all take hold of opportunities, if we are going to work towards helping to change the directions that so many are taking, that leads to dead ends.

Make no mistake about it, unless we take clear directions, it may be helpful to be cautious just before we try to move forward, other wise we may have to repeat our steps before we get going, because we are all on this journey through life, the question is what destination are we expecting.

To carve out a place and to get a slice of this pie, we should firstly know that there is a pie out there for the taking, that may even give you a good reason to pursue, it just doesn't help a bit to not having a sense of direction, that can prove to be disastrous thereby leaving you with some thing far greater to deal with, than first thought.

As you try to make a way for your self, there will be many ups and downs, but don't allow that to discourage you, just keep the end results in clear sight, so that you may have a vision of what it is that you are hoping to find.

Expectations are all at times, no matter what it is that you are doing, if you don't have an expectation of what it is that you are after, it becomes pointless, after a while.

When I was a little boy I had a thought deep inside of me, and that I wanted to have a house with a long and, wide drive way, with a car in the yard, the next one was I wanted to have a family, of four, all the way through my life I thought that way, until at one time I realized that my expectations were being realized, and that I would have exactly what I wanted.

Need less to say, that I had a pre conceived notion that things were going to go well for me if that were going to happen, but steadfastness were the name of the game for me, and no matter what happened I was not going to have it any other way.

In order for us to have all of our expectations materialized we should just stay the course, and work towards our goals, it may not be the end of the world if we didn't accomplish some of the things that we hoped for, but as they say you may aim for the moon, but hit the stars, at least you have made it way past your endeavor, and that becomes a rather good story to tell.

No matter what may happen, for God sake please don't ever say no to your self, because if you do are saying the same to every one else, this is called self incrimination, and that means that you are doomed to what we call failure, not the best situations to ever find your self in.

I often tell people that if I can rise to where I am today, after the expedition that I made, with all of the many uncertainties that I had to subject my self to then any one, any where can make it for sure.

Of all of the things that I love to do, one of them is listening to bright, educated, and influential people, because they inspire me to do all of the things that are important to me, which I hope would be just as important to you and all others.

As I spent some of my time reading up on materials here is what I came across. It is no doubt that by now you are fully aware that there are countless of all over the world that is trying to do some thing to help them selves in one way or the other, some times we make our selves feel that we can make it from where we are, although that may be true in some ways, yet in other ways it may not be so.

Personally I believe that there are way too many of us trying to make ends meet, and have been doing so for many years, some how it seems that this method has been fruitful to as many of those that have tried.

One day as I was looking at television, I heard a commercial playing, what it was saying in the form of a question, it goes like this, have you ever noticed that in your sleep you had a dream but when morning came you just couldn't remember your dream, at the very end the answer came, and it said it's because we dream too small.

As some one you may know, or only heard about, but love, respect, and admired for their work as a major world leader, Madeleine Albright, the first female U.S. Secretary of State, Here is what she said. As you go along your road in life, you will, if you aim high enough, also meet resistance...but no matter how tough the opposition my seem, have courage still- and persevere.

Those words spoke volumes to me, for as a man who has worked tirelessly to make a dent for my self, I know exactly what she is saying, because I have personally met all sorts o oppositions in my trial to become what I always to be, I know how difficult it could be for any one like me who did not have a great start.

Some times the very best thing that we can do is to start despite all that you are not, because it is by starting that ultimately brings on the end results, I could of been still at my zero point and not have done any thing, so yes, what I had to resort to was courage, for the tirelessly journey ahead.

I am quite sure that may hear many leaders saying that when you begin, just keep in mind that the prize is ahead of you, and not the other way around, unless you have decided to return to your starting point, I well knew that I was to go back it wouldn't be with out what I went for.

I think what we should all do is when tempted to do nothing is to think of what might have happened if they didn't go, but at the very same time I do take this opportunity to sermon leaders to consider their leadership, for if you falter the rest will inevitably do the same, remember that leadership is for sure, if you are going to lead make darn sure that you are going to take me some where good, I am depending on you for that.

My father led me to the place that am in today, I am very thankful and, appreciative for his leadership, so in return I am giving him all of the credits for a job well done, because with out him, it's hard to say just what could of been.

Not every one that is in front can be classified as a leader, after all at any given time just about any one will be in front, that is very common, so it's best to search out just who is worth while following after, and while you are there you better watch out for pitfalls along the way.

In this complex world you have got to have all of your priorities in order right from the start, know where you are going, and what you are going for, it is just what I had to do as I started, it is difficult to set out and reach half of the way, just to realized that you now have questions about what you are going to find.

As we enter into the twenty first century, my desire is to think more of every thing long before I engage my self into any thing, and that is because I have seen too many of us failing ascertain what might be the highlight of our journey.

As for me I like the way that I think, and is a strong believer in alternative thinking which can provide a much better way forward for us to accomplishing the goals that we set for our selves, I really try to take the lead in my life, because I am my very own trusted leader, simply because I trust my self for getting me there.

With that kind of well adjusted attitude , I knew that would be the very best approach if I was going to lead any one, I am the very first to tell you that I am not perfect, because I am human, but I will try all that I can to get you there for sure, after all life is a learning experience, and that is why I am prepared to lead with what I know for sure.

As we go through life, just know that you can enrich your self with admonition of all those great men and, women who has helped greatly to lay the foundations for us all.

Frankly I just think that it is my turn to return the favors and do all of the things that I can do as I take my position in this world, and that is despite all what the others have done, for they have done theirs, but that is not enough in this great big world.

As a sense of responsibility each person should prepare to shoulder his/ her share of the burden which as we know is just too heavy for one to carry, especially as we hoping to see all of the benefits that comes as a direct result from their efforts.

I for one have never been quite interested to stand and watch people work as hard as they could just to provide my comfort, some how I just get the feeling that I must do all that I can to take care of my self in the very best way that I can.

Help is always available to those that need it, in most cases we are the ones to call out for the kind of help that may suit our needs, so when you feel like you are going to drown as you make way to paddle your way through just let your voice be heard, signaling your need for help.

Look, it is the same just about every where, I remember there was a time that my dad wanted me to carry some thing, but before I could he has to help me to lift it to my shoulders in order that I could do my share, while at the same time helping him to do his.

All through life I try to keep my eyes wide open as wide as I could, just that I may see all that there are to be seen, simply because I thought, if I can see I will know for sure, because I don't like second guessing, for it's up to all of us to see the real picture, before we may decide to change.

In my case I wanted to have empowerment, so I learnt what I needed to know, and implement the knowledge from most of the things that I learnt, once I accomplished that I began to research ways that would enable me to use my powers towards changing what I could.

As we all have heard the saying, that knowledge is power, that is very true, but only when we use it to affect any situation that would help to make things better.

When I was a boy it was my determination to work towards change, so what I did was first to find out how necessary that change would be, for there is no need to go about changing every thing in our sight just in the name of change, the change must be real, and purposeful.

May be this might be a none issue, but I will tell you any way, one day I went to the barber to have my hair trim, all along I had a feeling that the barber was just not doing what I really wanted, but I sat there, he was through, and I left for home.

As I entered the house I headed straight to the powder room, where I checked my hair job, I really didn't like one bit, so right then I decided to fix it once and for all.

That was when I reached for the razor and began the job all over again, only this time was to save him the hassle of having to make the same mistake again, I shaved it to a bald, and I made a promise that I from here on will do it all for my self.

In this whole episode I accomplished two things, all in one slue, I saved my self a lot of money and frustration I am a winner, in that regard.

In this life one has to play hard to win in every thing, some times it's like no more mister wise guy and, I really don't mean this harshly, what I mean is that you should face up to the challenge, and do it like it is the very last day of your life.

Look, I did the very same thing at the very beginning of my journey, it is said that nice guys come last, if you take a closer look at life, you just can't help but to agree, just imagine that some placed two very nice flower pots in the front of their yard, with a note that said, this is good, please take, and make good use of it.

You walked by several times of the day, but playing that you are so nice, in the eyes of those people around, and may be you are just too good to let some one se you picking up those lovely pots, but as they say, you snooze, you loose.

The very next time you thought of taking it with you, it's gone, some one else took those lovely pots, now you feel regretful that you didn't take it, now it's gone, this is exactly why we say nice guys comes last.

If you want some thing that will work for you why wait, go for it, and you just stop your pretending, if the opportunity is there for you, make the very most of the time that you have to seize those precious moments, because when they are gone, they are gone and, is not coming back this way any time soon.

It is just like me, I did not finish high school before I traveled, as I traveled, I realizes that I needed to have more education, so I made the decision, to get what I thought was the most important thing for me, it was back to school, only this time it was attending college in my chosen field.

Today I can stand strong, and say I am very glad that I did, don't get caught in indecision   decide on what it is that you need, then feel that void with the desire to succeed, I really cannot over state that if you didn't succeed it is because of you own lack of will power to go past your complacency.

Develop the now mentality, waiting for too long only sets you back and, now you are light years behind.

It is way too hard to try to catch up to the crowd ahead, now you feel like giving up, you are tired, and it is pulling you back, to avoid that just make a plan that you know for sure , you can deliver on, there are those that may try to climb the tree from the top, well, you already know just what can happen by now, you will fall and hurt your self, and by then it's game over.

Do things in a sort of chronological way, complete the first task, then start the next one, before you know it , they are all completed and, you are happy with what you have done so far.

Quit wasting precious time and, work with time to accomplish all of your objectives, it is also one of the very best ways to finish on a high note, trust me you will be proud of your self for doing so, and after you are through it will be the perfect time to start boasting to your friends.

It a true saying that people loves stories, this is you time to tell yours to them, and see if you can inspire them to roll up their sleeves and, get to work.

When I set my self on my journey, to take charge of my destiny, it simply because I realized that I had choices to be made, it was either I went all of the way or not go at all, both had consequences so I chose the one that would help me to realize my dreams.

To me it is the only way to go and, as they say the very best way is up.

Life is about having some fun too, but there are people that has gotten carried away, and had just a little too much fun, while they do very little to sustain their livelihood, and ultimately every thing just fell apart.

Here is what I would like to have you consider, drop a raw egg onto the floor, with out question it smashes into a million pieces, now what I would like you to do is to put it back together, any way before you try, you can call it the impossible task, I don't know of any one that has tried it and succeeded at any attempt, so don't waste your time, nor frustrate your self at the same time.

The reason why I went into that kink of analogy, is simply because there are some one out there that may agree with it, the opportunities that you face each day are exactly what is suppose to change things for you, so what you do? you play careless and , let it sleep through your fingers, now you are able to think straight every one that had to do with putting this into motion, has changed their minds for good, now it is impossible to do this again.

Look, I take all of this time to relate to you on all sorts of levels, find a place that makes you aware of the things that would bring lasting change in your life, once and for all. No one is going to change things for you but you, remember, you are master of your destiny, and you are the single most important person to you, so learn to take care of you, the very best way that you can.

This life teaches us that unless we accomplishes any thing, chances are we are going to be envious of what others have done, don't let that be you, we all have the very same chances to every thing that is out there, all that you have to do is to set your sight on it, then work towards it.

Just know that you are not different to any else that have first tried and, succeeded, that could of been you, so get inspired, take matters into your own hand, and do the things that no one else would do for you, which is like to succeed for you.

I love gardening immensely, I get the greatest thrills from planting flowers and, shrubs, and at the right time to see all of the variety of flowers, nothing feels better in this whole wide world.

But, not only that I also take pleasure in planting some vegetables too, what ever I can find I just stick it into the ground, the best thing is they grows well and, bears bountiful crops too.

What is even better is my neighbor and I get into competition, and at harvest time we trade off some of our yields, for instance at one time I was surprised at the amount of winter squash that I have gotten, and because I just didn't know what to do with them I gave some away to good use.

You, see this is just how I love to live, there is nothing quite like sharing with others some of the things that we love, and not only that , but it is also a very good way to build better relations with even those that you are not quite sure about.

There are all sorts of opportunities, but some how I love any thing that has to do with bringing people closer together, sharing our space, and enjoying a little part of God's earth, you see, we live is a very nice ,and quiet neighborhood, and we love it that way, but there is something that take pride in and that is as I walk the streets, it not uncommon to hear us call out from across the other side of the street just to say hello, it gives me that wonderful feeling that puts every thing into perspective, like the way it should be.

There are just so many ways to teach people, and we should not expect to be in a class room, to expect to be taught, our lives should be a constant teacher, passing on some of the wonderful qualities that we are made up off.

I told you so, that if you only gave me the opportunity to take you on a journey with me, I can guarantee you that your life could be changed forever, that is just how I started, and the purpose was to make an impact on ever one every where, although it's hard at times to judge your self, but I just can't help it, simply because I promised to try to do the most good that I can, and I think that I am doing fine thus far.

What ever you do allow, life to take you to the highest high that you can attain too, and give credit to time for taking you there, every thing that we do is based on the time that we committee too, for it is only with time on our side that we can accomplish any thing.

I just want to keep doing things, because of the purpose, and passion that is contained within me, especially because every thing is towards the greater good, that will benefit some thing, or some one, some where.

My life so far has been has taken many turns, fortunately to say, they were all for the better, because really I did not enter into this thing for just to be here, and waited it out on a breeze, I expected to find all sorts of obstacles, because they were inevitable,

all because of the time that I came into this world.

As I take a look back, just to see how far I have traveled, I can only be amazed at where I am now, as usual I find my self on a tread mill and, as far as I am concern I must realize just what I am doing there, but to keep moving, and although there is no exist on that moving machine, yet I will keep going.

One thing that I keep abreast of is that, I must go, but not with out a destination in sight, or in mind, but for darn sure that major stop, must be the reason why I have gotten started to begin with, it's like I have an unquenchable thirst burning inside of me, fueling me to reach my goal.

I set the standard, I set the pace, I know what I am looking for, and I mush find it, nothing is going to stand in my way, it's all good, and I am good to go, it's been too many times, now hearing people saying that you only go around this bend once, whether you believe it or not it is really true, just prepare to take all that you can, but don't forget to help the others to find theirs. Remember? purpose, and passion, let it be your fuel, as you move forward.

To this day all of the events that helped me to compiled my experiences to bring them to you, was all based on my own willfulness, and curiosity, the fact of the matter is I have gone through layers, after layers of learning all that I knew that would need as I entered this journey of my life time.

Every thing was planned as I saw the opening, my main goal was to enter into the gates that would eventually take me to the mansion that willfulness prepared.

I well knew that there would be many obstacles, especially to some of the things that I wanted to do, it was not doubt that I knew I was able to succeed, because I knew what I was capable of.

Under going some of those events was no doubt questionable by some, but there are times when one must break some of the rules in order to pursue important goals.

I still remember the day that I said to my mom, that I was going away, and that if she didn't se me come back, just know that I am okay, that was particularly heart breaking for her, but in any account she gave me her blessing, and I was on my way to the greatest expedition of my life, well, mom is long gone, but never be forgotten (mom R.I.P.) since then all that I do I never loose that indelible picture of her in my mind, and that I will take with me till I see her again.

I hope that by now you can really see, just what kind of person I am, it is my intention to hold my self accountable for all that I do, and that is why I am spending this time with you, this is a very special time in my life, so I hope you will take it as a building block to your life.

One thing that I take is pride in my work and my life, I feel very inspired to do the work that I do, it took me a very long time, and I can only thank God, that he gave me sustained life so that I can do good things, which is motivating ,and inspiring people every where to do all that they can to live a prosperous life.

Now here are some tips that may help you to succeed:

Focus your dreams

Develop common sense in your quest for success

Choose carefully the things that you wish to pursue

Stay determined to win at all cost

Be realistic

Make plans to succeed

Ask questions, get answers

Take no lightly

Follow through to the end

Do not give up on your self.

Spend enough time to think, about what ever it is you are going to do, rather than doing first, then start thinking later, ride the horse the right way, it will surely get you home.
It is my expectation that you become very successful, after reading this book, I succeeded in getting it to you.

Think on these things:

 Right thinking produces the right results

The right answers comes from the right questions

A mirror always reflects the truths

Climbing may be difficult, but coming descending is down right dangerous

Very seldom people laugh because of their pains

Most people carries around an indelible picture of those that they loves in their minds

Positive steps get you closer

Negative steps takes you right on the brink of disaster

Never say yes if you did not hear the questions.

Together we thrive that we all may be a much better people, loving , and caring and doing the very best for each other, I now urge us all to use alternative thinking to provide a better way forward.

Notes:

Tracking your dreams...

Taking notes of the:

The Past

The Present

The Future

It may be time for you to begin your journey....

About the Author

Paul G. Utley is the author of from," Pitfalls to progress," a book dedicated to help you to with stand all of the hard knocks in life , and yet survive despite of them, you will notice, first hand some of the various things, that Paul had to endure in order that he may make it to his journey's end.

Paul acknowledges that tough times will always be there, whether you want them or not, so may be the very best thing to do is to use them as stepping stones as you make your way up, and while you are on your way, keep in mind that the very first word to remove from your vocabulary should be " easy" in life there is no easy way in or out of any thing.

The other book in his series is Prosperity: "The Fruit of Challenge" this book offers you a glimpse into the life of Paul's the real expedition that led him to where he is today.

Al of the stories in his two books are real, and true, Paul does not like fiction, in his writing you will come face to face with Paul, and his perilous journey, in a recent conversation with Paul he said to me, every thing is possible, as long as you are determine, and willing to pursue.

At the very beginning, Paul has done some thing that most people call, simply out of your rockers, and in most cases destined to fail, imagine you standing right at the very brink of a dangerous pitfall, that was just where he established his faith in God, and as he said is the reason to be felt guided each step of the way.

Conclusion

One thing that I know for sure is that every one loves a story, I am telling mine, hopefully to inspire you to move beyond where you are, to a place that will make you feel that you have not just lived life, instead you live life to help other lives.

At this time I feel very excited because I have gone through the very worst to achieve the very best, and this best is not about lining my pockets with money, instead I love the opportunity that I have to spend some quality time with you.

I fulfilled the past, I accomplished the present, and I imagine the future.

To connect with Paul, go to paulottley@rogers.com
Or you may reach Paul at aimhighermotivation.com

Here is some thing that I prepared especially for you, as you think of making this life more exciting for your self.

This thing about succeeding is not about, because you may be facing a little tough time, isn't that not life is all about, determining to challenging your self for the success that you want.

I have noticed time and time again, athletes competing for that gold medal, and that nothing could ever come in their way of winning.

After all they have invested many years preparing for this event, so winning is paramount in their minds.

So may be some time you may want to consider, pretending that you are an athlete, investing time preparing to succeed, despite the efforts of all of the others.

Success is very sweet, especially after working so hard so very hard as you make a push towards the goals that you have set.

Remember that life as we know it is simply not going any where, only we are, and the very same is true, that life needs simply nothing from us, instead we need all that life has to offer, and that is why we should do all that we can with the little time that we have.

If you are going to reap a harvest, hurry and sow your seeds now, then plant your trees,

then you have all the rights to expect a harvest, from the seeds that became trees.

Keep in mind that every thing matured in it's fullness of time, just as we should as we go from thoughts to things.

I know that many of you wants to succeed, but you seems to be afraid of the many curves on the roads ahead.

When ever you get that feeling, just imagine just how sweet success feels, that is the exact time you may change your mind, and wish for nothing but the very best that you can have, thereby leaving you feeling very satisfied, and well accomplished.

My greatest hope for all, is that you succeed way beyond your unwillingness, that you may enjoy all of the benefits of you labor, and the short time that we all have on this precious earth.

To be honest, any thing other than winning and, succeeding in life should be the ultimate goal of each and, every one of us, otherwise life as we know it is really not quite worth living, why would you want to be in a place that you are just not enjoying being there.

I am really not suggesting any thing, all that I know is that this life was meant to be lived to the fullest and, having a lot of fun doing so at the same time.

I don't know about you, but I am just beginning to enjoy my self, I have no plane to stop any time soon, this feel too good to give up now, just follow some of the tracks that I have made, they will lead you to a place where you always dreamt of being, and guess what, you will find me there waiting for you, it is the place that I call progress.

Here are some sayings that I love.

When your disappointments seems too much to handle, press on one more time, it may be getting better soon

When people fail and, disappoint you, press on one more time, and give them more time to change their minds

When it becomes difficult to see the light, keep moving forward, you might be closer than you think.

If you know that with God all things are possible, then why are you giving up now, for you may be sorry that you did.

You are here for a reason, until you have found your purpose, it's no time to stop, there is still good work to be done.

I searched and just couldn't find any thing quite as sweet as life, if you could find any thing better please let me know.

And that is why I can never stop having the fun that I am having, don't stand on the side lines watching, join in the fun.

When you feel that you have given 100% and, feel spent, take a rest and start all over again, don't miss a moment.

Look, we are all in this together let's keep comforting each other on this journey call life.

These are people that I would love to say thanks too: My dear mother, who has taken to that part of the bible that says, I can do all things through Christ who strengthens me, thank you mom for being there for me, when I needed you most.

Today I am saying, I have done all of these things because He strengthened me.

My wife, and all of those wonderful people and, friends that has had any thing to do, with every thing that I have done.

My Doctors, my Dentists, all of you played a key role in my life, and health. thank you.

My publishers, and all of my consultants, thank you all, may God richly bless your lives.

CPSIA information can be obtained at www.ICGtesting.com
Printed in the USA
LVOW031913220911

247454LV00004B/28/P